Emeril's DELMONICO

Other books by Emeril Lagasse

Emeril's Potluck

Emeril's There's a Chef in My Family

From Emeril's Kitchens

Emeril's There's a Chef in My Soup

Prime Time Emeril

Every Day's a Party with Marcelle Bienvenu and Felicia Willett

Emeril's TV Dinners with Marcelle Bienvenu and Felicia Willett

Emeril's Creole Christmas with Marcelle Bienvenu

Louisiana Real & Rustic with Marcelle Bienvenu

Emeril's New New Orleans Cooking with Jessie Tirsch

Emeril's DELMONICO

A RESTAURANT WITH A PAST

EMERIL LAGASSE

WM
WILLIAM MORROW
An Imprint of HarperCollins*Publishers*

HarperCollins books may be purchased for educational, business, or sales promotional use. For information please write: Special Markets Department, HarperCollins Publishers, 10 East 53rd Street, New York, NY 10022.

FIRST EDITION

Designed by Jaime Boyle

Printed on acid-free paper

Library of Congress Cataloging-in-Publication Data
Lagasse, Emeril.
Emeril's Delmonico : a restaurant with a past / Emeril Lagasse — 1st ed.
p.   cm.
Includes index.
ISBN-10: 0-06-074046-9 ISBN-13: 978-0-06-074046-7
1. Cookery, American—Louisiana style. 2. Cookery—Louisiana—New Orleans.
3. Emeril's Delmonico (Restaurant : New Orleans, La.) I. Emeril's Delmonico (Restaurant : New Orleans, La.) II. Title.
TX715.2.L68L33 2005
641.5976—dc22
2005041445

05 06 07 08 09 ❖ / QW 10 9 8 7 6 5 4 3 2 1

Dedication

For Angie Brown and Rose Dietrich, two gracious ladies, who not only gave me the opportunity to take their beloved restaurant into a new era but also inspired me to continue the traditions that generations of New Orleanians hold in such high esteem.

It was with great honor that I accepted the challenge of carrying on the torch to continue to maintain the high standards of attention to food, wine, and personal service that is so essential for the success of a great restaurant. I hope that I have made the ladies proud.

Tribute

I would like to take the opportunity to pay tribute to the old Delmonico cooks, the unsung heroes as far as I'm concerned, who were the backbone of the kitchen staff for many, many years. Here is my personal salute to Ernest "Jitterbug" Rome, Elmer Decquir, Irene Polk, Atwood Davis, and the late Kennis Leonard. Long before chefs were visible "in the front of the house," the cooks in earlier times labored long and hard "in the back of the house" without much fanfare or accolades. A tip of my toque to all of you!

I also want to salute the longtime waiters and waitresses of old Delmonico who were always diligent in taking care of the generations of customers who frequented the establishment.

CONTENTS

Acknowledgments

Like a great restaurant with a great staff, a great cookbook also takes a great team. And what a culinary team I am blessed to have at Emeril's Homebase.

Chef David McCelvey for great drive, vision, and dedication to this project.

Marcelle Bienvenu for her patience and her talent in capturing the spirit of both the old and new Delmonico.

Trevor Wisdom for her culinary tastes and hard work.

Chef Bernard Carmouche, Charlotte Armstrong Martory, Alain Joseph, and Laura Martin for all your friendship and culinary support.

I also must thank:

My friend and editor Harriet Bell for seeing the total vision of the amazing history of the restaurant.

My immediate family—my always-supportive parents, Miss Hilda and Mr. John. My amazing, loving wife, Alden, for her support. My lovebug children, Jessie, Jilly, E.J., and Meril, who are very special to me. And my brother, Mark, and his wife, Wendy, and my sister, Dolores, and her son, Jason.

Marti Dalton for her creativity, support, and vision on this project.

Mara Warner, who always keeps me on track.

My manager, agent, and friend Jim Griffin, thanks.

My comrades Eric Linquist, Tony Cruz, Mauricio Andrade, Scott Farber, and Tony Lott—some of my favorite people in the world.

Jim McGrew and Mark Stein for their expert legal advice and friendship.

Damion Michaels and Ivan Bryant for some big Web dreams.

Chaye Larsen, Marti Dalton's assistant, for tirelessly keeping us on schedule during the photo shoots.

Russ Bergeron, head bartender at Emeril's Delmonico, for his expertise of the cocktail.

Everyone at Emeril's Homebase and the amazing people who make it happen every day.

The hardworking staffs at all of my restaurants: Emeril's New Orleans, NOLA, and Emeril's Delmonico in New Orleans, Emeril's New Orleans Fish House and Delmonico Steakhouse in Las Vegas, Emeril's Orlando and Emeril's Tchoup Chop in Orlando, Emeril's Atlanta, and Emeril's Miami Beach.

My friend and awesome photographer Kerri McCaffety, who captured the soul of Emeril's Delmonico.

And all the folks at William Morrow/HarperCollins who worked so hard to make this special book a reality.

Former Delmonico proprietors Rose LaFranca Dietrich (left) and Angie LaFranca Brown with Chef Emeril

And those who helped in our research:

Judge Dennis J. Waldron, who so graciously and generously shared his memories and memorabilia collection of old Delmonico.

Nancy Burris, head librarian at The Times-Picayune Library in New Orleans.

Mark Cave, curator of manuscripts, The Historic New Orleans Collection.

Pamela Arceneaux, reference librarian, The Historic New Orleans Collection.

Tom Fitzmorris, host of The Food Show on WSMB Radio and publisher of *The New Orleans Menu Daily*.

Gene Bourg, a food writer who knows just about everything there is to know about New Orleans restaurants.

Emeril's
DELMONICO

Introduction

In 1895 New Orleans recorded eight inches of snow on Valentine's Day. In the same year Charles "Buddy" Bolden, who some believe gave birth to improvised music that later became known as jazz, was at the peak of his career. The third Hotel St. Charles, designed by architect Thomas Sully, was completed. The Hennen Building, at the corner of Common and Carondelet, was finished, and at ten stories high, became the city's first skyscraper. The Dr. Tichenor Antiseptic Waltz was written by Louis Blake and published by the Sherrouse Medicine Company, Ltd., based in New Orleans. It was also in the year 1895 that Delmonico opened its doors at the corner of St.

Charles Avenue and Erato Street in what is now the Lower Garden District. Seventy years after the original Delmonico's, of New York opened, Anthony Commander, who owned a saloon on Magazine Street in New Orleans, was able to obtain the blessings of the New York family to open an independent branch of the renowned New York City establishment in the Crescent City. It was destined to become one of the most popular and best-loved restaurants in the city, especially by local residents.

The Delmonico's Restaurant in New York, which began in 1827 as a small café and pastry shop at 23 William Street in what is now the Financial District in lower Manhattan, expanded next door and by March 1830 had the distinction of becoming the first restaurant or public dining room to open in the United States. Their policy from the very beginning was to serve the finest quality foods in an impeccable manner. The "Great Fire" of 1835 destroyed much of lower Manhattan, including the restaurant on William Street, so the brothers set about remodeling part of the lodging house to accommodate the restaurant while they began construction nearby for a new building to house their restaurant, which opened in 1836. The three-and-a-half story construction featured inlaid floors and grand dining rooms decorated with expensive furnishings. The kitchen was one of the finest in the city and the wine cellar held sixteen thousand bottles of wine.

The restaurant was always on the cutting edge, serving an extensive menu of 370 items, and celebrities from around the world found their way to this magnificent establishment. Many classics of American cuisine are said to have originated at Delmonico's during the tenure of chef Charles Ranhofer, including lobster Newburg, Chicken à la King (p. 154), eggs benedict, and Baked Alaska (page 227).

It enjoyed grand times and great success, but the continuing escalation of food costs, the deaths of family members that led to changes in ownership and managers, as well as battles between siblings and owners, and then the final blow—Prohibition—brought the business to its knees. On May 21, 1923, a final dinner was held, and just less than a century since the first Delmonico's Restaurant was opened in New York, the institution died. (Note: Neither the current Delmonico's Restaurant at Beaver and South William streets nor the Delmonico Hotel on Park Avenue has any connection with the Delmonico family or the original business.)

But the independent Delmonico in New Orleans lived on and thrived.

Not much is known about Anthony Commander. We do know that he was the youngest brother of Emile Commander, who opened a saloon that he dubbed Commander's Palace in 1880 on the corner of Washington Avenue and Coliseum Street in the Garden District in New Orleans. The establishment is now the famed Commander's Palace, owned and operated by the Brennan family.

A third brother, Charles J., was a prominent businessman, who with Emile and their grandfather Peter owned a grocery business, a broom factory, and at one time had a commercial orange grove in Metairie, a suburb of New Orleans.

We also know that Mr. Commander opened the New Orleans Delmonico in a building built in 1890 as a one-story dairy creamery that later gained a second story by 1911. The top floor served as a gymnasium where gentlemen in bow ties boxed to work off some of the luncheon specials. (Photographs of this era grace the walls of the elegant bar at Emeril's Delmonico today.)

The menu under Mr. Commander's ownership reflected his association with Delmonico's in New York, featuring steaks and French-style dishes, but also included classic New Orleans–style dishes.

The restaurant became a favorite dining spot for local businessmen who had offices in the neighborhood, but because of some personal business problems, Mr. Commander handed the torch of ownership to Anthony LaFranca in 1911.

LaFranca, at age twelve, came from Sicily to New Orleans where he began working at Tranchina's Restaurant on Carondelet Street and Howard Avenue. It was there that LaFranca met his bride, Marie Masset. Her grandfather was the proprietor of the restaurant. With the help from the Eureka Homestead Society and a short-lived partnership with Joseph Smurchich, who lived on Euterpe Street behind the restaurant, LaFranca purchased Delmonico.

When LaFranca began active management of the restaurant, the two-door entrance to the ornate Edwardian building was highlighted by the words *Restaurant Café*. A corner lamppost of three globular lights stood at the entrance at Erato and St. Charles. The windows and fanlights over the entrance were of leaded glass and the floors were of an intricate tile design in the pattern of an Oriental carpet, which created an elegant atmosphere.

When Anthony married Marie Masset in 1916, the gymnasium was converted to a residence where their daughters, Angela (Angie) and Rose Marie, were born.

The restaurant thrived. Diners enjoyed Italian, French, and New Orleans dishes along with cocktails and good wine.

But in 1943 Anthony died and Marie, as hostess and owner, took over the reins of the restaurant. In 1944, the exterior façade was changed.

A prominent local architect, August Perez, was hired to do structural work, and another local architect, Merlin McCullar, changed the interior to French Provençal, adding oak wainscoting and large oak doors to create a more formal atmosphere. Elegant furniture and chandeliers from Henry Stern's antiques shop in Royal Street in the French Quarter graced the dining rooms, which had seventeen-foot ceilings. The bar area, popular with male customers, provided an informal club atmosphere.

It was during this period that Mrs. LaFranca commissioned John McCrady, who was probably the best exponent of regionalism working in the South, to paint the large oil painting *Steamboat 'Round the Bend*, depicting the dramatic race of the paddle wheelers *Natchez* and *Robert E. Lee* steaming down the Mississippi River in the 1860s, to hang behind the bar. McCrady was paid with dinners, drinks, and an unknown fee for his work, which took a year to complete. (The painting was sold at auction for $280,000 in 1997.)

The menu was revised and expanded, and included such classics as Oysters Rockefeller and Oysters Bienville, as well as the restaurant's signature oyster sampler—Oysters Delmonico—topped with crabmeat and melted cheese. Creole specialties such as shrimp remoulade, turtle soup, trout amandine, and pompano *en papillote* were featured, as well as Kansas City beef—filet mignon, Kansas City strip, and rib eye. Italian specialties included spaghetti and *daube*, spaghetti *à la bordelaise*, and chicken cacciatore with noodles.

Mrs. LaFranca, known for her graciousness and creativity, guided the restaurant into its golden years that followed World War II. It became a favorite haunt of old-line New Orleans families, local businessmen, and theater stars such as Helen Hayes, Agnes Moorehead, and June Havoc, who came in to dine when they were in the city.

When Mrs. LaFranca died in 1975, Angie Brown and Rose Dietrich took over the business and did so with great graciousness. One or both of the ladies were always at the front door to meet and greet their loyal customers. Being born and raised in the restaurant, they were well aware of their customers' likes, dislikes, and special needs.

One customer didn't like his oysters on the half shell to be watery, so when the ladies knew he was coming, they would drain the oysters on crushed ice just for him. Another local gentleman, Mr. Manheim, always wanted to sit at Table 16 and he favored frog's legs. And yet another regular customer loved roast beef sandwiches, but didn't want the gravy to drip, so, of course, that was taken care of before it left the kitchen.

It was this attention to detail and their genuine concern for their customers that made the establishment so well loved by their guests, many of whom became lifelong personal friends.

The restaurant maintained its customer base and remained a timeless Creole dining haven, celebrating its one hundredth anniversary in 1995 with a multicourse feast featuring several signature dishes paired with wines.

Delmonico was one of the few restaurants in New Orleans (other than Antoine's and Galatoire's) that could claim a kitchen staff whose youngest staff member had been there for at least a quarter of a century. Ernest "Jitterbug" Rome, one of the cooks, began as a porter in 1939 and worked his way up. Elmer Decquir was with Delmonico for over forty years and has a daughter named Delco after the restaurant. Kennis Leonard started working in 1947. Irene Polk came in 1957, and later Atwood Davis. They worked together until 1997 when the ladies sold Delmonico.

After 102 years on St. Charles Avenue, the ladies decided that it was time for the restaurant to enter a new era. After the last of the Carnival parades on the Monday before Mardi Gras in 1997, the doors were closed.

For years Delmonico was closed to the public on Mardi Gras day. "We were always at the restaurant on Mardi Gras with our families to toast the captains of the parades who stopped in front. Pete Fountain and his Half Fast Marching Club would stop in front of the restaurant because we had food and drinks for them. We could repair their costumes if they had torn them along the way while they serenaded our guests," remembered Angie.

On that Mardi Gras day of 1997, Pete Fountain and his club halted, as usual, in front of the restaurant, now empty and quiet, and played taps in honor of his old friends.

The *Times-Picayune* restaurant writer Craig LaBan in his *Eating Out* column of February 11,

1997, noted, "dinner is over at Delmonico." Ron Chapman, a columnist for *The St. Bernard Voice*, another local newspaper, devoted his entire editorial on February 28, 1997, to the sad occasion of the restaurant's closing. "It was like losing a dear friend . . . a member of the family . . . a piece of New Orleans' rich history. When you walked into Delmonico, you were greeted as a family guest. There were no strangers. Regular customers grew to know one another and generated an even greater sense of family and intimacy."

Like so many other customers, he recalled the birthdays, anniversaries, weddings, and other cherished moments spent in this congenial setting. (Mention Delmonico to any number of New Orleanians of several generations, and they'll tell you a story about their many personal experiences at the restaurant.) Dennis J. Waldron, now a judge in the Orleans Parish Criminal District Court, frequented the restaurant with his mother when he was a young child. Later, after he married, he and his family often gathered for special occasions such as birthdays and anniversaries. Judge Waldron has collected a wealth of mementos, including photographs, menus, and correspondence, to confirm his attachment to the LaFranca family.

"On Mardi Gras day, the ladies, Angie and Rose, would offer drinks in Styrofoam cups to members of the marching clubs as they passed by the restaurant, which was on the route of just about every parade," he remembers.

"Ah, we had great times. The ladies were as much a draw as was the food then. They were so attentive to all the customers, who were like their extended family. I remember well when my mother was ill they sent a meal to her in the hospital on Mother's Day. The staff at the restaurant was also considered their family. There was little turnover because everyone was treated so well and everyone from the cooks to the waiters and waitresses and busboys knew all the customers' quirks, which table they preferred or their favorite drinks and dishes."

Many couples tell of their courting days, dining at the restaurant, then getting engaged there, having their wedding reception at the restaurant, and who continue to celebrate their anniversary at Delmonico. One such couple is Joan and Terry Walker, the parents of Mauricio Andrade's wife. (Mauricio is Director of Operations for Emeril's restaurants.)

"I had my bridesmaids' luncheon there the week before the reception that was held upstairs at the restaurant following our wedding at Incarnate Word Church," relates Joan. The Walkers remember that at the reception, drinks were passed on trays, as were hot hors d'oeuvres such as breaded veal tidbits, oyster patties, and shrimp canapés.

Joan remembers changing into her going-away suit upstairs, where Rose and her husband lived. "And we went back a year later for our first anniversary and continued to go often for special occasions. Of course, we still go there," says Terry.

In March 1997, it was announced that Chef Emeril Lagasse was the new owner of Delmonico. Lagasse, with two very successful restaurants (Emeril's and NOLA) under his belt in New Orleans, had plans to honor Delmonico's heritage and embrace its unique history, but it would indeed prove to be a challenge.

"When I took over ownership of Delmonico, I promised Rose and Angie I would make them proud," says Emeril. "It was my vision to preserve the traditional and classic origins of the restaurant and pay homage to an establishment that had been in the community for one hundred years. Here was a grand dame on stately St. Charles Avenue that just needed to be fluffed up, renovated, and redecorated to bring it into a new age, but I wanted to retain a certain uptown ambience and graciousness."

The building underwent an extensive historic renovation under the direction of Peter Trapolin of Trapolin Architects in New Orleans. The interior designers, Ann Holden and Ann Dupuy, of Holden & Dupuy, created a very elegant, yet understated design in keeping with the historic nature of the building. It took a year (a very hectic one) to ready the restaurant for its grand opening on July 26, 1998, but the time and effort was well rewarded.

"Rose and Angie were thrilled by the renovation and happy to see the restaurant reborn," says Emeril.

"Like Mrs. LaFranca, I wanted a stunning painting to hang in the restaurant, so we commissioned world-renowned still-life artist Amy Weiskopf to paint an oil painting that showcases the classic elements of Creole cuisine. The bar area on the first floor pays homage to Anthony LaFranca's love for the sport of boxing with several original photographs of his second-story gymnasium, dating back to the early 1900s.

"The style of cuisine at Delmonico is Creole, and I wanted to keep many of the classic items from the former menu while adding inventive flavors of my own. We started tableside service and preparation in keeping with the classic style of Creole cuisine in New Orleans," says Emeril.

"Like the first Delmonico's in New York City and at the Delmonico of New Orleans, I want to keep the vision alive. There was always great attention to the quality of food, the consideration of the customers, fine wines, great art, and faultless service. The ambience of the renovated restaurant is exactly as we dreamed it to be—elegant, yet understated, luxurious, but comfortable. It is these tremendous responsibilities that give me the inspiration to keep this restaurant alive and well for many years to come.

Thanks, Rose and Angie, for giving me your blessings; a table is always here for you. I hope you and everyone will enjoy this homage to the past and continue these traditions into the future."

COCKTAILS & LIBATIONS, OLD AND NEW

There is much speculation as to how and when the cocktail originated. Stanley Clisby Arthur, in his book *Famous New Orleans Drinks*, claims that the cocktail was born in New Orleans. His account tells us that a gentleman by the name of Antoine Amedée Peychaud fled San Domingo in 1793 during the slave uprising and sought refuge in New Orleans. He brought with him a secret family recipe for a liquid tonic that was to become known as bitters. Peychaud, an apothecary, set up shop in a building that still stands in the 400 block of Royal Street in the French Quarter, where he dispensed his bitters combined with cognac to remedy stomach ailments.

Arthur tells us in the book:

"He poured portions into what we now know as an egg-cup, the old-fashioned double-end egg-cup. This particular piece of crockery, known to the French-speaking population as a *coquetier* (pronounced 'ko-k-tay'), was, in all probability, forerunner of the present jigger—the name given the double-end metal contraption holding a jigger (1½ ounces) in the big end, and a pony (1 ounce) in the little end, which we now use to measure portions for mixed drinks." Arthur goes on to explain that the pronunciation of the *coquetier* may have changed due to the "thickened tongues of the imbibers."

I don't know about you, but I like Arthur's theory!

The Sazerac, a New Orleans favorite, was created in New Orleans in the 1870s. Other local cocktail standards include Old Fashioneds and Manhattans (probably a favorite in the New York Delmonico in its heyday), as well as what we call eye-openers—bloody Marys, milk punches, and gin fizzes.

Take my advice, don't gulp the cocktails; rather, sip and enjoy them.

Absinthe Frappé

You'll find that New Orleans–style mixed drinks are as complex and distinctive as the food, and many call for absinthe or its modern-day substitutes.

Absinthe was a distilled aromatic liquor first commercialized in France in the early 1800s, achieving the height of its popularity in the 1850s. It was popular in New Orleans—most probably due to the city's busy port and French influences—and a popular French Quarter establishment still is called the Absinthe Bar from long ago. Many countries banned absinthe in 1915 due to the supposed toxicity and addictive properties of thujone, a chemical in the ingredient wormwood, although it was later determined that the combination of high alcohol with the thujone was probably to blame.

Other strong anise-flavored and herb-infused liquors were created when the wormwood-containing absinthes were banned. Of these anise-flavored liquors are the French Pernod and Ricard, and the American-made Herbsaint.

Crushed ice
1½ ounces Pernod or Herbsaint
¾ ounce Simple Syrup (page 23)

Put the crushed ice into a small rocks glass. Add the Pernod and the simple syrup along with a splash of water. Serve immediately.

Absinthe Suissesse

The Swiss Absinthe is a reference to one of the three categories of absinthe made in the 1800s. The name refers not to the manufacturing locale but to the highest grade of absinthe made.

In this cocktail, the anise-flavored liqueur is combined with cold half-and-half, but you can certainly use chilled milk or heavy cream. Orgeat syrup is made with almonds, sugar, and rose water or orange-flower water. It's available at most wine and liquor stores, and also can be found through online retailers.

1½ **ounces Pernod or Herbsaint**
¾ **ounce orgeat syrup**
1 **large egg white**

4 **ounces cold half-and-half**
Crushed ice

Combine all the ingredients in a cocktail shaker and shake vigorously. Strain into a chilled martini glass or white wine goblet and serve.

Delmonico Bloody Mary Mix

Spicy Bloody Marys are a favorite New Orleans eye-opener, particularly during Carnival season. Here's our recipe for a large batch that can be made in advance and kept chilled in the refrigerator until ready to use.

Four 32-ounce bottles tomato juice
8 ounces Worcestershire
3 tablespoons fresh lemon juice
1 tablespoon Emeril's Original Essence or Creole Seasoning (page 260)

1 tablespoon prepared horseradish, or to taste
1 teaspoon celery salt
1 teaspoon freshly ground black pepper

Combine all the ingredients in a gallon container. Shake well, adjust the seasoning to taste, and refrigerate until ready to serve.

*{ Bloody Mary Cocktail

MAKES 1 COCKTAIL

1½ ounces vodka
4 ounces Delmonico Bloody Mary Mix

Crushed ice
Lime or lemon wedge, for garnish

Combine the vodka and Bloody Mary mix in a large Old-Fashioned glass. Add the crushed ice to fill the glass, stir, and garnish with a lime or lemon wedge. Serve immediately.

Café Brûlot

I've heard that a visitor to New Orleans once described a version of *café brûlot* as "tasting the delights of Heaven while beholding the terrors of Hell." Let me tell you why.

The coffee, brandy, and spices are flamed tableside, usually with the house lights dimmed, for a dramatic effect and the taste is, well, heavenly.

Most restaurants that serve this have a special decorative *brûlot* bowl that is heated over a flame. The liquor is flambéed in the bowl and then ladled down long orange and lemon peel spirals back into the bowl, and then hot black coffee is added. A specially designed metal *brûlot* ladle has a small strainer at the end of it so that the citrus peel and spices can be filtered out. The finished drink is served either in demitasse cups or tall footed mugs often decorated with a full-length portrait of the devil, a reference to a similar flamed coffee drink called *café diable*, which has only lemon peel rather than both orange and lemon.

If you don't have a *brûlot* bowl, you can certainly use a chafing dish with a flame underneath.

1	medium thin-skinned orange	3	ounces brandy
1	medium thin-skinned lemon	1½	ounces Grand Marnier, Triple Sec, or other orange-flavored liqueur
10	whole cloves		
Two	2-inch cinnamon sticks, broken in half	2	cups hot, freshly brewed black coffee

1. Using a small, sharp knife, remove the peel from the orange in a long intact spiral, about 1 inch wide. Remove the peel from the lemon in the same manner, but about ½ inch wide. Discard the fruit or reserve for another use.

2. Stud the orange and lemon peels each with 5 cloves at intervals and place in a *brûlot* bowl or chafing dish with the flame on low. Add the cinnamon sticks, brandy, and liqueur and carefully ignite with a match. Hold the orange and lemon spirals with the prongs of a fork over the bowl, and, while the mixture is still flaming, ladle the flaming mixture down the peel 4 times into the bowl. Add the hot coffee and stir well with the ladle.

3. Ladle the hot coffee mixture into 4 or 6 demitasse cups, leaving the peels, cloves, and cinnamon sticks in the bowl. Serve immediately.

Ramos Gin Fizz

I understand that Henry C. Ramos invented the gin fizz at the Imperial Cabaret in New Orleans in 1888. It's said that the original formula was never disclosed, but this recipe is our take on it. This is another cocktail that is popular to serve at brunch and is reputed to have been a favorite of former Louisiana governor Huey P. Long. The half-and-half and egg white when shaken are what give the drink its frothy appearance. Orange-flower water is usually available at liquor stores or gourmet shops.

1½ ounces gin	Splash of fresh lemon juice
½ ounce Simple Syrup (page 23)	Splash of fresh lime juice
2 ounces half-and-half	Crushed ice
1 large egg white	Club soda
2 to 3 dashes of orange-flower water	1 lime wedge, for garnish

Combine all the ingredients except the ice, club soda, and lime wedge in a cocktail shaker and shake vigorously. Strain into a Collins glass filled with crushed ice and top off with a splash of club soda. Garnish with the lime wedge and serve.

Milk Punch

One of my favorite brunch libations, milk punch can be made with brandy, bourbon, Scotch, or dark rum, or a combination of these. This is the fun part—experiment to find your personal preference.

We use brandy, unless otherwise specified by the customer, and half-and-half, but you also can use whole milk or heavy cream. Oh, and never serve it over ice as that will water down the drink—a definite no-no.

4 ounces half-and-half	4 to 5 dashes of pure vanilla extract
1½ ounces brandy, bourbon, Scotch, or dark rum	Cracked Ice
	Pinch of grated nutmeg
½ ounce Simple Syrup (page 23)	

Combine the ingredients, except the nutmeg, in a cocktail shaker filled with cracked ice and shake vigorously for 30 seconds. Strain into a large Old-Fashioned glass, garnish with the nutmeg, and serve.

Manhattan Cocktail

MAKES 1 COCKTAIL

It is difficult to find the origin of the Manhattan cocktail. One source tells us that it was first made at the old Delmonico's Restaurant in New York during the 1890s. There it was made with Italian vermouth and bourbon whiskey. Another source says that it originated in New York City at the Manhattan Club in the 1870s. Like with food, local tastes differ so much from region to region, city to city, that every drink has dozens of variations.

In New Orleans the drink was, for a time, made with rye whiskey and sweet vermouth as well as a couple of dashes each of Peychaud and angostura bitters, garnished with a lemon peel. Some bartenders choose to garnish it with a maraschino cherry. You may also find a Manhattan made with brandy rather than whiskey in some parts of the country. Some experts tell you that it should be stirred not shaken. It really is all a matter of personal preference—experiment to find yours. Here is our version.

2 ounces Maker's Mark bourbon	Dash of maraschino cherry juice (from the jar)
½ ounce sweet vermouth	Crushed ice
Dash of angostura bitters	1 maraschino cherry (with stem), for garnish

Combine the bourbon, vermouth, bitters, cherry juice, and crushed ice in a cocktail shaker. Stir or shake. Strain into a chilled martini glass, garnish with the cherry, and serve.

Old-Fashioned

Some New Orleanians prefer rye whiskey to bourbon in their Old-Fashioneds. I sometimes like Scotch in mine. Your call!

1 orange slice	4 to 5 dashes of Peychaud bitters
1 maraschino cherry	Crushed ice
½ ounce Simple Syrup (page 23)	1½ ounces bourbon

Put the orange slice and cherry in a large Old-Fashioned glass, add the simple syrup and bitters, and muddle with a cocktail spoon. Add the ice and bourbon, and top with a splash of water. Serve immediately.

Planter's Punch

MAKES 1 COCKTAIL

Enjoy this on a hot summer afternoon when you can relax and sip away. Russ, our head bartender, says this recipe was originated by the Myer's Rum Company in the late nineteenth century.

1½ ounces Myer's dark rum
 1 ounce cranberry juice
 1 ounce fresh orange juice
 1 ounce grenadine
 ½ ounce fresh lemon juice

 ½ ounce fresh lime juice
    Crushed ice
 1 thin orange wedge, for garnish
 1 maraschino cherry, for garnish

Combine all the ingredients, except the orange and cherry, in a Collins glass. Toss into a cocktail shaker, shake once, and then pour back into the Collins glass. Skewer the orange and cherry on a toothpick and garnish the drink. Serve immediately.

Rob Roy

This is sometimes called a Scotch Manhattan because Scotch is substituted for the bourbon whiskey, with a lemon peel for the cherry garnish.

2 ounces Scotch
½ ounce sweet vermouth
Dash of angostura bitters, optional

Crushed ice
Lemon peel

Combine the Scotch, vermouth, and bitters, if using, in a cocktail shaker with ice and stir to chill. Strain into a small cocktail or martini glass. Twist the lemon peel over the drink, drop it in, and serve.

Sazerac

There is no question that this drink originated in New Orleans. When it was first created, it contained an imported Cognac, a brand that was made by a company called Sazerac-deFlorge et fils of Limoges, France. The mixture was changed in the late 1870s, when American rye whiskey was substituted for the brandy to please the tastes of New Orleanians. We use Old Overholt rye whiskey, but any good rye will do.

Splash of Herbsaint or Pernod
1½ ounces Old Overholt rye whiskey
½ ounce Simple Syrup (page 23)
3 dashes of Peychaud bitters

3 dashes of angostura bitters
Crushed ice
Lemon twist, for garnish

1. Splash the Herbsaint in a small rocks glass and twirl the glass around to evenly coat it.

2. Combine the rye, simple syrup, both bitters, and ice in a cocktail shaker. Stir and then strain into the glass with the Herbsaint. Garnish with the lemon twist and serve.

Delmonico Martini

When we reopened Delmonico I wanted to offer a classic gin martini, but I knew we had to adjust the ratio of gin to vermouth to accommodate modern tastes. We like to use Hendrick's dry gin, which is distilled and bottled in Scotland. Unlike other high-end gins, Hendrick's uses five simple botanicals—coriander, citrus peel, cucumber, juniper, and rose petals—sublime in my opinion.

Russ Bergeron, our head bartender, uses this trick: put the vermouth in a spray bottle and, rather than splash it in, spray the martini glass with it. Of course, add the vermouth to your personal taste.

2½ ounces Hendrick's gin
     Crushed ice

Splash or spray of dry vermouth
2   queen pimento-stuffed olives

Combine the gin and ice in a cocktail shaker and shake vigorously for 30 seconds. Mist a chilled martini glass with vermouth. Strain the gin into the martini glass, garnish with the olives, and serve.

Whiskey Sour

As far as I'm concerned, you can't go wrong with this drink. It's always popular and particularly great in that you can use bourbon, Scotch, Canadian whiskey, or Irish whiskey—whatever makes you happy.

1½ ounces whiskey
 4 ounces Sour Mix (recipe follows)

Crushed ice
1 maraschino cherry, for garnish

Combine the whiskey and sour mix in a large Old-Fashioned glass with ice. Stir, garnish with the cherry, and serve.

*}Sour Mix

Combine equal parts of fresh lemon juice and sugar, then dilute it with water to the desired concentration and personal taste. Stir to dissolve the sugar. (The sour mix will keep refrigerated in an airtight container for up to 1 week.)

Simple Syrup

This syrup is great to have on hand for sweetening all manner of drinks—from cocktails to iced tea. The recipe doubles and triples easily to suit your needs.

1 **cup sugar**
1 **cup water**

1. Combine the sugar and water in a small saucepan and bring to a boil. Reduce the heat to medium-low and simmer until the sugar dissolves, about 4 minutes. Remove from the heat and let cool.

2. Pour the syrup into a clean container and refrigerate until well chilled, 1 to 2 hours. (The syrup will keep refrigerated in an airtight container for up to 2 weeks.)

TO BEGIN

Not long after I opened Emeril's Delmonico, I received a book from René Nichlaus, who had been the executive chef in 1964 at the Roosevelt Hotel (now the Fairmont Hotel) in New Orleans. With the gift was also an old meat hook that the longtime butcher A. J. "Tony" Fasola used in the kitchen at the Roosevelt. Needless to say, I was touched by the thoughtfulness of Chef René. The book, *The Epicurean*, by Charles Ranhofer, onetime chef of Delmonico's in New York City, greatly influenced some of my ideas for the menu at Delmonico in New Orleans.

The thick volume (more than one thousand pages) was published in 1894 and I was amazed by its content. I can easily understand why Ranhofer was considered the greatest chef in America during his more than three decades (1862–1896) at the helm of the New York restaurant. I was so impressed with the book I went in search of another copy, which I found in New York City, and that one holds a place of honor in a shadow box in the foyer at Emeril's Delmonico today. (Ranhofer was trained in Paris before coming to America. He first worked in New York City, then spent time in Washington, D.C., and even a short time working in New Orleans before returning to New York, where he was hired by Lorenzo Delmonico in 1862.)

The book has pages of menus, then called Bills of Fare, which reaffirmed my intentions and ideas for the dishes I wanted to offer on our *carte du jour*.

Ranhofer's appetizers included oysters, escargots, shrimp, and crabmeat prepared in numerous ways. Here are some first courses that show some old and new techniques.

Shrimp Remoulade

Here's the old Delmonico restaurant's interpretation of this classic Creole dish. This sauce was so popular among New Orleanians that when the LaFranca sisters hosted the restaurant's one hundredth anniversary party in 1997, they gave each attendee a jar of this delicious sauce to take home!

1   small head iceberg lettuce, trimmed and shredded
2   dozen large shrimp, boiled, peeled, and deveined

1   cup Remoulade Sauce (recipe follows)
4   lemon wedges, for garnish

Mound the shredded lettuce on 4 chilled salad plates and arrange 6 shrimp on each. Spoon ¼ cup of the sauce on each serving and garnish each plate with a lemon wedge. Serve immediately.

⁎} Remoulade Sauce

There are two types of remoulade sauce—the classic French mayonnaise-based white sauce (more like what we Americans think of as tartar sauce) and the red-colored New Orleans Creole variety, of which this recipe is one.

The New Orleans–style sauce has whole-grain Creole mustard as its base, with a variety of chopped vegetables and spices giving it texture and piquancy. Some sauces have a loose consistency that's more like a salad dressing, while others, like this one, are tighter emulsion-based sauces. Some sauces contain a little mayonnaise or an egg as a thickener, and others use ketchup to deepen the color and sweeten the flavor; some are spicy, although others are mild. How they're made is a matter of house style or personal preference.

Remoulade sauce was served at the old Delmonico on boiled and peeled shrimp for Shrimp Remoulade, but it's a great complement to any type of boiled or fried seafood—from crawfish tails to catfish and soft-shell crabs. A variation on this is the fried green tomatoes with lump crabmeat and two remoulade sauces, one of the more popular of Emeril's Delmonico offerings, where both red and white remoulade sauces top the crabmeat and tomatoes.

½ cup Creole mustard or other mild whole-grain mustard	2 tablespoons sugar
	1½ tablespoons paprika
½ cup prepared horseradish	1½ teaspoons Worcestershire
¼ cup finely chopped yellow onions	1 teaspoon granulated garlic
¼ cup finely chopped green onions	¼ cup vegetable oil
¼ cup finely chopped celery	¼ cup red wine vinegar

1. Combine the mustard, horseradish, yellow onions, green onions, celery, sugar, paprika, Worcestershire, and garlic in the bowl of a standing mixer, and mix on medium speed until well blended. With the machine running, slowly add the oil in a steady stream and continue to mix until the mixture is thick and emulsified. Slowly add the vinegar in a steady stream and mix well to blend.

2. Transfer the sauce to an airtight container and refrigerate until well chilled before using, at least 2 hours. (Stored in an airtight container, this sauce will keep refrigerated for up to 5 days.)

Oysters Rockefeller

MAKES 2½ DOZEN OYSTERS, 4 TO 6 SERVINGS

This renowned baked oyster dish was created at Antoine's Restaurant in New Orleans in 1899, by then proprietor Jules Alciatore. According to legend, the dish was created as a substitute for baked snails, which were hard to obtain from France. It was named in honor of John D. Rockefeller, one of the world's wealthiest men, due to the sauce's intense richness.

The original Antoine's recipe is a secret, but New Orleans restaurants and home cooks have made variations on the dish for the last one hundred years. This is the old Delmonico restaurant's take, with the Rockefeller sauce base used not only to make the Oysters Rockefeller appetizer but also to spread on toast for canapés. The base, without the addition of oysters, can be made in advance and refrigerated, tightly covered, for up to three days.

Rock salt, for baking
2½ dozen oysters in their shells,
    freshly shucked and drained, and
    deeper bottom shells rinsed and
    reserved for baking

1   recipe Rockefeller Sauce Base
    (recipe follows)

1. Preheat the oven to 400°F. Spread a ½-inch-thick layer of rock salt on a large baking sheet and across the bottoms of 4 to 6 large plates. (Alternatively, if you have heat resistant plates, spread the plates with rock salt and place on a large baking sheet.) Set aside.

2. Arrange the reserved oyster shells on the prepared baking sheet (or on the prepared plates). Put 1 oyster in each shell and top with approximately 1½ tablespoons of the sauce, spreading the sauce evenly out to the edges of the shell to completely cover the oyster. (Alternatively, transfer the sauce to a pastry bag fitted with a plain tip and pipe the sauce over the oysters.) Bake until the sauce is lightly browned and the oysters begin to curl around the edges, about 20 minutes.

3. Using tongs or a spatula, carefully transfer the hot shells to the salt-covered plates (or onto cool base plates) and serve immediately.

*{Rockefeller Sauce Base

MAKES 2¾ CUPS

6 ounces fresh spinach, stems removed and rinsed	2 tablespoons Herbsaint or other anise-flavored liqueur, such as Pernod or pastis
8 tablespoons (1 stick) unsalted butter	¾ teaspoon salt
½ cup finely chopped yellow onions	¼ teaspoon freshly ground black pepper
¼ cup finely chopped celery	½ cup cracker meal or cracker crumbs
1 tablespoon minced garlic	5 drops of green food coloring, optional

1. Bring 1 quart of water to a boil in a medium pot. Add the spinach and cook until very tender and the water is green, 5 to 6 minutes. Drain the spinach in a colander set over a large bowl and reserve 2¾ cups of the cooking liquid. Let the spinach sit until cool enough to handle, finely chop, and set aside.

2. Melt the butter in a medium pot over medium-high heat. When the butter is foamy, add the onions, celery, and garlic and cook, stirring, until soft, about 3 minutes. Add the reserved spinach water, bring to a boil, and cook for 1 minute. Add the chopped spinach, Herbsaint, salt, and pepper and simmer, stirring occasionally, until the mixture reduces slightly, 10 minutes. Remove from the heat, add the cracker meal and food coloring, if using, and stir well to combine. Cool completely before using.

Oysters Rockefeller Canapés

MAKES 40 TO 52 CANAPÉS

Miss Angie remembers that these delicious canapés were served at the original Delmonico for special events such as weddings and birthday parties.

The number of canapés this recipe yields depends upon the size of the sliced bread and how thickly you spread the Rockefeller mixture on each piece. For a different look, cut the toasted bread into rounds with a cookie cutter before spreading on the Rockefeller mixture.

10 to 13 **slices white sandwich bread**
1 **dozen oysters, drained**
One **2-ounce can oil-packed anchovies**
2 **tablespoons Herbsaint or other anise-flavored liqueur, such as Pernod or pastis**

1½ **cups Rockefeller Sauce Base (page** 29**)**
1 **tablespoon freshly grated Romano**
½ **teaspoon Tabasco sauce**
⅓ to ½ **cup Fish Stock (page** 259**) or Shrimp Stock (page** 267**)**

1. Lightly toast the bread, remove the crusts, and set aside.

2. Bring a medium saucepan of water to a low boil. Add the oysters and poach until firm and the edges of the oysters curl, 1 to 2 minutes. Drain and transfer to an ice bath. Pat the oysters dry and finely chop.

3. Drain the anchovies, reserving the oil, and finely chop.

4. Combine the oysters, anchovies, anchovy oil, Herbsaint, Rockefeller Sauce Base, Romano, and Tabasco in a medium bowl and stir to combine. Add ⅓ cup of the stock and mix to a spreadable paste, adding more stock as needed to achieve a paste-like consistency.

5. Adjust the oven rack to the upper third of the oven and set the oven setting to broil.

6. Spread 3 to 4 tablespoons of the oyster mixture onto each slice of toasted bread, spreading all the way to the edges and smoothing the top. Cut diagonally to make 4 small triangles, or cut horizontally to make 4 small squares, and place on an ungreased baking sheet. Broil until the tops are lightly browned and the topping is hot, 1 to 3 minutes.

7. Remove from the oven and transfer with a spatula to a platter. Serve immediately.

Oysters Bienville

Both Antoine's and Arnaud's, two other long established New Orleans restaurants, are said to have originated this local baked oyster favorite. No matter who named it, it is a tribute to Sieur de Bienville, Jean Baptiste le Moyne, French founder of the City of New Orleans.

At Delmonico, we serve our hot oyster dishes on preheated plates lined with beds of rock salt. The hot salt ensures that the baked oysters stay hot and it also keeps the shells from sliding across the plates. If you don't have heat-resistant plates, spread a thick layer of rock salt on a baking sheet to bake the oysters, and then transfer the baked oysters to plates spread with a rock salt layer. Another preparation is to bake the shucked and drained oysters in shallow gratin dishes, topped with the sauce.

Rock salt, for baking	1/2 pound medium shrimp, peeled, deveined, and chopped
4 strips bacon, finely chopped	
1 cup finely chopped yellow onions	1/4 cup finely grated Parmigiano-Reggiano
1/2 teaspoon salt	4 teaspoons fresh lemon juice
1/4 teaspoon cayenne	1/4 cup chopped green onions (green parts only)
2 tablespoons unsalted butter	
1 teaspoon minced garlic	4 teaspoons finely chopped fresh parsley
3 tablespoons all-purpose flour	2 large egg yolks, lightly beaten
1 cup whole milk	2 dozen oysters in their shells, shucked, drained, and deeper bottom shells rinsed and reserved for baking
1/2 cup dry white wine	
1/2 cup finely chopped white button mushrooms	

1. Preheat the oven to 400°F. Spread a 1/2-inch-thick layer of rock salt on a large baking sheet and across the bottoms of 4 to 6 large plates. (Alternatively, if you have heat resistant plates, spread the plates with rock salt and place on a large baking sheet.) Set aside.

2. Fry the bacon in a large skillet over medium-high heat until just crisp, about 3 minutes. Add the yellow onions, salt, and cayenne and cook, stirring, for 2 minutes. Add the butter and garlic and cook, stirring, until the butter melts and the garlic is fragrant, 30 seconds to 1 minute. Add the flour and, stirring slowly and constantly, cook to form a light roux, 2 minutes. Add the milk and wine, stir to blend, and bring to a boil. Reduce the heat to medium, add the mushrooms and shrimp and stir to blend. Cook, stirring, until the mixture is thick, 3 to 4 minutes. Add the cheese, lemon juice, green onions, and parsley and stir to blend. Remove from the heat, add the egg yolks, and blend well. Let cool to room temperature.

3. Arrange the reserved oyster shells on the prepared baking sheet (or on the prepared plates). Place 1 oyster in each shell and top with about 1½ tablespoons of the sauce, spreading the sauce evenly out to the edges of the shell to completely cover the oyster. (Alternatively, transfer the sauce to a pastry bag fitted with a plain tip and pipe the sauce over the oysters.) Bake until the sauce is lightly browned and the oysters begin to curl around the edges, about 20 minutes.

4. Using tongs or a spatula, carefully transfer the hot shells to the salt-covered plates (or onto cool base plates) and serve immediately.

Oysters *on the* Half Shell *with* Shallot–Black Pepper Mignonette *and* Grapefruit Sorbet

Louisiana oysters have been harvested commercially since the 1880s and today the state is the number one domestic oyster producer, accounting for 30 percent of the American market. It's no wonder that oysters, prepared a number of ways, have long been popular on New Orleans menus. I like them any which way, but especially raw on the half shell. Instead of the ketchup-based cocktail sauce that's usually served with raw oysters in New Orleans, the French mignonette sauce is more appropriate in our elegant restaurant. Cold, plump salty oysters on the half shell drizzled with the cool sauce and topped with the cold sorbet—what a great starter!

¼ cup Champagne vinegar	6 tablespoons kosher salt
3 tablespoons dry red wine	2 dozen freshly shucked oysters
1 tablespoon finely chopped shallots	on the half shell
2 teaspoons finely crushed white pepper	½ cup Grapefruit Sorbet (recipe follows)
6 cups finely crushed ice	

1. Combine the vinegar, wine, shallots, and white pepper in a small bowl and whisk to blend. Set aside.

2. Put 1 cup of the ice in each of 6 shallow rimmed soup bowls and press down gently to make a level bed. Sprinkle each bed of ice with 1 tablespoon of the kosher salt and arrange 4 oysters in their shells on top.

3. Whisk the mignonette once more before drizzling 1 teaspoon over each oyster.

4. Using a teaspoon dipped in hot water, scoop out small spoonfuls of the sorbet. Place 1 teaspoon of sorbet on each oyster and serve immediately.

✻ Grapefruit Sorbet

MAKES ABOUT 1 QUART

A few years back, then Emeril's Delmonico chef Neal Swidler and pastry chef Blair Kolb created this sorbet as a tart counterpart to briny oysters. It's easily made in a home ice cream maker and is a refreshing treat on its own, particularly on a hot summer afternoon.

1 cup sugar	4 cups fresh grapefruit juice
1 cup water	1 teaspoon salt

1. Combine the sugar and water in a medium, heavy saucepan over high heat. Reduce the heat to medium-low. Simmer, stirring, until the sugar is completely dissolved, 6 to 8 minutes. Remove from the heat and cool to room temperature. Add the grapefruit juice and salt and stir to blend.

2. Pour the mixture into an ice cream machine and churn according to the manufacturer's instructions. Pack the sorbet into an airtight container and freeze for at least 2 hours before serving. Keep frozen until ready to serve. (Alternatively, pour the mixture into a 2-quart plastic container or metal baking pan. Put into the freezer and allow the mixture to get very cold. Stir vigorously with a fork every 45 minutes until it is completely frozen, about 4 hours. Transfer to an airtight container and freeze until ready to serve.)

Crabmeat Remick

MAKES 6 SERVINGS

Crabmeat Remick has been a New Orleans menu standard since the 1920s, when it first appeared on the menu at the Pontchartrain Hotel's Caribbean Room, another fine New Orleans establishment down the street from Delmonico on St. Charles Avenue. The popularity of the dish spread and, from what I can understand, it also was a favorite of the celebrities who packed the Stork Club and the Eden Rock in New York over fifty years ago.

Crabmeat Remick is such a local classic that I put it on the menu when we reopened Delmonico in 1998. It can be made several hours ahead, refrigerated, and then baked just before serving.

1½ teaspoons unsalted butter
1 cup Mayonnaise (page 264) or store-bought mayonnaise
½ cup chili sauce
2 tablespoons finely chopped green onions
1 tablespoon fresh lemon juice
1 teaspoon minced garlic
1 teaspoon dry mustard
1 teaspoon tarragon vinegar
1 teaspoon paprika

1 teaspoon hot sauce
1 pound lump crabmeat, picked over for shells and cartilage
6 ounces (7 strips) bacon, crisply fried and crumbled
6 tablespoons freshly grated Parmigiano-Reggiano
1 recipe Large Croutons (page 263) or toast points

1. Preheat the oven to 400°F. Grease six 4-ounce ramekins with the butter, place on a baking sheet, and set aside.

2. Combine the mayonnaise, chili sauce, green onions, lemon juice, garlic, mustard, vinegar, paprika, and hot sauce in a large bowl and mix well. Fold in the crabmeat and mix until well coated with the sauce, being careful not to break up the lumps. Divide the mixture among the prepared dishes and top each portion with 1 tablespoon each of the bacon and cheese. Bake until the crabmeat is hot and the cheese is golden brown on top, 8 to 10 minutes.

3. Carefully transfer the ramekins to 6 plates and serve immediately with croutons on the side.

Crabmeat Imperial

MAKES 4 SERVINGS

Crabmeat Imperial was on the menu as an entrée when I was appointed executive chef at Commander's Palace twenty years ago. Fresh lump crabmeat combined with a tart mayonnaise mixture was served in a large deep shell and it was very popular. But as the menu evolved when guests began asking for lighter dishes, this old favorite fell by the wayside.

I wanted to bring it back when I reopened Delmonico, but I changed the ingredients a bit, adding fresh herbs and a gratinée of bread crumbs and cheese. It's a great beginning for any meal.

2 teaspoons olive oil

2 tablespoons finely chopped green bell peppers

2 tablespoons finely chopped red bell peppers

2 tablespoons minced shallots

1 teaspoon minced garlic

1 cup Mayonnaise (page 264) or store-bought mayonnaise

1 tablespoon finely chopped fresh parsley

1½ teaspoons finely chopped fresh tarragon

½ teaspoon salt

¼ teaspoon ground white pepper

1 pound lump crabmeat, picked over for shells and cartilage

¼ cup fine dry bread crumbs

¼ cup finely grated Parmigiano-Reggiano

Chopped fresh parsley, for garnish

1 recipe Large Croutons (page 263) or toast points

1. Preheat the oven to 350°F. Lightly grease four 4-ounce scallop shells or shallow ramekins and place on a baking sheet. Set aside.

2. Heat the oil in a small skillet over medium heat. Add the green and red bell peppers and the shallots and cook, stirring, for 1 minute. Add the garlic and cook until fragrant, about 30 seconds. Let cool slightly.

3. Combine the mayonnaise, bell pepper mixture, finely chopped parsley, tarragon, salt, and white pepper in a medium bowl. Gently fold in the crabmeat, being careful not to break up the lumps. Divide the mixture equally among the prepared scallop shells or ramekins. Sprinkle each serving with 1 tablespoon of the bread crumbs and 1 tablespoon of the cheese. Put the shells on a baking sheet and bake until the crabmeat is hot and the tops are light golden brown, 8 to 10 minutes.

4. Place the shells on 4 plates, garnish with parsley, and serve immediately with croutons or toast points on the side.

The crabmeat is usually baked inside a large scallop shell. If you don't have such shells on hand, use a shallow 4-ounce baking dish. And don't be misled by the seemingly small portion size of this dish—the rich sauce is very filling.

Lump Crabmeat *and* Brie Strudels
with Herbsaint Cream Glaze

MAKES 4 SERVINGS

Since crabmeat is a staple on Creole menus because of its availability from the Gulf of Mexico, I love to find different ways to use it on our Delmonico menu. The kitchen staff and I played around with different combinations and came up with a mixture of crabmeat and herbs to wrap in phyllo, then drizzled with a cream sauce flavored with Herbsaint.

Herbsaint is an anise-flavored liqueur with complex herb-infused flavors and bright yellow color that was developed as a substitute for absinthe—an earlier addictive liqueur—when it was banned. It is no longer produced here; however, it remains a popular ingredient in Creole cooking, such as Oysters Rockefeller (page 28), and in local cocktails, such as the Sazerac (page 20).

⅓	cup Clarified Butter (page 257) or olive oil	½	teaspoon chopped fresh tarragon
½	pound lump crabmeat, picked over for shells and cartilage	¼	teaspoon salt
		⅛	teaspoon ground white pepper
1	tablespoon extra virgin olive oil	8	sheets phyllo pastry, thawed
1½	teaspoons fresh lemon juice	Four	1-ounce pieces Brie cheese with rind, ½ inch by 2½ inches each
½	teaspoon chopped fresh chervil		
½	teaspoon chopped fresh parsley	1	recipe Herbsaint Cream Glaze (recipe follows)

1. Preheat the oven to 375°F.

2. Using a pastry brush, lightly coat the bottom of a large baking sheet with clarified butter and set aside.

3. Combine the crabmeat, olive oil, lemon juice, chervil, parsley, tarragon, salt, and pepper in a bowl and stir, being careful not to break up the lumps. Set aside.

4. Stack the phyllo sheets on a work surface and cut into a 9-inch square. Discard the trimmed phyllo or reserve for another use. Lay 1 phyllo sheet on the work surface, with one of the points toward you. Using a pastry brush, lightly brush the top with clarified butter. Stack a second phyllo sheet on the first and brush the top lightly with clarified butter. Place 1 slice of Brie just below the center of the wrapper, above the bottom point. Spread one-quarter of the crabmeat filling evenly over the Brie. Pull the bottom point up over the filling, fold over the sides, and roll up to completely enclose the filling. Brush the seam lightly with clarified butter to seal, and place the strudel seam side down on the prepared baking sheet. Continue with the remaining phyllo, Brie, and crabmeat filling. Lightly coat the top of each crab strudel with the remaining clarified butter and bake until golden brown and the cheese is melted, 20 to 22 minutes. Cut each pastry in half on the diagonal.

5. To serve, spoon the cream glaze onto the center of 4 plates. Stand 1 pastry half vertically and lay the other across the plate in the sauce. Serve immediately.

❊{ Herbsaint Cream Glaze

MAKES ABOUT 1½ CUPS

We created this particular sauce to go on the Crabmeat and Brie Strudels, but believe me, it's fantastic to use with oysters. You might want to try poaching drained freshly shucked oysters in the sauce and serving them on Large Croutons (page 263) for another type of appetizer.

3 tablespoons cold unsalted butter	3 ounces fresh spinach, rinsed, patted dry, and coarsely chopped (about 1 cup packed)
¼ cup minced shallots	
½ cup plus 1 teaspoon Herbsaint or other anise-flavored liqueur, such as Pernod or pastis	1 teaspoon fresh lemon juice
	⅜ teaspoon salt
	¼ teaspoon ground white pepper
2 cups heavy cream	

1. Melt 2 tablespoons of the butter in a medium pot over medium-high heat. Add the shallots and cook, stirring, until soft, 2 minutes. Add ½ cup of the Herbsaint, bring to a boil, and cook for 2 minutes. Add the cream and return to a boil. Reduce the heat to medium and simmer until reduced to about 1½ cups, about 20 minutes. Add the spinach and cook, stirring, until wilted, about 1 minute. Add the lemon juice, salt, pepper, and the remaining 1 tablespoon butter and stir to incorporate.

2. Remove from the heat and purée with a handheld immersion blender, or in batches in a blender or food processor. Strain through a fine-mesh strainer into a medium saucepan, add the remaining 1 teaspoon Herbsaint, and serve immediately, or cover to keep warm until ready to serve.

Pan-Fried Crab Cakes *with* Chili-Lime Dressing, Mango-Cucumber Relish, *and* Mixed Greens

MAKES 4 TO 8 SERVINGS

Crab cakes, usually served with tartar sauce, have long been a popular dish on the New Orleans table, but when our chef de cuisine, Shane Pritchett, began experimenting with different toppings he came up with this combo—fresh lime juice and chili garlic sauce—to bring this dish up to another level. The cool cucumber relish smoothes out the tangy lime sauce.

4½ tablespoons unsalted butter, melted and cooled slightly

3 tablespoons Mayonnaise (page 264) or store-bought mayonnaise

1½ tablespoons fresh lemon juice

1½ tablespoons extra virgin olive oil

1 tablespoon chopped green onions (green parts only)

1 tablespoon chopped chives

1 tablespoon chopped fresh parsley

¾ teaspoon salt

½ teaspoon freshly ground black pepper

⅛ teaspoon cayenne

1 pound jumbo lump crabmeat, picked over for shells and cartilage

6 tablespoons fine dry bread crumbs

⅓ cup all-purpose flour

1 large egg

2 tablespoons milk

1½ cups panko (Japanese bread crumbs)

½ cup vegetable oil

1 recipe Mango-Cucumber Relish (recipe follows)

1 recipe Chili-Lime Dressing (recipe follows)

1 cup mesclun or assorted baby greens, for garnish

Emeril's Delmonico crab cakes are made with jumbo lump crabmeat from locally caught blue crabs. This meat consists of the largest chunks that come from the hind leg area of the crabs. Jumbo lump is the most expensive type of crabmeat available and sometimes can be hard to obtain. If you use lump crabmeat, claw meat, or canned crabmeat, the meat will not be as chunky and also will be moister, requiring more bread crumbs for the mixture to hold together.

Panko are Japanese bread crumbs. Their coarser texture and larger, flakier crumbs absorb less grease during cooking for a lighter, crisper breading that we prefer for our crab cakes. They can be found in the Asian food section of supermarkets and at Asian markets, and also can be ordered online. If you can't find panko, substitute regular bread crumbs.

One crab cake per serving probably is ample, depending on your appetite and at which course these are served. Or make small cakes from this recipe to serve as hors d'oeuvres.

1. Line a baking sheet with parchment paper and set aside.

2. Combine the butter, mayonnaise, lemon juice, olive oil, green onions, chives, and parsley in the bowl of a food processor and process until well blended and slightly thickened. Add the salt, pepper, and cayenne and process for 15 seconds to blend. Transfer to a medium bowl with the crabmeat and bread crumbs and fold gently to mix, being careful not to break up the lumps.

3. Form the crabmeat mixture into eight 2½ to 3-inch-round cakes, about 2½ ounces each, and pack gently but firmly. Place on the prepared baking sheet, cover with plastic wrap, and refrigerate until well chilled, 1 to 2 hours.

4. Place the flour in a small shallow dish. In a separate bowl, whisk together the egg and milk to make an egg wash. Place the panko in a third shallow dish.

5. Dredge each crab cake in the flour, then in the egg wash, and then in the panko crumbs, shaking to remove any excess breading. (Note that the crab cake mixture will be slightly wet and should be handled carefully. If the crab cakes become too loose during the breading, they can be refrigerated again until firm.) Set aside.

6. Heat ¼ cup of the vegetable oil in a large, heavy skillet over medium heat. Pan-fry the crab cakes 3 or 4 at a time until golden brown, about 4½ minutes per side. Add more oil as needed. Drain the crab cakes on paper towels.

7. To serve, arrange 2 crab cakes on each of 4 plates and top with 2 tablespoons of the Mango-Cucumber Relish. Drizzle the Chili-Lime Dressing around the crab cakes, garnish each plate with greens, and serve immediately.

✳{ Mango-Cucumber Relish

MAKES 1¼ CUPS

½ cup peeled, seeded, and diced mangoes	1 tablespoon rice wine vinegar
½ cup peeled, seeded, and diced cucumbers	1½ teaspoons extra virgin olive oil
¼ cup seeded and diced red bell peppers	

Place the mangoes, cucumbers, and bell peppers in a medium bowl and toss gently with the vinegar and oil to coat. Cover and chill until ready to serve. (The relish can be made up to 2 hours in advance.)

*{Chili-Lime Dressing

There are several commercially available brands of chili garlic sauce available at Asian markets. Made from coarsely ground chiles and garlic, this medium-hot sauce can be used as a condiment or in cooking, and is delicious added to marinades, stir-fries, and sauces.

6 tablespoons chili garlic sauce	¾ teaspoon sesame oil
2 tablespoons fresh lime juice	¼ cup olive oil
2 teaspoons sesame seeds, lightly toasted	

Combine the chili garlic sauce, lime juice, sesame seeds, and sesame oil in a medium bowl and stir well to combine. Whisking, slowly add the olive oil in a steady stream and whisk to combine. Set aside until ready to serve. (The chili-lime dressing will keep, covered, in the refrigerator for up to 3 days.)

Crawfish *in* Spicy Cream Sauce

Crawfish, those delicate freshwater crustaceans, can be prepared in all kinds of ways, and when they're plentiful in Louisiana, from January to June, we like to include them on our menu. Served in puff pastry with a kicked-up hot sauce, this is one of my personal favorites.

One 17¼-ounce package puff pastry
(2 sheets), thawed

½ pound peeled crawfish tails

1 teaspoon Emeril's Original Essence or
Creole Seasoning (page 260)

1 tablespoon olive oil

1 tablespoon minced shallots

1½ teaspoons minced garlic

1 cup heavy cream

1½ teaspoons hot sauce

1½ teaspoons Worcestershire

¼ teaspoon salt

⅛ teaspoon ground white pepper

2 tablespoons finely chopped green onions
(green parts only)

1 tablespoon unsalted butter

8 whole chives, for garnish

1. Preheat the oven to 400°F. Line a baking sheet with parchment paper and set aside.

2. Roll out the puff pastry on a lightly floured surface to a 13 x 12-inch rectangle. Trim the pastry to a 10-inch square and cut into quarters to make four 5-inch squares.

3. Fold 1 square diagonally in half to form a triangle and place on a work surface with the folded side closest to you.

4. Starting ½ inch from the bottom corners of the triangle, cut a ½-inch border along the top two sides, leaving the two bottom corners intact. Unfold the triangle and using your finger, brush the ½-inch strips with water. Fold the right strip underneath the left strip and the left strip over the right strip, wet sides down, and press firmly into place to make a diamond shape with raised borders. Repeat the process with the remaining squares. Place the pastries on the prepared baking sheet and bake until set and light golden brown, 18 to 20 minutes.

5. Transfer the pastries to a wire rack to cool.

6. Season the crawfish with the Essence.

Rather than serving the crawfish in these puff pastry boxes, you can certainly use store-bought pastry shells or phyllo cups, or serve these on split Herb Biscuits (page 156). Or toss the crawfish sauce with linguine or angel hair for a flavorful pasta course.

7. Heat the olive oil in a large skillet or sauté pan over medium-high heat. Add the shallots and garlic and cook, stirring, until fragrant, about 30 seconds. Add the crawfish and cook, stirring, for 1 minute. Add the cream, hot sauce, Worcestershire, salt, and pepper and bring to a boil. Reduce the heat and simmer until the sauce is thick and the volume is reduced by half, 2 to 3 minutes. Add the green onions and butter, stir, and remove from the heat. Adjust the seasoning to taste.

8. To serve, spoon about 1 tablespoon of the sauce into the center of 4 plates and arrange the pastries on top. Fill the pastries with the crawfish and the remaining sauce, garnish the top of each with 2 chives, and serve immediately.

Escargots *with* Garlic Butter *and* Parsley *and* Puff Pastry Cheese Sticks

MAKES 4 SERVINGS

There's no way around it—escargots are snails, of which there are 116 edible varieties raised around the world. But keep in mind that snails have been considered a culinary delicacy since Roman times and particularly in France, where they are a renowned specialty of the Burgundy region. This classic preparation of snails cooked in garlic butter often is found on menus by its French name, *Escargots Bourguignonne* (snails in the Burgundian style).

Escargots have long been a favorite of New Orleans diners. Typically, escargots are served in specially designed porcelain dishes that have six indentations along the bottom for placing the snails and butter, but you can substitute shallow gratin dishes..

One 7.5-**ounce can escargots**
  (2 dozen snails)
1 **recipe Garlic Compound Butter**
  (recipe follows)

½ **recipe Puff Pastry Cheese Sticks**
  (recipe follows)

1. Preheat the oven to 400°F.

2. Place the escargots in a colander, rinse well under cold running water, drain, and pat dry.

3. Place 1 snail in each of the 6 indentations of 4 snail dishes, or arrange 6 snails in each of four 6-ounce shallow gratin dishes or ramekins. Place the dishes on a large baking sheet.

4. Thinly slice the garlic butter into 24 thin slices, 1 teaspoon each. Arrange 1 butter slice on each snail and bake until the butter is melted and bubbly, about 10 minutes.

5. Carefully place the hot dishes on 4 serving plates, arrange 3 cheese sticks on each plate, and serve hot.

⁕}Garlic Compound Butter

MAKES ½ CUP

8	tablespoons (1 stick) unsalted butter, at room temperature	
2	tablespoons chopped fresh parsley	
1	tablespoon minced garlic	
2	teaspoons fresh lemon juice	
¼	teaspoon salt	
	Pinch of freshly ground black pepper	

1. Combine all the ingredients in a food processor and mix well. (Alternatively, place the butter in a medium bowl and cream with a wooden spoon or rubber spatula. Add the remaining ingredients and mix well.)

2. Spoon the butter mixture into the center of a large sheet of parchment or wax paper, or plastic wrap, forming a log 1 to 1½ inches in diameter. Fold the wrap over the butter and gently push in and under to form a smooth cylinder. Twist the ends to seal. Refrigerate until firm, about 1 hour. (Refrigerate for up to 1 week or freeze for up to 1 month.)

*⟩ Puff Pastry Cheese Sticks

MAKES 2 DOZEN CHEESE STICKS

These cheese sticks also are a marvelous accompaniment to salads and soups, and they make easy and quick hors d'oeuvres for the cocktail hour.

One-half 17¼-ounce package puff pastry (1 sheet), thawed	¼ cup grated Parmigiano-Reggiano
1 large egg	¼ teaspoon Emeril's Original Essence or Creole Seasoning (page 260)
1 tablespoon water	

1. Preheat the oven to 400°F.

2. Roll out the pastry sheet to a 12 x 18-inch rectangle on a lightly floured surface.

3. Beat together the egg and water in a small bowl to make an egg wash. Lightly brush the top of the pastry with the egg wash. Sprinkle the cheese and Essence over half of the sheet. Fold the other half over the cheese, pressing firmly to adhere, then lightly roll with a rolling pin. With a knife, trim the edges.

4. With the long edge facing you, cut the dough crosswise using a pizza wheel or a long thin knife into 24 individual strips, about ½ inch wide. Twist each 3 times to make a spiral and place on an ungreased baking sheet at least 1 inch apart. Bake until golden brown and risen, 10 to 12 minutes.

5. Serve hot or at room temperature. (The cheese sticks will keep in an airtight container at room temperature for up to 2 days.)

Frog's Legs Bordelaise

MAKES 4 SERVINGS

The regulars of the old Delmonico restaurant were known for their favorite dishes as well as their preferred tables. According to Miss Rose, "Mr. Manheim loved frog's legs and always had to eat at Table Sixteen in the downstairs dining room." Frog's legs have fallen somewhat out of fashion on today's menus, although they make a delicious appetizer when sautéed in a New Orleans–style garlicky bordelaise sauce that is quite different from the classic French one, which is made with red wine, shallots, beef stock, parsley and other herbs, and commonly served with broiled meats. Here in New Orleans, the garlic sauce has been known to appear on steaks, be tossed with pasta, or used in cooking oysters and frog's legs.

16	large frog's legs, about 1½ pounds	2	tablespoons dry white wine
2	teaspoons salt	1	tablespoon fresh lemon juice
½	teaspoon plus ⅛ teaspoon ground white pepper	1	tablespoon heavy cream
1	cup all-purpose flour	6	tablespoons cold unsalted butter, cut into pieces
½	cup olive oil	1	tablespoon chopped fresh parsley
2	teaspoons minced garlic		Pinch of freshly ground black pepper

1. Lightly season the frog's legs with ½ teaspoon of the salt and ⅛ teaspoon of the white pepper.

2. Combine the flour with the remaining 1½ teaspoons salt and ½ teaspoon white pepper in a large shallow dish. In batches, dredge the legs in the seasoned flour, shaking to remove any excess.

3. Heat the olive oil in a large sauté pan or large deep skillet over medium-high heat. Add the legs in 2 batches and cook, turning constantly, until golden brown, 2 to 3 minutes per side. Drain on paper towels.

4. Carefully drain all but 1 tablespoon of the oil from the pan and return to medium-high heat. Add the garlic and cook, stirring, until fragrant, about 30 seconds. Add the white wine and lemon juice and bring to a boil. Cook until reduced by half, about 1 minute. Add the heavy cream and cook for 30 seconds. Reduce the heat to medium-low and add the butter, several pieces at a time, stirring constantly, until all the butter has been incorporated. Remove from the heat and stir in the parsley and black pepper. Return the frog's legs to the pan and cook over medium heat to warm through, shaking the pan back and forth to coat evenly with the sauce, 30 seconds to 1 minute.

5. Divide the legs among 4 plates or arrange on a large platter and drizzle with the sauce. Serve immediately.

Morris Kahn's Steak Tartare
in Parmesan Cups

MAKES 4 SERVINGS

Morris Kahn, a local attorney and wine aficionado, has been a loyal customer of Emeril's Delmonico since we reopened the restaurant in 1998. He dines frequently with us and he loves steak tartare!

The secret to making steak tartare successfully is to use the very best quality meat and to prepare it immediately before serving—when the meat is freshly cut and well chilled. At the restaurant we mix steak tartare to order, one serving at a time. For ease of preparation, we've written this recipe to serve four, but you can cut it down to two servings or an individual serving. We serve our tartare with all the traditional garnishes on the side, but these are optional; add them to suit your taste.

We serve the tartare in a cup made of Parmesan cheese, but you can simply shape the meat into patties or balls. An alternative presentation can be made using a ring mold. To do this, place a two-and-a-half-inch ring mold in the middle of each plate, gently pack with one portion of the meat mixture and remove.

If you have meat-loving friends, steak tartare makes a great passed hors d'oeuvre. Place large dollops (about two teaspoons each) of the steak on small toasted bread rounds.

12 ounces prime beef tenderloin, cut into ¼-inch cubes
¼ cup minced yellow onions
2 tablespoons plus 2 teaspoons extra virgin olive oil
4 teaspoons capers, drained
4 cornichons, drained and minced
4 teaspoons chopped fresh parsley
1 oil-packed anchovy fillet, drained and minced

¼ cup Tartare Mayonnaise (recipe follows)
½ teaspoon salt
½ teaspoon freshly ground black pepper
1 recipe Parmesan Cups (recipe follows)
Kosher salt to taste
Traditional garnishes, such as grated egg whites, grated egg yolks, diced red onions, diced capers, and chopped fresh parsley, optional
1 recipe Large Croutons (page 263)

1. Combine the beef, onions, olive oil, capers, cornichons, parsley, and anchovy in a small bowl, tossing to combine. Gently stir in the tartare mayonnaise, salt, and pepper.

2. Divide the tartare among the 4 Parmesan Cups. (Alternatively, divide the tartare among 4 medium-size plates and shape with a 2½-inch ring mold.) Repeat with the remaining meat. Sprinkle kosher salt lightly over the top of each portion.

3. Arrange the desired garnishes around each portion, and place 4 croutons on each plate. Serve immediately.

*{ Tartare Mayonnaise

1	large egg yolk	³⁄₄	teaspoon Worcestershire
2½	tablespoons Dijon mustard	½	teaspoon salt
2	teaspoons fresh lemon juice	½	cup vegetable oil
1½	teaspoons hot sauce	¼	cup ketchup

1. Place the egg yolk, mustard, lemon juice, hot sauce, Worcestershire, and salt in the bowl of a food processor or blender and process for 20 seconds. With the motor running, slowly add the oil in a thin stream through the feed tube, processing until all of the oil is incorporated and the mixture is emulsified. Add the ketchup and process until completely incorporated, 20 to 30 seconds. Adjust the seasoning to taste.

2. Cover and refrigerate until ready to use. (The mayonnaise will keep, stored in an airtight container, for up to 1 day.)

*{ Parmesan Cups

MAKES 4 CUPS

These Parmesan cups are traditional to the Friuli region of northern Italy, where they are known as *frico* and are said to be so delicious they can make the dead breathe again! *Frico* can be shaped into flat disks, cups, or curved like crisp taco shells. Be sure to use a nonstick skillet and cook them until they reach a golden color. Be careful not to overcook these or they will taste bitter.

At Delmonico, we serve Steak Tartare inside these crisp cheese cups, but you might want to use them as edible bowls for a Caesar Salad (page 86), or form them into cones or leave them flat for snacks.

2	teaspoons unsalted butter
2	cups coarsely grated Parmigiano-Reggiano, Montasio, or Asiago cheese

1. Melt ½ teaspoon of the butter in an 8-inch nonstick skillet over medium-low heat. When the butter is foamy, sprinkle ½ cup of the grated cheese in an even layer over the bottom of the pan and shake the pan to evenly distribute the cheese, as if you were making an omelet. Cook slowly until the cheese melts and forms a light golden brown crust, 6½ to 7 minutes. Continue to cook until the edges set and the crisp turns golden brown, 30 seconds to 1 minute. Using the tines of a fork, gently lift the edges of the crisp and turn with a thin spatula. Cook until light golden brown on the second side, 45 seconds to 1 minute, being careful not to let it burn.

2. Carefully lift the crisp from the pan and shape it inside a small bowl or ramekin (3 to 3½ inches in diameter) to cool and harden, blotting with a paper towel to remove any excess oil. (Alternatively, set flat on a paper towel to make a flat crisp or drape over a rolling pin or dowel to make a curved shape.) Repeat with the remaining ingredients.

3. Carefully lift the hardened crisps from the cups and serve. (The cups will keep in an airtight container at room temperature for up to 2 days.)

Soupes du Jour

S oups have long been the introduction to meals in just about every cuisine and especially in the French style of service. The fine restaurants of New Orleans always have featured *potages* made with local ingredients such as turtle, shrimp, crabmeat, or oysters, and more likely than not they also offer a robust gumbo or two to satisfy the taste buds of local customers.

When I came to New Orleans in 1985, I realized that hearty soups and gumbos were often the main course for many meals. And when accompanied by toasty French bread lathered with creamy butter, I can understand why.

These soups featured at Delmonico, then and now, demonstrate the different types that appeal to the dining public. Some, like turtle soup and gumbo, are simmered long and slow to allow the flavors to come together. Others get their flavor from fresh herbs and local seafood. We've also included a cold soup—ideal to serve on hot summer days.

Oyster-Artichoke Soup

Oysters and artichokes are an unbelievably delicious combination that you'll find often in New Orleans and that New Orleanians really love. I've found this pairing in appetizers and casseroles, as well as in a soup when I was at Commander's Palace. Warren Le Ruth is credited as the first chef to combine oysters and artichokes in a soup at his long gone, famed New Orleans restaurant, Le Ruth's.

2½ quarts water	¼ teaspoon chopped fresh thyme
2 tablespoons plus ½ teaspoon salt	1½ tablespoons all-purpose flour
1 teaspoon black peppercorns	2 cups Chicken Stock (page 254)
3 bay leaves	or canned low-sodium chicken broth
2 large artichokes, 1 to 1¼ pounds each	1 pint oysters, with their liquor
1 lemon, halved	¼ cup dry vermouth
4 tablespoons (½ stick) unsalted butter	2 tablespoons dry white wine
¼ cup chopped yellow onions	2 tablespoons half-and-half, or more
3 tablespoons finely chopped celery	as needed
(about ½ rib)	1½ teaspoons Worcestershire
3 tablespoons peeled and finely	1½ teaspoons fresh lemon juice
chopped carrots	2 teaspoons grated lemon zest
½ teaspoon minced garlic	¼ teaspoon fennel seeds
1½ teaspoons chopped fresh parsley	¼ teaspoon cayenne

1. Combine the water, 2 tablespoons of the salt, peppercorns, and 2 of the bay leaves in a large pot and bring to a boil.

2. Trim the tough outer skin from the artichoke stems and remove the bottom row of leaves. Carefully add the artichokes and lemon halves to the boiling water and return to a boil. Using tongs, place a heavy heat-resistant plate on top of the artichokes to keep them submerged, reduce the heat, and cook at a low simmer until the artichokes are tender and a paring knife inserted into the heart pierces easily, about 20 minutes. Drain in a colander and let sit until cool enough to handle.

This recipe can be doubled to obtain a larger yield; simply multiply the ingredients by two, except the lemon zest, which should be added to taste. The consistency of the soup will vary depending upon the size of the artichokes used. Thin the soup to a desired consistency with additional half-and-half.

3. Remove the large outer leaves from the artichokes and scrape the meat from each into a small bowl. Remove and discard the spiky inner leaves. Scrape the hairy choke from the hearts and discard. Roughly chop the artichoke hearts and the stems, if available, and add to the bowl of artichoke meat. Set aside.

4. Melt the butter in a Dutch oven or large heavy pot over medium-high heat. Add the onions, celery, and carrots and cook, stirring, until soft, 2 to 3 minutes. Add the garlic, parsley, thyme, and the remaining bay leaf and cook, stirring, until the garlic is fragrant, 30 seconds.

5. Add the reserved artichoke meat, chopped artichoke hearts, and the flour and cook, stirring constantly, until the flour is incorporated into the mixture. Add the remaining ingredients, stir well, and bring to a boil. Reduce the heat to medium-low and simmer, uncovered, stirring occasionally, for 30 minutes. Remove the bay leaves and discard.

6. Remove the soup from the heat and using a handheld immersion blender or in batches in a food processor or blender, purée the soup until smooth. Adjust the seasoning to taste.

7. Ladle the soup into bowls and serve immediately.

St. Paul's Seafood Gumbo

MAKES 5 QUARTS

St. Paul Bell is one of those amazing culinary success stories. He and I first met at the Commander's Palace kitchen, where he became one of my first apprentices, and he has risen through the ranks to become sous chef at Emeril's Delmonico.

St. Paul's seafood gumbo is a bit unusual in several respects. First, he warms the stock before adding it to the roux (usually cold stock is added to a hot roux). Second, he cooks filé powder (ground sassafras root) with the gumbo; filé normally is sprinkled onto the soup at the table. Also, he uses both okra and filé powder in this gumbo; usually only one is added as a thickening agent. I tell you what, though, this gumbo is rich tasting and absolutely delicious, no matter how unusual!

1 cup vegetable oil	½ pound okra, stem ends trimmed and cut crosswise into ½-inch-thick slices (about 1½ cups)
1¼ cups all-purpose flour	
10 cups Shrimp Stock (page 267) or Fish Stock (page 259)	
	2 tablespoons chopped fresh parsley
2 cups chopped yellow onions	1½ tablespoons filé powder, plus more for serving (see Source Guide)
1 cup chopped green bell peppers	
1 cup chopped celery	1 teaspoon liquid crab boil (see Source Guide)
1 tablespoon chopped garlic	
½ cup lager beer	1¾ pounds medium shrimp, peeled and deveined
1¼ pounds andouille or other hot, smoked sausage, sliced ¼ inch thick	
	1 teaspoon Emeril's Original Essence or Creole Seasoning (page 260)
3 tablespoons tomato paste	
1 tablespoon dried basil	1 pint oysters, with their liquor
1 tablespoon dried thyme	Salt to taste
2 bay leaves	Freshly ground black pepper to taste
1 pound gumbo crabs without the legs, rinsed well and quartered (see Source Guide)	½ recipe White Rice (page 121)

1. Heat the oil in a large Dutch oven or heavy pot over medium heat. Add the flour and cook, stirring constantly with a large wooden spoon, to make a light brown roux, 10 to 15 minutes.

2. Meanwhile, bring the stock to a simmer in a medium heavy pot over medium-high heat. Reduce the heat to low and cover to keep warm.

3. Add 1 cup of the onions, ½ cup of the bell peppers, ½ cup of the celery, and 1½ teaspoons of the garlic to the roux, and cook, stirring, over medium-high heat until the vegetables are softened, 4 to 5 minutes. Add the beer and stir to blend. Add the heated seafood stock, 1 cup at a time, stirring well after each addition and letting the mixture return to a simmer before adding the remaining stock. Simmer over medium-high heat while preparing the remaining ingredients.

4. Cook the andouille in a large skillet over medium-high heat until browned and the fat is rendered, about 5 minutes. Add the remaining 1 cup onions, ½ cup bell peppers, ½ cup celery, and 1½ teaspoons garlic and cook, stirring, until the vegetables are soft, about 3 minutes. Add the tomato paste, basil, thyme, and bay leaves and cook, stirring, for 1 minute.

And here's a tip about adding that hot stock to the roux—add the stock a cup or so at a time and then let the mixture return to a simmer before adding more stock. Otherwise, your roux will break. Gumbo crabs are small blue crabs that have been cleaned and are ready for the soup pot. They are available both fresh and frozen, and can be found at reputable seafood retailers or by special order. St. Paul doesn't add salt to the pot until after the oysters have been added. This is because of the saltiness of the oysters, which will vary depending upon the time of the year. Same thing with the pepper—both the andouille and crab boil are spicy, so, depending upon your taste, you might not need additional pepper.

5. Add the andouille mixture to the seafood stock mixture and stir to mix. Add the crabs, okra, parsley, 1½ tablespoons filé powder, and crab boil and stir well. Reduce the heat to medium-low and simmer for 20 minutes, skimming occasionally to remove any foam that rises to the surface.

6. Season the shrimp with the Essence in a medium bowl.

7. Add the shrimp and the oysters and their liquor to the gumbo, stir well, and cook until the shrimp are pink and just cooked through and the edges of the oysters start to curl, about 5 minutes.

8. Remove from the heat and season with salt and freshly ground black pepper. Remove the bay leaves and discard.

9. Spoon the rice into large soup bowls, about ½ cup per serving, and ladle the gumbo over the rice. Serve immediately, passing additional filé powder at the table, as desired.

Chicken and Smoked Sausage Gumbo
with Roasted Green Onion
Rice–Stuffed Quail

This unusual presentation is typical of the variations on local culinary themes that we present at Emeril's Delmonico. Consider this, if you will, a "dressed up" gumbo, with the rice-stuffed quail taking the place of the white rice usually found in gumbo bowls throughout south Louisiana.

While the gumbo and stuffed quail are fantastic together, each also is delicious on its own. Remember to add a big scoop of hot White Rice (page 121) to each bowl of gumbo before serving if you choose not to serve the quail.

1½ tablespoons unsalted butter	1 bay leaf
4 ounces chicken livers, drained, patted dry, and chopped	½ teaspoon dried thyme
	½ teaspoon Worcestershire
2 ounces smoked ham, chopped	¼ cup chopped green onions
¼ cup chopped yellow onions	2 teaspoons minced fresh parsley
1 teaspoon minced garlic	Six 3½ to 4-ounce quail
2 tablespoons brandy	3 tablespoons melted unsalted butter
¾ cup long-grain white rice	2 teaspoons Emeril's Original Essence or Creole Seasoning (page 260)
¼ teaspoon salt	
¼ teaspoon freshly ground black pepper	½ recipe Chicken and Smoked Sausage Gumbo (recipe follows)
⅛ teaspoon cayenne	
1½ cups Rich Chicken Stock (page 256), canned low-sodium chicken broth, or water	2 teaspoons thinly sliced green onions (green tops only), for garnish

1. Melt the butter in a medium saucepan over medium-high heat. Add the chicken livers, ham, yellow onions, and garlic and cook, stirring, until the livers are browned and the onions are soft, about 3 minutes. Add the brandy, remove from the heat, and ignite with a match. Carefully return to the heat and cook until the alcohol is burned off, about 2 minutes. Add the rice, salt, pepper, and cayenne and cook, stirring, until the rice is glassy, about 2 minutes. Add the chicken stock, bay leaf, thyme, and Worcestershire, stir, cover, and reduce the heat to medium-low. Cook undisturbed at a bare simmer until the rice is tender and the liquid is absorbed, 18 to 20 minutes.

2. Remove from the heat and let sit for 5 minutes. Discard the bay leaf. Fluff the rice with a fork, add the green onions and parsley, and stir to mix. Let cool.

3. Preheat the oven to 400°F.

Chef Emeril with Shane Pritchett

4. Place the quail breast side down on a baking sheet. Divide the stuffing into 6 equal portions and form into firm balls. Insert 1 ball in the cavity of each quail and bring the meat and skin up and around to cover completely. Turn the birds, breast side up, on a large baking sheet.

5. Combine the melted butter and the Essence in a small bowl. Brush the seasoned butter with a pastry brush over the tops and sides of the birds. Roast until cooked through and an instant-read thermometer registers an internal temperature of 160°F, about 20 minutes.

6. To serve, ladle the gumbo into each of 6 large shallow bowls and place 1 stuffed quail in the center of each bowl. Garnish each serving with green onions and serve immediately.

*}Chicken and Smoked Sausage Gumbo

MAKES 3 QUARTS, 10 TO 12 SERVINGS

For a different gumbo, substitute Roasted Duck (page 81) for the smoked or roasted chicken that we call for here.

1 cup vegetable oil	3 bay leaves
1 cup all-purpose flour	8 cups Chicken Stock (page 254) or
1½ cups chopped yellow onions	canned low-sodium chicken broth
1 cup chopped celery	1 pound boneless smoked or roasted
1 cup chopped green bell peppers	chicken meat, or 1 recipe Quick Cooked
1 pound smoked sausage, such as	Chicken (page 156), cut into ½-inch
andouille or kielbasa, cut crosswise	chunks or shredded
into ½-inch slices	½ cup chopped green onions
1½ teaspoons salt	2 tablespoons chopped fresh parsley
¼ teaspoon cayenne	

1. Heat the oil in a large pot or Dutch oven and cook over medium heat. Add the flour and cook, stirring slowly and constantly with a heavy wooden spoon, to make a dark brown roux the color of chocolate, 20 to 25 minutes. Add the yellow onions, celery, and bell peppers and cook, stirring, until soft, 4 to 5 minutes. Add the sausage, salt, cayenne, and bay leaves and cook, stirring, for 5 minutes. Add the stock and stir until the roux mixture and stock are well blended, and bring to a boil. Reduce the heat to low and cook at a very low simmer, uncovered, stirring occasionally, for 1 hour. Add the chicken, stir, and simmer, stirring occasionally, for 2 hours.

2. Remove from the heat and discard the bay leaves. Stir in the green onions and parsley and cover to keep warm until ready to serve.

Cream of Chicken Soup

MAKES ABOUT 2 QUARTS, 6 TO 8 SERVINGS

Ernest "Jitterbug" Rome, who began working at old Delmonico at the age of fifteen, created this soup as well as many of the dishes that appeared on the menu. Under the tutelage of Marie LaFranca, he learned the skills that earned him the position of head cook. This soup is so creamy you'll never believe there's no milk or cream in it! The secret to achieving this texture is the light roux that's the base for the soup.

The LeGoût Chicken Base has a very yellow hue that gives this soup a beautiful color. If the color of the soup is too pale, the cooks recommend that you add a little yellow food coloring to brighten it up.

4 boneless, skinless chicken breasts (about 1½ pounds)	1 tablespoon plus ½ teaspoon LeGoût Chicken Base or other thick chicken base
¾ cup chopped celery	7 drops yellow food coloring, optional
½ cup chopped yellow onions	⅓ cup thinly sliced carrots
2 quarts water	½ cup finely chopped pimientos
8 tablespoons (1 stick) unsalted butter	½ teaspoon salt
½ cup all-purpose flour	Pinch of freshly ground black pepper

1. Put the chicken in a medium stockpot or Dutch oven with the celery and onions, add the water, and bring to a boil over high heat. Reduce the heat to medium-low and simmer until the chicken is cooked through and tender, about 12 minutes. Remove from the heat and transfer the chicken to a plate until cool enough to handle. Finely chop the chicken. Strain the chicken broth into a clean pot, reserving the vegetables.

2. Melt the butter in a medium saucepan over medium-high heat. Add the flour, whisking constantly, and cook to make a light roux, about 2 minutes. Slowly add the reserved broth, chicken base, and yellow food coloring, if desired, and whisk to blend.

3. Place the reserved cooking vegetables and the carrots in the bowl of a food processor and pulse to coarsely chop. Add the vegetables to the soup with the pimientos, chopped chicken, salt, and pepper and bring to a boil. Reduce the heat to medium-low and simmer, uncovered, until the mixture is slightly thick and creamy, 20 to 25 minutes.

4. Ladle into soup bowls and serve immediately.

Chilled Cucumber, Tomato, *and* Avocado Soup

MAKES 6½ CUPS, 6 SERVINGS

This refreshing soup makes appearances on the summer menu, when tomatoes and cucumbers are at their most flavorful. You might want to offer this soup as part of a buffet spread at a spring or summer party, served in small cups instead of soup bowls.

3 tablespoons unsalted butter	¼ teaspoon ground white pepper
1 cup roughly chopped yellow onions	3 cups Chicken Stock (page 254) or
2 tablespoons all-purpose flour	canned low-sodium chicken broth
2 pounds ripe tomatoes, peeled, seeded, and chopped (about 3 cups)	1 cup heavy cream
	One 8-ounce Hass avocado, peeled, pitted
3 cups peeled, seeded, and chopped cucumbers (2 large cucumbers)	and cut into small dice, for garnish
	1½ teaspoons snipped fresh chives,
¾ teaspoon salt	for garnish

1. Melt the butter in a medium saucepan over medium heat. Add the onions and cook, stirring, until soft, about 5 minutes. Add the flour, and cook, stirring constantly, for 2 minutes. Add the tomatoes, stir well, and cook, stirring, for 2 minutes. Add the cucumbers, salt, and pepper and stir well. Add the chicken stock and bring to a boil. Reduce the heat to medium-low and simmer, stirring occasionally, for 15 minutes.

2. With a handheld immersion blender or in batches in a blender, puree the mixture and chill in an ice bath, stirring occasionally. Cover and refrigerate until well chilled, at least 4 hours or overnight.

3. Stir in the cream and adjust the seasoning to taste. Ladle the soup into large 6 shallow soup bowls and garnish each serving with diced avocado and ¼ teaspoon of the chives.

4. Serve immediately.

Creamy Carrot *and* Apple Soup *with* Ginger Crème Fraîche

MAKES 1 QUART, 4 SERVINGS

Calvados is an agricultural area within the Normandy region of France, known for apples, butter, and cheese. Calvados also is the name of the apple brandy that gives this soup a pronounced apple flavor. Brandy or cognac make fine substitutes if you cannot find Calvados.

2 tablespoons unsalted butter	3 cups heavy cream
¾ cup thinly sliced yellow onions	½ cup Chicken Stock (page 254) or
Two 5 to 6-ounce carrots, peeled, halved	canned low-sodium chicken broth
lengthwise, and quartered crosswise	1 teaspoon honey
2 tablespoons Calvados or brandy	1 teaspoon fresh lemon juice
1 Granny Smith apple, peeled, cored,	½ teaspoon salt
and sliced ¼ inch thick	¼ teaspoon ground white pepper
¼ cup crème fraîche	1 teaspoon chopped fresh tarragon,
1 teaspoon minced fresh ginger	for garnish

1. Preheat the oven to 350°F.

2. Melt the butter in a medium ovenproof saucepan or casserole over medium heat. Add the onions and cook, stirring occasionally, until soft, 6 to 8 minutes. Add the carrots and Calvados and stir well. Remove from the heat, cover tightly, and bake until the vegetables are very tender, about 45 minutes. Add the apple, stir, cover tightly, and bake until tender, about 20 minutes.

3. Combine the crème fraîche and ginger in a small bowl and mix well. Set aside.

4. Remove the pan from the oven. Add the heavy cream, chicken stock, honey, lemon juice, salt, and pepper, bring to a simmer over medium heat, and cook, stirring, until the mixture is heated through, 2 to 3 minutes. Remove from the heat.

5. Puree the soup using a handheld immersion blender, or in batches in a food processor or blender, until smooth.

6. Ladle the soup into 4 large shallow bowls. Spoon 1 tablespoon of the ginger crème fraîche into the center of each bowl and garnish with ¼ teaspoon of the tarragon. Serve immediately.

Turtle Soup

MAKES ABOUT 3½ QUARTS, 10 TO 12 SERVINGS

This soup was so popular at the old Delmonico that the turtle meat from Wiley's Turtle Farm in Jonesville was delivered one hundred pounds at a time! (To give some perspective, this recipe using one pound of meat serves ten to twelve people.)

As is common New Orleans practice, this soup has quite a bit of sherry added in the kitchen before service. It's also typical to add more sherry to the soup at tableside. So, small pitchers of dry sherry were placed on the Delmonico dining room tables so that diners could add more to taste. Some, according to Miss Angie, not only would help themselves but also would sip on it!

Longtime Delmonico cook Elmer Decquir showed us how to make this soup in the test kitchen. She emphasized that the chopped hard-boiled eggs not be added to the entire batch of soup but instead spooned into individual bowls just before serving. This is done because the eggs get tough if the soup is kept warm for any length of time or is reheated.

One 28-ounce can chopped tomatoes, with their juice
1 pound boneless turtle meat (see Source Guide)
2 ribs celery, finely chopped
1 large green bell pepper, cored, seeded, and finely chopped
½ cup chopped yellow onions
½ lemon, seeded and chopped
3 quarts water
½ cup ketchup

2 tablespoons A1 Steak Sauce
1 bay leaf
½ teaspoon salt
⅛ teaspoon hot sauce
¾ cup all-purpose flour
3 tablespoons LeGoût Chicken Base or other thick chicken base
1 tablespoon Kitchen Bouquet
1 cup dry sherry, plus more for serving
1 recipe Hard-Boiled Eggs (page 260), peeled and finely chopped, for garnish

1. Place the tomatoes in a food processor and pulse to coarsely chop.

2. Combine the turtle meat, tomatoes and their juice, the celery, bell pepper, onions, lemon, 2 quarts of the water, ketchup, steak sauce, bay leaf, salt, and hot sauce in a large heavy pot and bring to a boil over high heat. Reduce the heat to medium and cook uncovered until the turtle meat is slightly tender, about 35 minutes. Transfer the turtle meat with a slotted spoon to a platter to cool. Finely chop the meat and return to the pot.

3. Combine 2 cups of the remaining water and the flour in a 2-quart measuring cup and whisk until smooth. Add the chicken base and Kitchen Bouquet and whisk until well combined. Add the remaining 2 cups water, whisk to combine, and slowly stir into the soup. Bring the soup to a gentle boil, reduce the heat, and simmer, uncovered, stirring occasionally, until thickened slightly, 2½ to 3 hours.

4. Remove the soup from the heat and stir in the 1 cup sherry. Ladle the soup into bowls, garnish each serving with chopped hard-boiled eggs, and top with an additional teaspoon of sherry, as desired. Serve immediately.

Hearty Vegetable Soup

MAKES 4½ QUARTS

Gene Bourg, a former restaurant critic for the *Times-Picayune* in New Orleans, noted in one of his columns about old Delmonico that the vegetable soup was "one of the best around. What separates it from the crowd is its subtle turnip taste. Any Southern vegetable soup worthy of the name needs a turnip or two in the pot, and this one has just the right level of turnip taste in the beef-and-tomato broth."

Cook Elmer Decquir put it on in the morning when she arrived in the kitchen and let it simmer until lunchtime. During the LaFranca era, the cooks often used a chicken base to flavor soups, sauces, and other dishes. The favored brand was LeGoût, which is still available in supermarkets in the New Orleans area. You can certainly substitute another brand, but be aware that some of those bases are quite salty, so adjust your seasoning to taste.

3 quarts water	2 cups sliced carrots
1 tablespoon salt	5 red potatoes, peeled and diced
2 teaspoons freshly ground black pepper	1½ cups chopped cabbage
2 pounds top round with bones, cut into 1-inch pieces	1 cup chopped celery
3 to 4 cups tomato juice, to taste	One 1-pound bag frozen mixed vegetables, optional
3 cups canned chopped tomatoes, with their juice	½ cup chopped green bell peppers
2½ cups chopped yellow onions	¼ cup chopped green onions
3 medium turnips, peeled and cubed (about 2½ cups)	1 tablespoon LeGoût Chicken Base or other thick chicken base

1. Combine the water, salt, black pepper, and soup meat and bones in a large heavy pot or Dutch oven and bring to a boil over medium-high heat. Add the tomato juice and tomatoes and their juice and bring the mixture to a boil. Reduce the heat to medium-low and simmer, uncovered, until the meat is very tender, about 1½ hours, stirring occasionally. Add the yellow onions, turnips, carrots, potatoes, cabbage, celery, and the frozen vegetables, if using, and simmer, stirring occasionally, until the vegetables are very tender, about 30 minutes. (If the soup gets too thick, add up to 1 cup water.) Add the bell peppers, green onions, and chicken base, stir, and simmer for 15 minutes.

2. Remove from the heat and adjust the seasoning to taste.

3. Ladle the soup into large shallow bowls and serve immediately.

SALADS:
LETTUCE AND BEYOND

Cold service, or *service froid*, as the French call it, includes delicate and elegant dishes such as aspics, *ballotines*, and *chaud-froids*, which are rarely found on contemporary menus in America since they require a great deal of skill and a lot of time to pull them off correctly. Salads also fall into the cold service course and that's what modern-day customers prefer before their meal or as a main course.

For so long salads were not the strong suits in many establishments because, I think, they were not given as much attention as were other courses. So many of us thought a salad was simply one kind of lettuce or greens, maybe some sliced tomatoes, and flavorless oily dressing.

But now all that has changed since there are all kinds of salad greens, fresh herbs, and other options, such as duck, chicken, seafood, and vegetables, to accent salads. I have long advocated creativity in salads in my restaurants, introducing fresh fruit and cheese as well as good dressings to liven up otherwise ho-hum dishes.

The salads included here are the ones that I think will more than satisfy as the cold course of any meal.

Delmonico House Salad

MAKES 4 SERVINGS

This is probably the most requested recipe from the old regime. The salad came to the table in a crisp globular leaf of iceberg lettuce in which was finely chopped lettuce, blanched broccoli, and carrots, garnished with sliced beets and wedges of tomatoes, and drizzled with the house salad dressing. The cooks tell us that blanched green beans, blanched cauliflower, and thin slices of fresh green bell peppers also can be added.

2 cups trimmed broccoli flowerets
1 cup ¼-inch-thick round carrots
4 large iceberg lettuce leaves
1 cup finely chopped iceberg lettuce

1 small canned beet or roasted beet, cut into 4 thick slices
One 6-ounce tomato, cut into 12 wedges
1 recipe Delmonico Salad Dressing (recipe follows)

1. Bring a medium pot of salted water to a boil. Add the broccoli and blanch until tender, 2 minutes. Remove with a slotted spoon and place in an ice bath. Drain and pat dry.

2. Return the water to a boil, add the carrots, and blanch until tender, 1 minutes. Remove with a slotted spoon and place in an ice bath. Drain and pat dry.

3. Place 1 large lettuce leaf on each of 4 salad plates and arrange ¼ cup of the chopped lettuce in the center of each lettuce leaf. Chop one-quarter of the broccoli and arrange equal amounts inside each lettuce leaf. Arrange the remaining broccoli flowerets and the carrots in each of the lettuce leaves. Cut each beet slice into 4 sticks and arrange inside the lettuce leaves, alternating with the tomato wedges. Drizzle each salad with 2 tablespoons of the dressing and serve immediately.

Delmonico Salad Dressing

MAKES ABOUT ½ CUP

2½ tablespoons Creole mustard or other mild whole-grain mustard
2 tablespoons ketchup
2 tablespoons vegetable oil
2 tablespoons water
¾ teaspoon A1 Steak Sauce
½ teaspoon sugar

½ teaspoon Worcestershire
¼ teaspoon lemon juice concentrate or fresh lemon juice
⅛ teaspoon salt
Pinch of garlic powder
2 tablespoons red wine vinegar

1. Combine all of the ingredients except the vinegar in a medium bowl and whisk well to blend. Whisking, slowly add the vinegar and whisk until emulsified.

2. Transfer to an airtight container and refrigerate until ready to use. (The dressing will keep refrigerated in an airtight container for up to 1 week.)

Delmonico Jumbo Lump Crab Salad *with* Bibb Lettuce, Cucumbers, Caper-Herb Dressing, *and* Crispy Garlic Toast

MAKES 4 SERVINGS

This salad is a very popular main course item on our Emeril's Delmonico lunch menu, although it would make a fitting first course for a dinner party if served in smaller portions. We make the salad with jumbo lump crabmeat, but use whatever is available fresh in your area.

The caper-herb dressing makes an outstanding tartar sauce—like accompaniment to seafood—from broiled salmon to boiled or Cornmeal Fried Shrimp (page 137).

1 pound jumbo lump crabmeat, picked over for shells and cartilage	4 large leaves or 8 medium leaves Bibb lettuce
1 recipe Caper-Herb Dressing (recipe follows)	4 ounces seedless cucumber, peeled, cut in half lengthwise, and sliced ¼ inch thick
Salt to taste	4 teaspoons extra virgin olive oil
Freshly ground black pepper to taste	1 recipe Crispy Garlic Toast (recipe follows)

1. Combine the crabmeat and dressing in a large bowl, gently folding so as not to break up the lumps. Adjust the seasoning to taste with salt and pepper.

2. Arrange 1 large lettuce leaf or 2 medium leaves in the center of 4 large plates and spoon the crabmeat into the center of the leaves. Arrange the cucumber slices to one side of the crabmeat and drizzle each portion lightly with 1 teaspoon olive oil.

3. Serve immediately with 2 pieces of the garlic toast on the side of each salad.

⁂{ Caper-Herb Dressing

MAKES A GENEROUS ¾ CUP

Use a good-quality salad oil, such as vegetable oil or canola oil for this dressing. Olive oil is too strongly flavored and will overpower the flavor of the capers and herbs. If you cannot obtain small capers, chop larger ones for this recipe.

1 large egg	¼ teaspoon salt
1½ teaspoons red wine vinegar	¼ teaspoon freshly ground black pepper
1½ teaspoons fresh lemon juice	1½ teaspoons drained small capers
¼ teaspoon strained caper juice	1 teaspoon chopped fresh dill
¾ cup vegetable oil	1 teaspoon chopped fresh tarragon

Combine the egg, vinegar, lemon juice, and caper juice in a blender or the bowl of a food processor and process for 10 seconds. With the machine running, add the oil in a steady stream through the feed tube and process until all the oil has been added and the mixture is thick and emulsified. (If the mixture becomes too thick, add water, 1 teaspoon at a time to thin, pulsing to incorporate.) Add the salt and pepper and pulse to incorporate. Transfer to a bowl and fold in the remaining ingredients. Adjust the seasoning to taste, cover, and refrigerate until well chilled, about 2 hours. The dressing will keep, tightly covered in the refrigerator, for up to 1 day.

⁕{ Crispy Garlic Toast

MAKES 8 TOASTS, 4 SERVINGS

Once you've tried this garlic toast, you'll find yourself pairing it with soups, salads, steaks—you name it!

8 tablespoons (1 stick) unsalted butter, at room temperature	½ cup freshly grated Parmigiano-Reggiano (about 1 ½ ounces)
1 tablespoon minced garlic	
One 12-inch-long thin French baguette, ends trimmed and cut in half lengthwise	

1. Preheat the oven to 350°F. Line a large baking sheet with aluminum foil and set aside.

2. Cream the butter and garlic in a medium bowl using a wooden spoon or rubber spatula.

3. Spread both halves of the bread evenly with the garlic butter and top with the grated cheese. Cut each half crosswise into quarters, arrange on the prepared baking sheet, and bake until fragrant and golden brown, about 12 minutes. (Alternatively, broil until golden brown, 1 to 2 minutes.)

4. Serve hot.

Arugula, Duck, and Strawberry Salad
with Balsamic Brown Sugar Vinaigrette
and Candied Pecans

MAKES 4 SERVINGS

Here's a delicious way to use leftover duck, although if you want to kick this up another notch, make this instead with duck confit. If you don't have duck on hand, substitute roasted chicken.

1 recipe Roasted Duck (recipe follows), or 3 cups shredded roasted chicken or Quick Cooked Chicken (page 156)	4 cups arugula, washed and spun dry, tough stems removed
1 cup fresh strawberries, rinsed and thinly sliced	¾ cup Candied Pecans (recipe follows), or lightly toasted pecan halves
1 recipe Balsamic Brown Sugar Vinaigrette (recipe follows)	4 ounces goat cheese, crumbled

1. Preheat the oven to 400°F.

2. Remove the skin from the cooled duck and discard. Remove the meat from the bones and discard the bones. Shred the meat with your fingers or 2 forks. Place the meat on a baking sheet and warm in the oven, 2 to 3 minutes. Remove from the oven.

3. Combine the strawberries and vinaigrette in a large bowl. Add the arugula and toss to coat.

4. Divide the salad among 4 salad plates. Top each portion with shredded duck, candied pecans, and goat cheese and serve immediately.

Roasted Duck

MAKES 1 DUCK, ABOUT 3 CUPS OF MEAT

Try this simple roasting technique. This duck also would make a terrific dinner for two. Cut it in half by slicing along either side of the breastbone and remove the bone, then remove the breast-plate and rib cage. Try the White Rice (page 121) or the Rosemary-Gruyère Bread Pudding (page 204) alongside, and the Barolo Syrup (page 191) or Apple Chutney (page 108) as accompaniments.

One 5-pound domestic duck, rinsed and patted dry	1 teaspoon salt
	½ teaspoon freshly ground black pepper

1. Preheat the oven to 500°F.

2. Remove all visible fat from the duck. With a fork, prick the skin all over without piercing the meat. Sprinkle the duck with the salt and pepper. Place on a rack in a roasting pan and roast for 40 minutes.

3. Reduce the oven temperature to 400°F and roast until the thigh juices run clear when pierced, about 30 minutes more. Remove from the oven.

4. The duck can be stored, tightly covered, in the refrigerator for up to 3 days.

Balsamic Brown Sugar Vinaigrette

MAKES ABOUT 1/2 CUP

3 tablespoons balsamic vinegar	1/8 teaspoon finely ground black pepper
2 teaspoons light brown sugar	1/2 cup extra virgin olive oil
1/4 teaspoon salt	

Combine all the ingredients in a small bowl and whisk until well blended and the sugar is dissolved. Serve immediately or store refrigerated in an airtight container for up to 3 days.

Candied Pecans

MAKES 2 CUPS

You'll find these addictive nuts also make ideal cocktail fare.

2 cups water	Vegetable oil, for frying
2 cups plus 1 teaspoon sugar	1/2 teaspoon salt
1/4 teaspoon plus 1/8 teaspoon cayenne	1/4 teaspoon ground cinnamon
2 cups pecan pieces	

1. Line a baking sheet with parchment or wax paper.

2. Combine the water, 2 cups of the sugar, and 1/4 teaspoon of the cayenne in a medium heavy saucepan over medium-high heat. Cook, stirring occasionally with a wooden spoon, until the mixture comes to a boil and becomes slightly thick, about 5 minutes.

3. Add the pecans and cook for 5 minutes, stirring often. Drain the pecans in a colander set over a bowl, shaking off the excess liquid.

4. Heat enough oil to come halfway up the sides of a medium pot to 360°F. Add the pecans and fry, stirring often, until they are a deep mahogany color, 4 to 5 minutes. Transfer with a slotted spoon to the prepared baking sheet and stir with a fork to prevent the nuts from sticking together.

5. Combine the remaining 1 teaspoon sugar, the salt, the cinnamon, and the remaining 1/8 teaspoon cayenne in a small bowl and sprinkle over the pecans. Cool completely before serving. (The pecans can be stored in an airtight container at room temperature for up to 1 week.)

Tomato and Watercress Salad
with Shaved Red Onions, Avocado,
and Blue Cheese Vinaigrette

MAKES 4 SERVINGS

I'm always bragging about our delicious local Creole tomatoes that appear in late May or early June. But any vine-ripened tomatoes will do just fine in this salad that also includes heady watercress, sweet red onions, buttery avocado, and creamy blue cheese. Now that's a salad with lots of flavor!

4 ounces watercress, stems trimmed, leaves washed and spun dry

1 firm-ripe avocado, peeled, halved, seeded, and cut into ¾-inch dice

½ cup thinly sliced red onions

1 recipe Blue Cheese Vinaigrette (recipe follows)

Three 5 to 6-ounce tomatoes, trimmed and cut into 4 slices each

1. Combine the watercress, avocado, and onions in a large bowl and toss with enough vinaigrette to lightly coat.

2. Arrange 3 tomato slices around the outside edge of 4 salad plates and drizzle lightly with additional vinaigrette. Divide the watercress mixture among the plates, drizzle with additional vinaigrette, as desired, and serve immediately.

We use Danish blue cheese—a rich and somewhat mild cow's milk cheese—in our vinaigrette. But if you're really into blue cheese, crumble extra over the top of each salad.

This salad was developed for the 2003 Easter Sunday menu and makes an occasional special appearance on our lunch and dinner menus. It is a delicious start to a hearty steak meal, although I think it's a great meal on its own, served with hot French bread and sweet butter on the side.

⁑⟩ Blue Cheese Vinaigrette

MAKES ABOUT 1 CUP

3 tablespoons red wine vinegar

1 tablespoon snipped fresh chives

2 teaspoons minced shallots

1 teaspoon Dijon mustard

½ teaspoon minced garlic

½ teaspoon chopped fresh thyme

Pinch of salt

Pinch of freshly ground black pepper

6 tablespoons extra virgin olive oil

2 ounces Danish blue cheese or other mild blue cheese, crumbled (about ¼ cup)

Whisk together the vinegar, chives, shallots, mustard, garlic, thyme, salt, and pepper in a medium bowl. Add the oil in a slow, steady stream, whisking constantly until the mixture is thick and an emulsion is formed. Add the cheese, whisk to incorporate, and adjust the seasoning to taste. Cover tightly and refrigerate until ready to use. (The vinaigrette will keep tightly covered in the refrigerator for up to 3 days.)

Caesar Salad

I wanted to bring back tableside service when we reopened the restaurant because I felt that guests would love excitement and drama in the dining rooms. Caesar salad, supposedly created by Caesar Cardini, an Italian restaurateur in Tijuana, Mexico, in 1924, is classically prepared tableside, in large wooden bowls, by our dining room captains.

One	18-ounce bag hearts of Romaine lettuce, torn into pieces or left whole, as desired	1	recipe Small Homemade Croutons (recipe follows)
1	recipe Creamy Parmesan Dressing (recipe follows)	½	cup finely grated Parmigiano-Reggiano cheese

Put the lettuce in a large bowl, toss with the dressing to taste, and divide among 4 large salad plates. (Or arrange the hearts on the plates and drizzle the dressing over the lettuce.) Top with the croutons and cheese and serve.

Creamy Parmesan Dressing

No one ingredient dominates in a good Caesar salad, in spite of the fact that the individual dressing ingredients all are fairly strong tasting on their own. It is said that Cardini's original salad included Worcestershire sauce instead of anchovies. And while some Caesar salad dressings include raw egg yolks, we instead include one whole coddled egg in our creamy Parmesan dressing.

1	large egg	1	tablespoon fresh lemon juice
2	anchovy fillets, drained	1	teaspoon Dijon mustard
½	teaspoon chopped garlic	¼	cup extra virgin olive oil
¼	teaspoon kosher salt	1	teaspoon Worcestershire
¼	teaspoon freshly ground black pepper	2	dashes of hot sauce
2	tablespoons freshly grated Parmigiano-Reggiano		

1. Bring a small saucepan of water to a boil. Add the egg and cook for 30 seconds until coddled. Drain.

2. Combine the anchovies, garlic, salt, and pepper in a small bowl and mash with the back of a fork. Break the egg into the mixture and whisk well to blend. Add the cheese, lemon juice, and mustard and whisk well. Add the olive oil in a steady stream, whisking constantly to form a thick emulsion. Add the Worcestershire and hot sauce and whisk well to blend. Cover tightly and refrigerate until ready to use. (The dressing will keep refrigerated for 1 day.)

⁕⟩Small Homemade Croutons

MAKES 1 CUP

1 cup ½ to ¾-inch cubed French bread ¼ cup extra virgin olive oil	2 teaspoons Emeril's Original Essence or Creole Seasoning (page 260)

1. Preheat the oven to 400°F.

2. Place the bread in a medium bowl and toss with the oil and Essence. Place on a baking sheet and bake, stirring occasionally, until light golden brown on top, about 6 minutes. Remove from the oven and cool slightly before serving.

Roasted Beet Salad *with* Goat Cheese *and* Pomegranate Molasses

MAKES 4 SERVINGS

Beets, grown in home gardens in New Orleans and also available at farmers' markets in the city, have long been used in salads or as garnishes. During the LaFranca era, they appeared as a side dish or in their popular house salad. Here is an updated salad that features roasted beets, goat cheese, and pomegranate molasses—an incredible combination of flavors.

4   medium beets (about 1 pound), trimmed and rinsed
1   cup water
½   cup white wine vinegar
4   sprigs fresh thyme
¼   teaspoon plus a pinch of salt
⅛   teaspoon freshly ground black pepper
¼   cup walnut pieces
¼   cup minced celery
¼   cup minced fresh parsley

2   tablespoons minced shallots
¼   cup pomegranate molasses, plus 1 teaspoon for garnish
3   tablespoons olive oil
4   ounces goat cheese, softened
2   tablespoons sour cream
½   cup microgreens, bean sprouts, or baby soft herbs, such as parsley, chervil, and chives

Roasted beets are amazingly sweet and the pomegranate molasses gives them an unbelievable flavor.
You'll find that beets are easiest to peel while still warm. The trick is to gently work the skin off using a small paring knife at the root end. Before you begin, rub a small amount of vegetable oil onto your fingers. Otherwise, your hands will be stained a lovely shade of maroon for the rest of the day.

1. Preheat the oven to 350°F.

2. Place the beets in an 8 x 8-inch-square baking dish. Add the water, vinegar, thyme, ¼ teaspoon of the salt, and pinch of the black pepper. Cover tightly with aluminum foil and bake until the beets are tender, about 90 minutes. Uncover and when cool enough to handle, slip off the skins. Cut the beets into medium dice, place in a large bowl, and let cool completely.

3. Meanwhile, spread the walnuts on a small baking dish and bake until fragrant and lightly toasted, 6 to 8 minutes. Let cool in the baking dish and then roughly chop. Set aside.

4. Add the celery, parsley, shallots, ¼ cup of the pomegranate molasses, the chopped walnuts, and 2 tablespoons of the olive oil to the beets and toss to coat evenly. Divide the salad among 4 medium plates.

5. Combine the goat cheese, sour cream, and the remaining pinch each of salt and pepper in a small bowl and stir to combine.

6. Combine the microgreens with the remaining 1 tablespoon olive oil in a small bowl, toss to lightly coat, and arrange 2 tablespoons of the mixture on top of each beet salad. Using 2 tablespoons, form the sour cream mixture into quenelles, or small ovals, and arrange 2 to the side of each salad. Garnish each plate with a few drops of the remaining teaspoon pomegranate molasses and serve immediately.

Ernest "Jitterbug" Rome, cook at the old Delmonico, testing the recipes at Emeril's Homebase.

BRUNCH:
A TIME FOR FAMILY

New Orleanians have never skimped on breakfast. A breakfast menu that appeared in *The Picayune's Creole Cook Book*, dating back over one hundred years, suggests sliced oranges, broiled trout with tartar sauce, broiled ham, scrambled eggs, French toast, grits and, of course, *café au lait*. This was not a restaurant menu but rather one to serve in your home!

This type of breakfast has evolved into grand brunches for which New Orleans has become famous. I witnessed that firsthand twenty years ago when I was named executive chef at Commander's Palace. Every weekend the place was packed with people enjoying Bloody Marys and Milk Punches, egg dishes of all kinds, while tapping their toes to the beat of old New Orleans jazz.

Now at Delmonico I'm thrilled to host a Sunday brunch with our signature dishes, which include omelets, quiches, house-made sausage, and the old New Orleans standby—*pain perdu* (French toast).

Miss Hilda's Asparagus
and Crabmeat Salad *on* Puff Pastry
with Saffron Crème Fraîche

MAKES 4 SERVINGS

This is a salad I developed for my mother, Miss Hilda, on Mother's Day several years ago when she came to dine at Delmonico. It combines two of her favorite ingredients—asparagus and crabmeat—with an elegant layered presentation on puff pastry.

1 **large egg**	1 **tablespoon snipped fresh chives**
1 **teaspoon milk**	1 **tablespoon fresh lemon juice**
One-half 17¼ **ounce package**	¼ **teaspoon salt**
puff pastry (1 sheet), thawed	¼ **pound jumbo lump crabmeat,**
1½ **teaspoons dry white wine**	**picked over for shells and cartilage**
⅛ **teaspoon saffron threads**	1 **ounce Sevruga caviar, optional**
½ **cup crème fraîche or sour cream**	12 **spears thin Blanched Asparagus**
¼ **cup Mayonnaise (page** 264**)**	**(page** 254**), patted dry**
or store-bought mayonnaise	12 **fresh whole chives, for garnish**

1. Preheat the oven to 400°F. Line a baking sheet with parchment paper and set aside. Beat together the egg and milk in a small bowl to make an egg wash and set aside.

2. Roll out the puff pastry to a 10-inch square on a lightly floured surface. Cut out four 3 x 5-inch rectangles and transfer to the prepared baking sheet. Using the tip of a paring knife, lightly score the tops of the puff pastry in a grid pattern, as desired, being careful not to cut all the way through. Lightly brush the tops of the puff pastry with the egg wash and bake until puffed and light golden brown, about 15 minutes. Transfer to a wire rack to cool.

3. Combine the white wine and saffron in a small bowl, stir, and let infuse for 10 minutes. Add the crème fraîche and stir to blend. Cover and refrigerate until ready to use.

4. Combine the mayonnaise, snipped chives, lemon juice, and salt and stir well. Fold in the crabmeat and then gently fold in the caviar, if using, being careful not to break the eggs. Adjust the seasoning to taste.

5. Spoon 2 tablespoons of the crème fraîche into the center of 4 plates. Carefully cut each pastry lengthwise into 2 layers and discard any uncooked dough in the center. Place the bottom pastry layers in the middle of the crème fraîche. Divide the crabmeat mixture among the pastry bottoms and lay 3 asparagus spears over each portion. Arrange the pastry lids at an angle over the asparagus and garnish each serving with 3 chives. Serve immediately.

his would make a great first course for a dinner party. To make it easy on yourself, bake the puff pastry layers earlier in the day and keep them at room temperature, and make the crab-meat salad, cover, and refrigerate until you're ready to serve it.

Make your own homemade crème fraîche by combining 1 cup heavy cream and 2 tablespoons buttermilk in a bowl. Cover it with a clean kitchen towel and let it sit at room temperature until a thick, but still pourable, consistency, 12 to 24 hours. Stir, cover with plastic wrap, and refrigerate until ready to use.

Citrus-Cured Gravlax *with*
Lemon-Caper Creole Cream Cheese

MAKES 12 TO 16 SERVINGS

We put gravlax, the Swedish specialty of cured salmon, on our brunch menu because I wanted to match it up with one of our New Orleans specialties—Creole cream cheese. I had a hunch that it would interest the local palates. My instinct paid off and it's one of our more popular brunch appetizers. Served with house-made bagels, this is a great starter.

One 8-ounce orange, washed, wiped dry, and cut into eighths

One 4-ounce lemon, washed, wiped dry, and cut into eighths

One 4-ounce lime, washed, wiped dry, and cut into eighths

2 cups kosher salt

2 tablespoons cracked black peppercorns

One 3 to 3½-pound side of salmon fillet, skin and pinbones removed, rinsed under cool water, and patted dry

1 cup roughly chopped fresh basil

1 cup roughly chopped fresh dill

1 cup roughly chopped fresh mint leaves

1 cup roughly chopped fresh parsley

1 recipe Lemon-Caper Creole Cream Cheese (recipe follows)

Assorted breads or crackers, Large Croutons (page 263), or toast points

Store-bought bagels, bagel chips, or Melba toast all would make good accompaniments to this. To serve gravlax for a crowd, thinly slice the salmon on the bias with a very sharp thin knife and serve atop crackers or sliced bread spread with this cream cheese sauce, or the more usual sour cream, capers, and chopped onions. Or serve your gravlax with ravigote sauce, as we did when we first opened Emeril's Delmonico.

Creole cream cheese faded from the local food scene for some years, but is being made again by small, independent New Orleans-area dairies. It has a unique tart flavor that seems a cross between plain yogurt and sour cream, and the texture is thick and creamy. Creole cream cheese is a common New Orleans breakfast item, served plain or over fruit, and it also makes a tasty spread when blended with regular cream cheese and other flavors, as we do here.

1. Combine the fruit, salt, and peppercorns and process to a paste in the bowl of a food processor.

2. Center a 2 x 3-foot piece of cheesecloth in a nonreactive baking dish or plastic container large enough to hold the fish flat, about 9 x 13 inches. Pack half of the citrus-salt mixture onto the skin side of the fish, spreading it out to the edges, and top with half of the herbs. Place the fish skin side down in the middle of the cheesecloth and spread the remaining salt mixture and herbs over the flesh. Fold the cheesecloth over the fish and carefully roll and turn the fish over into the cheesecloth to completely enclose.

3. Top with a second large nonreactive baking dish. Place weights or large heavy cans on the second dish to weight and press the fish. Let cure in the refrigerator for 48 hours, turning once.

4. Remove the weights and top baking dish and place the fish on work surface. Discard the wrap and scrape the salt and herb mixtures from the fish. Rinse the fish under cold running water for 1 minute to remove any remaining mixture and gently wipe dry with paper towels. Wrap in plastic wrap, place on a platter, and freeze until firm enough to slice easily, 30 to 45 minutes. (Alternatively, refrigerate until ready to slice.)

5. Remove the fish from the freezer, unwrap, and slice as thinly as possible at a slight angle. Arrange the slices decoratively on the platter or on individual plates and serve with the lemon-caper Creole cream cheese and assorted breads or toast on the side.

⁂{ Lemon-Caper Creole Cream Cheese

MAKES 1½ CUPS

8 ounces cream cheese, at room temperature	1½ teaspoons chopped, drained capers
4 ounces Creole cream cheese, at room temperature	1½ teaspoons snipped fresh chives
	½ teaspoon finely grated lemon zest
1 tablespoon fresh lemon juice	Pinch of freshly ground black pepper

1. Place all the ingredients in a medium bowl and cream together using a rubber spatula or heavy wooden spoon.

2. Spoon into a decorative bowl and serve immediately. (The cream cheese mixture will keep, tightly covered, in the refrigerator for 3 days.)

Ginger *and* Lemongrass—Marinated Fruit Salad *with* Basil Whipped Cream *and* Macadamia Nut Shortbread

MAKES 4 SERVINGS

This fruit salad makes an appearance on the Delmonico brunch menu in the summer, when the fruit is at the height of its ripeness. The ginger-lemongrass marinade and litchis give an unexpected but delightful Far Eastern twist to the salad.

Litchis (also spelled lychee) are small Chinese fruit, one to one-and-a-half inches in length, with a thin shell encasing a sweet pulp with a single seed. While it can be purchased fresh, this fragrant fruit most often is found dried or preserved in syrup in cans.

3 cups water	½ cup diced honeydew melon
2¾ cups granulated sugar	½ cup diced cantaloupe
2 ounces fresh gingerroot, peeled and thinly sliced	½ cup diced fresh pineapple
3 green cardamom pods, cracked	½ cup whole canned litchis in their syrup
1 stalk lemongrass	½ cup heavy cream
1 pod star anise	1½ teaspoons confectioners' sugar
½ cup fresh blueberries	4 leaves fresh basil, julienned
½ cup fresh blackberries	4 Macadamia Nut Shortbread Cookies (recipe follows)
½ cup fresh raspberries	
½ cup hulled and quartered fresh strawberries	

1. Combine the water, granulated sugar, ginger, cardamom, lemongrass, and anise in a medium saucepan and bring to a boil. Reduce the heat to medium and simmer, stirring occasionally, until the sugar is dissolved. Remove from the heat and let cool to room temperature. Strain the syrup and discard the solids.

2. Combine the fruit and litchis and their syrup in a large bowl and add the cooled syrup. Cover and marinate in the refrigerator for at least 1 hour and up to 8 hours.

3. Whip the cream in a medium bowl and beat with an electric mixer on medium speed or by hand until it becomes thick and frothy. Beating, add the confectioners' sugar and beat until soft peaks form. Fold in the basil and set aside.

4. Spoon 1 cup of the fruit salad with the syrup into four shallow bowls and top each serving with 3 to 4 tablespoons of the basil whipped cream. Arrange 1 shortbread cookie on the side of each bowl and serve.

❊{Macadamia Nut Shortbread Cookies

MAKES ABOUT 4 DOZEN COOKIES

The number of cookies you get from this recipe will be determined by how thickly you roll your dough. You can make this dough up to two days in advance and keep it, tightly wrapped, in the refrigerator until ready to cut and bake.

These are delicious when served with morning coffee or afternoon tea.

⅔ **cup roughly chopped macadamia nuts**	1 **small egg yolk**
½ **pound (2 sticks) unsalted butter,**	2⅔ **cups cake flour**
at room temperature	¼ **teaspoon salt**
¾ **cup plus 2 tablespoons confectioners'**	
sugar, sifted	

---

1. Preheat the oven to 350°F. Line 2 large light-colored baking sheets with parchment paper and set aside. Position the rack in the middle of the oven.

2. Spread the nuts on a small baking sheet and bake until fragrant and lightly toasted, about 8 minutes. Let cool on the baking sheet.

3. In the bowl of an electric mixer, cream together the butter and sugar, about 2 minutes. Add the egg yolk and beat to incorporate. Add the flour, nuts, and salt and gently mix until just blended, being careful not to overmix.

4. Spoon the dough onto a large sheet of plastic wrap or wax paper, forming a log about 2 inches in diameter. Fold the wrap over the dough and gently push in and under to form a smooth cylinder. Twist the ends to seal and refrigerate until firm, about 1 hour. (Alternatively, the cookies can be rolled out on a lightly floured surface and cut with a lightly floured 2-inch cookie cutter, and then refrigerated for 1 hour before baking.)

5. Slice the dough ¼ inch thick and arrange the rounds on the prepared baking sheets. Bake 1 sheet pan at a time until the shortbreads are set and the edges are light golden brown, about 20 minutes, rotating the pan after 10 minutes. Transfer to a wire rack to cool.

6. The cookies will keep in an airtight container for up to 1 week.

Steak *and* Eggs Delmonico
with Hash Brown Cakes *and* Tomato Chutney

MAKES 4 SERVINGS

Begin your meal with a Bloody Mary (page 11) or a Milk Punch (page 15), then order this hearty dish and you'll be set for the day.

Four **8-ounce boneless rib-eye steaks,**
 ³/₄ inch thick
 Salt
 Freshly ground black pepper
2 **teaspoons olive oil**

2 **tablespoons unsalted butter**
8 **large eggs**
1 **recipe Hash Brown Cakes (recipe follows)**
¹/₄to¹/₂ **cup Tomato Chutney (recipe follows)**

1. Generously season both sides of the steaks with salt and pepper.

2. Heat 2 heavy medium skillets over medium-high heat. Add 1 teaspoon of the oil to each skillet and when hot, place 2 steaks in each pan. Cook over medium-high heat to desired doneness, 4 to 5 minutes per side for medium-rare. Transfer the steaks to a large plate and tent to keep warm.

3. Pour out the drippings from each skillet and wipe clean with paper towels. Return the pans to medium-high heat and add 1 tablespoon of butter to each. When the butter is foamy, carefully crack 4 eggs, one at a time, into each skillet and season lightly with salt and pepper. Reduce the heat to medium-low, cover, and cook until the whites are firm and the yolks are just set but still soft, about 2 minutes. Uncover and using a spatula, separate the eggs from one another and gently flip. Cook on the second side until the yolks are firm and filmed over, 30 seconds. Remove from the heat.

4. To serve, arrange 2 slices of hash brown cakes in the center of each of 4 large plates and top with 1 steak. Cover each steak with 2 eggs, yolk side up, and spoon a heaping tablespoon of the tomato chutney between the eggs. Serve immediately.

Boneless rib-eye steaks cook quickly so they are convenient to serve for brunch or a crowd. Homemade Tomato Chutney tops this version of Steak and Eggs Delmonico. Some folks go crazy for this stuff and ask for extra; serve yours to taste. Or you can kick up your version by topping the eggs instead with Hollandaise Sauce (page 261) or Choron Sauce (page 135).

And cook the eggs to your liking. If you're in the mood for scrambled, then scramble them, or try poached (see Eggs Pontchartrain, page 101, for the method) for something altogether different.

✻{ Hash Brown Cakes

MAKES 4 SERVINGS

These potato cakes also can be served with any meat or poultry main course, or topped simply by fried or scrambled eggs.

If not cooking the potatoes immediately, place the shredded pieces in a large bowl of cold water to soak until needed, squeezing completely dry before cooking to prevent them from discoloring.

Two	12-**ounce Idaho potatoes**	½	**teaspoon salt**
6	**tablespoons Clarified Butter (page** 257**) or vegetable oil**	½	**teaspoon freshly ground black pepper**

1. Preheat the oven to 375°F.

2. Peel the potatoes and shred into matchstick pieces using a box grater. Squeeze in a clean kitchen cloth in batches to remove any excess liquid. Place the potatoes in a large bowl, add 2 tablespoons of the clarified butter, the salt and pepper, and toss to coat evenly.

3. Heat 2 tablespoons of the clarified butter in an 8-inch nonstick skillet over medium-high heat until hot but not smoking. Add half of the potatoes, pressing flat with the back of a spatula to flatten into a cake, and cook until set and starting to turn golden brown, 6 minutes on the first side and 3 to 4 minutes on the second side. Place on a baking sheet and repeat with the remaining clarified butter and potatoes. Bake the potato cakes until cooked through and crisp, about 10 minutes.

4. Place the potato cakes on a cutting board and cut each into quarters. Serve immediately.

*{Tomato Chutney

MAKES 1⅓ CUPS

You'll find this chutney is very versatile and provides a wonderful balance to just about anything—from grilled chicken or fish to a topping for cheese and crackers. I particularly like it as a side for fried fish and fried chicken. This recipe doubles well.

1½ **cups peeled, seeded, and chopped plum tomatoes (about 14 ounces)**	2 **tablespoons dried black currants**
¼ **cup finely chopped yellow onions**	½ **teaspoon mustard seeds**
One ½ x 1-inch-strip orange zest	⅛ **teaspoon salt**
2 **tablespoons packed light brown sugar**	⅛ **teaspoon cayenne**
2 **tablespoons apple cider vinegar**	⅛ **teaspoon ground allspice**
	⅛ **teaspoon cinnamon**

1. Combine 1 cup of the tomatoes and the remaining ingredients in a small nonreactive saucepan and bring to a boil. Reduce the heat to medium and simmer, stirring occasionally, until the mixture is thick and the liquid is nearly all evaporated, 10 to 12 minutes. Stir in the remaining ½ cup tomatoes and cook until warmed through, about 1 minute. Remove from the heat and discard the orange zest.

2. Cool slightly before serving. (The chutney will keep in an airtight container, refrigerated, for up to 6 week. Warm gently before serving or serve at room temperature.)

Eggs Pontchartrain

MAKES 4 SERVINGS

In 1699 French explorer Pierre le Moyne, Sieur d'Iberville, and his brother Jean Baptiste, Sieur de Bienville, traveled through Lake Pontchartrain (named for their French Minister of Marine) to found the city of New Orleans.

There are several interpretations of Eggs Pontchartrain in New Orleans. One features poached eggs atop crawfish and hash browns and another includes eggs on crab cakes and biscuits. Ours has poached eggs served with crispy-fried oysters and bacon, then drizzled with hollandaise flavored with tasso. Now that's what I call an over-the-top dish!

1 tablespoon white vinegar	1 recipe Tasso Hollandaise (recipe follows)
8 large eggs	
4 English muffins, split into halves and lightly toasted	1 recipe Fried Oysters (recipe follows)
	1 tablespoon chopped green onions, green tops only, for garnish
12 strips bacon, fried until crisp and strips broken in half	1 tablespoon chopped fresh parsley, for garnish

1. Pour cold water into a 10-inch sauté pan to a depth of about 2 inches. Bring to a simmer, then reduce the heat so that the surface of the water barely shimmers. Add the vinegar.

2. Break 4 of the eggs into individual saucers, then gently slide them out one at a time into the water and, with a large spoon, lift the white over the yolk. Repeat the lifting once or twice to completely enclose each yolk. Poach until the whites are set and the yolks feel firm yet soft when gently touched, 3 to 4 minutes. Remove the eggs with a slotted spoon and either serve immediately or place in a shallow pan or large bowl of cold water.

3. Repeat with the remaining eggs, adding more water as needed to keep the depth at 2 inches, and bringing the water to a simmer before adding the eggs.

4. To serve, reheat the eggs as necessary by slipping them into simmering water for 30 seconds to 1 minute. Place 2 toasted English muffin halves on each of 4 large plates and lay 3 half strips of bacon across each. Place 1 poached egg on top of each muffin half and drizzle with the tasso hollandaise. Arrange the oysters on top of the eggs and around each plate, garnish each serving with the chopped green onions and parsley, and serve immediately.

❋{Tasso Hollandaise

2 large egg yolks	1 tablespoon tepid water, as needed
1 tablespoon fresh lemon juice	¼ cup finely chopped tasso
2 teaspoons water	(about 2 ounces)
½ cup Clarified Butter (page 257), or 8	¼ teaspoon salt
tablespoons (1 stick) unsalted butter, melted	⅛ teaspoon cayenne

1. In the top of a double boiler or in a medium bowl set over a pot of barely simmering water, whisk the egg yolks with the lemon juice and 2 teaspoons water until the egg yolks are thick and pale yellow. Remove the double boiler or bowl and saucepan from the heat and gradually add the butter, whisking constantly to thicken. Add enough tepid water to thin to pouring consistency. Add the tasso, salt, and cayenne and whisk well to blend. Adjust the seasoning to taste.

2. Serve immediately, or cover to keep warm for up to 10 minutes, whisking occasionally to keep from separating.

❋{Fried Oysters

1 cup buttermilk	½ cup masa harina corn flour
2 tablespoons Emeril's Original Essence	½ cup all-purpose flour
or Creole Seasoning (page 260)	4 cups vegetable oil
16 freshly shucked oysters	
(about 1 pint), drained	

1. Combine the buttermilk with 1 tablespoon of the Essence in a medium bowl. Add the oysters and marinate for 5 minutes.

2. Combine the masa harina and flour with the remaining 1 tablespoon Essence in a shallow dish.

3. Heat the oil to 350°F in a medium heavy pot with high sides.

4. Dredge the oysters in the flour mixture and shake the pieces in a strainer to remove any excess. Carefully add to the hot oil in batches, and cook, turning occasionally, until golden on all sides, 2 to 3 minutes. Remove the oysters with a slotted spoon, drain on paper towels, and serve immediately.

Tasso is highly spiced, cured and smoked lean pork that is used as a seasoning in Cajun and Creole cooking. If you are unable to find tasso in your area, substitute chopped good-quality ham.

Chorizo *and* Manchego Cheese Omelet

There are several kinds of sausage, such as andouille and fresh pork, used in Louisiana cooking, but since I grew up on chorizo sausage, I like to use it as often as I can. Folding it in an omelet along with cheese makes a super brunch entrée or light supper.

Manchego is named for the Spanish region of La Mancha, home of Don Quixote, where this pasteurized sheep's milk cheese is made. Its mild, nutty flavor balances beautifully with the highly seasoned chorizo sausage. If you can't find manchego cheese, you can use Pecorino Romano, white Cheddar, or Monterey Jack.

Fluffy omelets are easier to make than you might think. The secret is to use a small preheated pan and to stir the eggs initially to form large, fluffy curds, such as when making scrambled eggs. Pat the eggs into an even layer, add the fillings, and then fold into a half-moon shape for a simple brunch or light supper treat.

4	ounces chorizo or hot Italian sausage, casings removed and chopped	2	tablespoons unsalted butter
6	large eggs	1/2	cup coarsely grated manchego cheese or Pecorino Romano
1/4	teaspoon salt	1/2	recipe Brabant Potatoes (page 201), optional
1/8	teaspoon freshly ground black pepper		

1. Heat a small nonstick omelet pan or 8-inch skillet over medium-high heat. Add the sausage and cook, stirring, until the fat is rendered and the sausage is browned, 5 to 6 minutes. Remove the sausage with a slotted spoon and drain on paper towels. Wipe the pan clean with paper towels.

2. Whisk the eggs, salt, and pepper in a medium bowl until frothy.

3. Return the pan to medium-high heat and add 1 tablespoon of the butter. When the butter is foamy, add half of the egg mixture and swirl to coat the bottom of the pan evenly. Using a heat-resistant rubber spatula or wooden spoon, stir the eggs lightly until almost set but still moist, 1 to 1½ minutes. Pat the egg curds into an even layer with the back of the spatula. Arrange half of the chorizo and half of the cheese across the omelet and cook undisturbed until the eggs are set but not colored, 30 seconds to 1 minute. Lift an edge of the omelet with the spatula and fold the omelet in half to enclose the filling. Slide the omelet onto a large plate and repeat with the remaining ingredients.

4. Serve the omelets immediately with Brabant potatoes on the side, as desired.

Pain Perdu *with* Homemade Pork *and* Chicken Breakfast Sausage, Cinnamon Sugar, *and* Apple Chutney

MAKES 4 SERVINGS

The Creoles who inhabited New Orleans long ago were frugal people who did not believe in wasting food. Stale or day-old French bread would reappear as bread pudding (page 236) or *pain perdu* (French for "lost bread"), the New Orleans version of French toast. No matter what you call it, this is a great way to start the day. And by finishing the bread in the oven, you'll find that it cooks all the way through and puffs up slightly.

This old-time favorite has appeared on the brunch menu since the restaurant's opening. However, the accompaniments are constantly changing; sometimes there's a sweet fruit chutney such as this one, other times the plate holds a homemade syrup or compote-like fruit sauce. Use whatever you like best, or simply dust the French toast with confectioners' sugar.

3 **large eggs**
¼ **cup sugar**
1 **teaspoon pure vanilla extract**
Pinch of salt
1 **cup heavy cream**
Eight ¾-**inch-thick slices day-old French or other crusty peasant-style bread**

2 **tablespoons vegetable oil**
2 **tablespoons unsalted butter**
1 **recipe Homemade Pork and Chicken Breakfast Sausage (recipe follows)**
1 **recipe Cinnamon Sugar (recipe follows)**
1 **recipe Apple Chutney (recipe follows)**
Syrup of choice, optional

1. Preheat the oven to 350°F.

2. Combine the eggs, sugar, vanilla, and salt in a large bowl and whisk to dissolve the sugar. Add the cream and whisk to blend.

3. Place 4 slices of the bread in the bowl with the batter and let sit until well moistened, about 2 minutes, turning once.

4. Heat half of the oil and melt half of the butter in a large nonstick skillet over medium heat.

5. Transfer the soaked bread to the pan and cook until golden brown, about 2 minutes per side, turning once. Transfer to a small baking sheet and repeat with the remaining bread.

6. Place the toast in the oven and bake until hot and cooked through, 6 to 8 minutes.

7. To serve, place 2 slices of toast on each of 4 large plates with 2 sausage patties. Sprinkle the toast with cinnamon sugar, spoon the chutney on the side, or drizzle with syrup as desired, and serve immediately.

Homemade Pork and Chicken Breakfast Sausage

MAKES 8 PATTIES, 4 SERVINGS

We've served a variety of homemade sausages at the restaurant through the years—everything from breakfast sausage and duck sausage to andouille and chorizo. You won't believe how easy this breakfast sausage is to make and it goes with all kinds of breakfast items.

- 8 ounces boneless, skinless chicken thigh meat, cut into ½-inch cubes
- 8 ounces pork butt, cut into ½-inch cubes
- 1 teaspoon minced garlic
- ½ teaspoon plus ¼ teaspoon salt
- ½ teaspoon plus ⅛ teaspoon paprika
- ½ teaspoon fennel seeds
- ¼ teaspoon chili powder
- ¼ teaspoon freshly ground black pepper
- ¼ teaspoon chopped fresh oregano
- ⅛ teaspoon cayenne
- ⅛ teaspoon chopped fresh thyme
- 2 teaspoons vegetable oil

1. Combine all the ingredients except the oil in the bowl of a food processor and pulse until the meat is finely chopped and the ingredients are well combined, scraping down the sides of the bowl as needed. (Alternatively, pass the meat through a meat grinder fitted with a fine metal plate, or according to the manufacturer's instructions.) Transfer to a medium bowl, cover, and refrigerate at least 4 hours or overnight.

2. Preheat the oven to 350°F. Cover a baking sheet with aluminum foil and set aside.

3. Form the meat mixture into 8 equal portions, 2 ounces each, about ½ inch thick.

4. Heat 1 teaspoon of the oil in a large nonstick skillet over medium-high heat. Add half of the patties and cook until browned, 2 minutes on each side. Transfer the cooked patties to the prepared baking sheet and repeat with the remaining teaspoon oil and sausage patties. Bake the patties until cooked through and an instant-read thermometer registers an internal temperature of 140°F, 10 minutes.

5. Serve hot.

✳︎ Cinnamon Sugar

MAKES ¼ CUP

You can use this cinnamon sugar on buttered toast and pancakes or sprinkle it on sugar cookies before they go into the oven for a crunchy texture and extra flavor.

¼ **cup sugar**
1 **teaspoon ground cinnamon**

Combine the sugar and cinnamon in a small bowl and stir to blend. Transfer to an airtight container until ready to serve. (The mixture will keep in an airtight container at room temperature for up to 3 months.)

✳︎ Apple Chutney

MAKES 4 CUPS

I like this chutney to be fairly chunky with the apples retaining most of their texture. If you prefer a soft texture, cook it a little longer to give you an applesauce-like consistency. The chutney is a great accompaniment to roasted or grilled pork chops or pork loin.

---

6 **Granny Smith apples (about 2½ pounds), peeled, cored, and cut into ½-inch dice**
½ **cup sugar**
½ **cup water**
½ **cup apple cider vinegar**
2 **tablespoons fresh lemon juice**
One **2 to 3-inch cinnamon stick**

---

1. Combine all the ingredients in a medium saucepan and bring to a boil. Reduce the heat to medium-low and cook, stirring occasionally, until the mixture is thick and nearly all the liquid is evaporated but the apples are still slightly chunky, 8 to 10 minutes. Remove the cinnamon stick.

2. Serve warm or at room temperature. (The chutney will keep in an airtight container, refrigerated, for up to 5 days.)

Jumbo Lump Crabmeat *and* Leek Quiche *with* Roasted Fennel *and* Arugula Salad *and* Chive Crème Fraîche

As far as I'm concerned, leeks are not used often enough and I think they're a natural for the New Orleans table. They're related to the onion and garlic, but the flavor is milder, making it perfect to pair with the delicate flavor of crabmeat.

We use fresh jumbo lump crabmeat for this brunch offering at Emeril's Delmonico, but you can use whatever crabmeat is available from your local market. Small boiled shrimp (or roughly chopped large boiled shrimp) also could be substituted.

- 1 recipe Flaky Butter Crust (recipe follows)
- 4 leeks (about 1½ pounds)
- 2 tablespoons unsalted butter
- 2 large eggs
- 1 tablespoon all-purpose flour
- 1 teaspoon salt
- ½ teaspoon ground white pepper
- ½ cup heavy cream
- ¼ cup milk
- 1 tablespoon chopped fresh soft herbs, such as chervil, tarragon, and chives
- ½ pound jumbo lump crabmeat, picked over for shells and cartilage
- ½ cup freshly grated Parmigiano-Reggiano
- 1 recipe Roasted Fennel and Arugula Salad (recipe follows)
- 1 recipe Chive Crème Fraîche (recipe follows)

1. Roll out the dough to an 11-inch circle on a lightly floured surface. Fit into a 9-inch fluted tart pan with a removable bottom and trim the edges. (Alternatively, a 9-inch pie pan can be used.) Refrigerate for at least 30 minutes.

2. Preheat the oven to 375°F.

3. Line the pastry with parchment paper and fill with pie weights or dried beans. Bake until the crust is set, 12 to 14 minutes. Remove the paper and weights and bake until golden brown, 8 to 10 minutes. Remove from the oven and cool on a wire rack. Leave the oven on.

4. Trim off the root ends and green parts from the leeks. Cut the leeks lengthwise in half and then crosswise into ¼-inch-thick slices. Place in a bowl of cold water and rinse well. Drain and rinse again in fresh water, as needed. Drain well.

5. Melt the butter in a medium skillet over medium-high heat. When the butter is foamy, add the leeks, reduce the heat to medium-low, cover, and cook until the leeks are very soft but not browned, about 15 minutes, stirring occasionally. Remove from the heat and drain in a fine-mesh strainer.

6. Combine the eggs, flour, salt, and white pepper in a large bowl and whisk to blend. Add the cream, milk, and herbs and whisk well.

7. Evenly distribute the leeks, crabmeat, and ¼ cup of the cheese across the bottom of the prepared pastry shell and pour in the custard mixture. Sprinkle the remaining ¼ cup cheese over the top and bake until the custard is set and the top is golden brown, 30 to 35 minutes.

8. Let rest on a wire rack for at least 30 minutes before serving.

*}Flaky Butter Crust

MAKES ONE 9-INCH TART OR PIECRUST

This crust can be made quickly, either in the food processor or by hand, and is ideal not only for quiches, but also for pot pies and empanadas. The recipe doubles easily and can be frozen, tightly wrapped, for up to two months.

1¼ cups all-purpose flour	4 tablespoons ice water, or more
¼ teaspoon salt	as needed
7 tablespoons unsalted butter, chilled and cut into pieces	

1. To make the dough in a food processor, combine the flour, salt, and butter in the processor and process until the mixture resembles coarse crumbs, about 10 seconds. With the machine running, add the ice water through the feed tube and pulse quickly 5 or 6 times, or until the dough comes together and starts to pull away from the sides of the container. Gather the dough into a ball, flatten it into a disk, and wrap in plastic wrap. Refrigerate for at least 1 hour.

2. To make the dough by hand, combine the flour, salt, and butter in a medium bowl, and mix with a pastry blender or your fingertips until the mixture resembles coarse crumbs. Add the water, 1 tablespoon at a time, and mix until the dough comes together and is no longer dry, being careful not to overmix. Form into a disk, wrap in plastic wrap, and refrigerate for at least 1 hour.

Roasted Fennel and Arugula Salad

MAKES 6 SERVINGS

I thought that fennel, with its delicate anise flavor, would perk up the taste buds of our local customers since they're used to Herbsaint, which is also anise flavored. It's perfect with the quiche.

2 fennel bulbs (1 to 1½ pounds), trimmed, cut in half, and then cut into ½ x 1½-inch strips, fronds reserved	½ teaspoon salt
	¼ teaspoon ground white pepper
	¼ teaspoon chopped fresh thyme
2 tablespoons olive oil	4 ounces fresh arugula, tough stems removed, rinsed, and patted dry
1 teaspoon minced garlic	
½ teaspoon sugar	1 tablespoon fresh lemon juice

1. Preheat the oven to 375°F.

2. Chop the fennel fronds to measure 2 tablespoons and set aside. Discard the fennel stems.

3. Arrange the fennel in the center of a large piece of aluminum foil and drizzle with the oil.

4. Sprinkle the garlic, sugar, salt, pepper, and thyme over the fennel and fold the aluminum to make a pouch, turning the edges under to seal. Place on a baking sheet and roast until the fennel is tender, 40 to 45 minutes.

5. Unwrap the foil packet and let the fennel cool to room temperature, reserving the fennel cooking juices.

6. Place the arugula in a large bowl and add the cooled fennel. Drizzle the salad with the reserved fennel cooking juices and the lemon juice. Season to taste with salt and pepper and serve.

Chive Crème Fraîche

MAKES 1 CUP

This sauce would make a great accompaniment to sliced smoked salmon or any caviar canapé. Or use it to top baked potatoes.

1 cup crème fraîche	¼ teaspoon salt
1 tablespoon finely chopped fresh chives	Pinch of ground white pepper
1 teaspoon dry white wine	

Combine all the ingredients in a small bowl and whisk to combine. Serve immediately or store, covered, in the refrigerator for up to 3 days.

Irene Polk, Elmer Decquir, and Atwood Davis, testing the old Delmonico recipes at Homebase

SEAFOOD:
DOWN BY THE RIVER

New Orleans is a seafood city. Mollusks, crustaceans (both freshwater and saltwater), and fish are prominently featured on home and restaurant menus in New Orleans and prepared every which way—fried, broiled, stuffed, and baked—and often are enveloped, drizzled, or sprinkled with sauces that add to the flavors that bounce around your lips.

The bills of fare in chef Charles Ranhofer's book *The Epicurean* often suggested oysters to begin the meal. Also on his menus were dishes that highlighted salmon, bass, trout, sole, crabs, shrimp, crayfish, and lobster.

At old Delmonico the chefs' specialties included soft-shell crabs (a local delicacy), both Maine and Florida lobsters, as well as flounder, trout, snapper, sweet lake shrimp, and crawfish. (And yes, crawfish and crayfish both are proper spellings; it's crawfish in the Creole vernacular.)

And on our menus, we pay special attention to our seafood dishes that range from jumbo shrimp, pompano, trout, flounder, and crabmeat from the Gulf of Mexico to plump salty oysters harvested in the bays along the Louisiana coast, as well as lobster, salmon, and other fresh seafood that our suppliers obtain specially for Emeril's Delmonico.

Seafood-Stuffed Shrimp
with Delmonico Lemon Butter Sauce

MAKES 32 STUFFED SHRIMP

These stuffed shrimp were Elmer's creation at old Delmonico, and were offered like this on the menu as an entrée. They were also served threaded on skewers with several pieces of fish and whole oysters and broiled, and could be found as well atop catfish meunière.

They would do well as hors d'oeuvres for cocktail parties. The stuffing mixture can be used to stuff soft-shell crabs or vegetables, such as eggplants, zucchinis, and bell peppers.

1 quart water	¼ cup chopped green onions
6 ounces small shrimp, peeled, deveined, and finely chopped	1 small bay leaf
4 ounces white or claw crabmeat, picked over for shells and cartilage	1½ tablespoons LeGoût Chicken Base or other thick chicken base
1 tablespoon salt	1 tablespoon A1 Steak Sauce
1 dozen freshly shucked oysters and their liquor	½ teaspoon Worcestershire
	½ teaspoon hot sauce
1 tablespoon unsalted butter	6 tablespoons cracker meal
½ cup chopped yellow onions	32 large shrimp (about 1¼ pounds), peeled and deveined
¼ cup chopped celery	
¼ cup chopped green bell peppers	1 teaspoon paprika
¾ teaspoon chopped garlic	½ recipe Delmonico Lemon Butter Sauce (recipe follows)

1. Line a large baking sheet with parchment paper or aluminum foil and set aside.

2. Combine the water, chopped shrimp, crabmeat, and salt in a large saucepan and bring to a gentle boil over high heat. Add the oysters and their liquor cook until the edges of the oysters curl, about 3 minutes.

3. Remove from the heat, drain, and reserve ½ cup of the cooking liquid.

4. Transfer the boiled seafood to a food processor and pulse to finely chop. Set aside.

5. Melt the butter in a medium pot over medium-low heat. Add the yellow onions, celery, bell peppers, and garlic and cook, stirring occasionally, until the vegetables are soft and golden, 5 to 10 minutes. Increase the heat to medium-high, add the green onions and bay leaf and cook, stirring, for 1 minute. Add the reserved seafood cooking liquid and cook until most of the liquid has evaporated, about 3 minutes.

6. Remove from the heat and stir in the chicken base. Add the chopped seafood mixture, steak sauce, Worcestershire, and hot sauce and stir to blend well. Discard the bay leaf. Fold in the cracker meal, stirring until the mixture binds together.

7. Transfer the mixture to a bowl, cover, and refrigerate until completely chilled, about 3 hours.

8. Using a small paring knife, carefully butterfly the large shrimp so that they open flat. Place a heaping tablespoon of the stuffing into each of the shrimp and roll from the tail end to the head end, pressing gently to seal. Arrange the stuffed shrimp 2 inches apart on the prepared baking sheet.

9. Adjust the oven rack to the top third of the oven and preheat the oven to broil.

10. Sprinkle the shrimp with the paprika, drizzle with ¼ cup of the lemon butter sauce, and broil until lightly browned, about 5 minutes. Reduce the oven temperature to 350°F, adjust the oven rack to the middle third of the oven, and bake until the shrimp are cooked through and the stuffing is hot, 10 to 12 minutes.

11. Remove the shrimp from the oven, arrange on a platter or plates, and drizzle with the remaining sauce. Serve warm.

⁑{ Delmonico Lemon Butter Sauce

MAKES 1¼ CUPS

This sauce accompanied many dishes at the old Delmonico—from Trout Delmonico (page 126) and Seafood-Stuffed Shrimp to vegetables. While similar sauces found at other New Orleans restaurants contain hot sauce or ground pepper, the Delmonico recipe has neither. About this, chef Ernest "Jitterbug" Rome says that "the fish or other items we cooked were seasoned (before being cooked), so no additional pepper was needed in the sauce."

½ pound (2 sticks) unsalted butter	¼ teaspoon salt
3 tablespoons fresh lemon juice	
2 tablespoons plus 2 teaspoons Worcestershire	

1. Combine all the ingredients in a medium saucepan, and cook over medium heat until the butter is melted. Increase the heat to medium-high and cook at a low boil for 2 minutes.

2. Remove from the heat and serve immediately.

Fried Soft-Shell Crabs Amandine

The blue crabs native to the Gulf South and Atlantic coastline shed their hard shells (or exoskeletons) many times as they grow. Before molting, the crabs form a soft new shell under the old one, which hardens within twelve hours. The crabs caught in this soft-shell state are a popular delicacy in south Louisiana.

When the LaFranca family operated the restaurant, the menu often offered soft-shell crabs broiled, fried, or stuffed, and served with lemon butter sauce or Creole meunière sauce. The classic French *beurre meunière* sauce is made by browning butter to a light hazelnut color and then adding lemon juice and parsley. Many New Orleans restaurants have their own particular version. Some meunière sauces are made by combining a rich brown stock with butter, lemon juice, Worcestershire sauce, and minced parsley. The LaFranca version was simple—their regular lemon butter sauce (page 117) was cooked just a bit longer to give it a richer color and deeper flavor.

4	soft-shell crabs, about 4 ounces each		Vegetable oil, for frying
1	cup all-purpose flour	12	tablespoons (1½ sticks) unsalted butter
1	teaspoon salt		
¼	teaspoon cayenne	½	cup blanched sliced almonds
1	cup buttermilk	2	tablespoons fresh lemon juice
2	large eggs	1½	tablespoons Worcestershire
1	cup cracker meal		Pinch of salt

1. Using kitchen shears, cut each crab across the face to remove the eye sockets and the lower mouth. Carefully lift up the apron and remove the gills. Gently rinse under cold running water, pat dry, and set aside.

2. Combine the flour with the salt and cayenne in a shallow bowl. Whisk together the buttermilk and eggs in another shallow bowl. Put the cracker meal in a third bowl.

3. Heat enough oil to come ½ inch up the sides of a large cast-iron skillet or Dutch oven over medium-high heat until hot but not smoking, about 350°F.

4. Dredge the crabs in the seasoned flour, and then dip in the buttermilk mixture, allowing any excess to drip off. Dredge the crabs in the cracker meal, making sure that the legs are well breaded.

5. In 2 batches, add the crabs to the pan, top side down, and cook until golden brown and just cooked through, 2 to 3 minutes per side. Drain on paper towels.

6. Pour the fat from the pan and wipe clean with paper towels. Return the pan to medium heat and add the butter. When the butter begins to foam, add the almonds and cook, stirring, until fragrant and beginning to brown, about 1 minute. Remove the almonds with a slotted spoon, reduce the heat to low, and cook the butter until it begins to brown and smell nutty, about 1 minute. Remove from the heat, add the lemon juice, Worcestershire, and salt and stir to combine. Return the pan to low heat and cook until the butter is browned, about 30 seconds. Remove from the heat, add the almonds, and swirl to coat with the sauce.

7. To serve, place 1 crab in the center of each of 4 large plates. Spoon the sauce over the crabs and serve immediately.

Crawfish Étouffée

In Louisiana, crawfish étouffée is usually served with steamed or boiled long-grain white rice, but it can be used for all sorts of things. At the old Delmonico restaurant it was used as a sauce on sautéed trout or red snapper. The restaurant also used this as a filling for crawfish omelets. What a great idea! Elmer Decquir made this dish whenever crawfish were in season.

One 28-ounce can chopped tomatoes, and their juice	1½ pounds peeled crawfish tails with their fat
8 tablespoons (1 stick) unsalted butter	2 bay leaves
1 cup chopped yellow onions	1 teaspoon Worcestershire
½ cup chopped celery	1 teaspoon A1 Steak Sauce
½ cup chopped green onions	½ teaspoon hot sauce
½ teaspoon minced garlic	1 recipe White Rice (recipe follows)
2 tablespoons LeGoût Chicken Base or other thick chicken base	

1. Place the tomatoes and their juice in a food processor and puree. Set aside.

2. Melt the butter in a medium pot over medium-high heat. When the butter is foamy, add the yellow onions, celery, green onions, and garlic and cook, stirring, until soft, about 4 minutes. Add the pureed tomatoes and the chicken base and bring to a boil. Reduce the heat and simmer for 5 minutes. Add the crawfish, bay leaves, Worcestershire, steak sauce, and hot sauce and return to a boil. Reduce the heat and simmer uncovered, stirring occasionally, for 15 minutes.

3. Remove from the heat, discard the bay leaves, and adjust the seasoning to taste. Ladle the étouffée into the center of 6 to 8 large bowls and place a large spoonful of hot rice in the center. Serve immediately.

*}White Rice

Did you know the state of Louisiana is the second greatest rice producer in the United States?

Here's a quick refresher recipe for basic rice that's great every time. Just don't stir it until it's had a chance to rest after cooking! In this cookbook, we call to serve rice with the Chicken and Smoked Sausage Gumbo (page 62) and St. Paul's Seafood Gumbo (page 60), as well as with this Crawfish Étouffée. Or, you can serve it as we do in south Louisiana, atop red beans or as a side to any fish or chicken dish.

2	cups long-grain white rice	1½	teaspoons salt
4	cups water or canned low-sodium chicken broth		

1. Combine the rice, water, and salt in a medium saucepan and bring to a boil over high heat. Reduce the heat to low, cover, and simmer undisturbed until all the liquid is absorbed, about 20 minutes. Remove from the heat and let sit, covered, for 5 to 10 minutes.

2. Fluff the rice with a fork. Serve hot.

Lobster Thermidor

I keep finding references to Napoleon Bonaparte in my food research. For example, did you know that the great French chef Antonin Carême is said to have made Napoleon's wedding cake? It is also believed that the dish Chicken Marengo (an old New Orleans favorite) is attributed to Napoleon's chef who created it to celebrate victory over the Austrians at Marengo in the Italian Piedmont. Then while traveling through the South of France, he decided to rest for the night near the town of Bessières. There he had a local innkeeper prepare him an omelet, which he enjoyed so much that he ordered the townspeople to gather all the eggs in the village to prepare a huge one for his army the next day. Then there is the fine Napoleon brandy as well as the delicious puff pastry dessert known as a Napoleon.

And now I find out legend has it that Napoleon named this dish after the month in which he first was served it. (Evidently, Thermidor was the eleventh month of the Republican calendar used for a short time after the French Revolution.) Well, if nothing else, Napoleon ate well. I have to agree that this dish, a real classic, is fit for an emporer.

2 lemons, halved	¼ cup heavy cream
1 medium yellow onion, quartered	¼ teaspoon plus ⅛ teaspoon salt
1 Bouquet Garni (recipe follows)	⅛ teaspoon ground white pepper
Two 1½ to 1¾-pound live Maine lobsters	½ cup plus 2 tablespoons finely grated Parmigiano-Reggiano
2 tablespoons unsalted butter	
2 tablespoons minced shallots	1 tablespoon Dijon mustard
½ teaspoon minced garlic	1 tablespoon finely chopped fresh tarragon
2 tablespoons all-purpose flour	
2 tablespoons cognac or brandy	2 teaspoons finely chopped fresh parsley, plus additional for garnish
¾ cup milk	

The basis for Thermidor sauce is a traditional French béchamel, which is composed of a light roux with milk added to make a creamy sauce. This one is thicker than usual as it is used to make a filling.

We suggest you make additional room for the Thermidor stuffing by pulling the crawlers or front legs from the head region of the lobster shells. Make sure you keep the tail and head portions of the shell intact while removing the meat, as the large half shells make an impressive presentation when stuffed.

1. Preheat the oven to 375°F. Line a baking sheet with aluminum foil and set aside.

2. Bring a pot of salted water containing the lemons, quartered onion, and bouquet garni to a boil. Add the lobsters and cook until red and firm, 8 to 10 minutes. Transfer the lobsters to an ice bath to stop the cooking process.

3. When the lobsters are cool enough to handle, cut in half lengthwise with a heavy sharp knife and carefully extract the tail meat. Remove the large claws from the body and gently crack with the back of a heavy knife to extract the meat. Gently pull the front legs from the shell and discard. Dice the tail meat and claw meat and set aside.

4. Place the halved lobster shells on the prepared baking sheet, cut sides down, and roast until dry, 5 to 6 minutes. Let cool on the baking sheet.

5. Melt the butter in a medium saucepan over medium heat. Add the shallots and garlic and cook, stirring, until fragrant, about 30 seconds. Add the flour and whisk to blend. Cook, stirring constantly with a heavy wooden spoon to make a light roux, about 2 minutes. Add the cognac and cook, stirring, for 10 seconds. Add the milk slowly, stirring constantly to incorporate. Bring to a boil, reduce the heat, and simmer until thick enough to coat the back of a spoon, 2 to 3 minutes. Slowly add the cream, stirring constantly, until all is incorporated. Cook, stirring, over medium heat for 1 minute. (The mixture will be very thick.) Add the salt and pepper and stir well.

6. Remove from the heat and stir in ½ cup of the cheese, the mustard, tarragon, and the 2 teaspoons of parsley. Fold in the lobster meat. Divide the mixture among the lobster shells and place stuffed side up on a clean baking sheet. Sprinkle the top of each lobster half with 1½ teaspoons of the remaining 2 tablespoons cheese and bake until the tops are golden brown, 14 to 15 minutes.

7. Place 1 lobster half on each of 4 large plates, garnish with additional parsley, and serve immediately.

*{Bouquet Garni

MAKES 1 BOUQUET

5 sprigs fresh thyme	10 whole peppercorns
2 bay leaves	3 sprigs fresh parsley

Put all the ingredients in the center of a 6-inch square of cheesecloth. Bring the corners together and tie securely with kitchen twine.

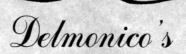

Delmonico's

100th Anniversary Dinner

Thursday, November 9, 1995

⚜ *Menu* ⚜

Wine & Cheese Upstairs in the Historic Home
Chimney Rock Fume Blanc, 1994

⚜ ⚜ ⚜

Shrimp Remoulade
Estancia Chardonnay, 1993

⚜ ⚜ ⚜

Turtle Soup
Estancia Chardonnay, 1993

⚜ ⚜ ⚜

Mixed Green Salad
with Rose's Special Creole Vinaigrette

⚜ ⚜ ⚜

Soft Shell Crab Meuniere with
Baked Creole Eggplant
Estancia Chardonnay, 1993

⚜ ⚜ ⚜

Lemon Ice

⚜ ⚜ ⚜

6 oz. Filet Mignon with Burgundy Sauce
and New Potatoes
Franciscan Cabernet Sauvignon, 1992

⚜ ⚜ ⚜

Cherries Jubilee
Mumm Napa Cuvee Blanc de Noir

Trout Delmonico

This signature dish from the LaFranca's Delmonico tenure is a celebration of local seafood, with large trout fillets topped by shrimp and oysters and lemon butter sauce—simple, elegant, and delicious.

4 tablespoons (½ stick) unsalted butter, melted	12 medium shrimp, peeled and deveined
1 tablespoon fresh lemon juice	12 medium freshly shucked oysters, drained
½ teaspoon plus ⅛ teaspoon salt	1 teaspoon chopped fresh parsley
½ teaspoon plus ⅛ teaspoon ground white pepper	4 fresh parsley sprigs, for garnish
Four 7 to 8-ounce trout fillets	4 lemon wedges, for garnish
	4 tomato wedges, for garnish

1. Preheat the oven to 350°F. Line a large baking sheet with parchment paper.

2. Combine the melted butter, lemon juice, ⅛ teaspoon of the salt, and ⅛ teaspoon of the white pepper in a small bowl.

3. Arrange the fish on the baking sheet without touching and place 3 shrimp on top of each fillet, spacing them about 1 inch apart. Using a pastry brush, lightly coat the tops of the fillets and the shrimp with the lemon butter mixture and season each with ⅛ teaspoon of the remaining salt and ⅛ teaspoon of the remaining white pepper. Bake, basting twice with the lemon butter mixture, until the fish is opaque and the shrimp are just pink, 8 to 10 minutes.

4. Remove the fish from the oven. Increase the heat to broil and move the top rack to the highest position. Place 3 oysters on top of each fillet, alternating with the shrimp. Brush the fish, shrimp, and oysters with the remaining lemon butter mixture, sprinkle each fillet with ¼ teaspoon of the parsley, and broil until the edges of the oysters begin to curl, 3 to 4 minutes.

5. Arrange 1 fillet on each of 4 serving plates. Garnish the plates with the fresh parsley sprigs and lemon and tomato wedges and serve immediately.

Trout Elmer

The cooks in the old Delmonico kitchen were always looking for ways to use what they had on hand. Elmer Decquir experimented with the anchovy dressing that was used to stuff artichokes and created a trout roulade that became a menu standard.

Six	8-ounce trout fillets	½	teaspoon paprika
1	recipe Elmer's Bread Crumb Stuffing (recipe follows)	½	recipe Lemon Butter Sauce (page 117) Chopped fresh parsley, for garnish

1. Preheat the oven to 350°F. Line a baking sheet with parchment paper and set aside.

2. One at a time, place the trout fillets between 2 sheets of plastic wrap and pound with the flat side of a meat mallet until ¼ inch thick. Place on the prepared baking sheet. Spread ¼ cup of the bread crumb stuffing over each fillet and roll to enclose, jelly-roll fashion. Sprinkle each fillet with ⅛ teaspoon of the paprika, then drizzle each with about 2 tablespoons of the lemon butter sauce. Bake until the fish flakes with a fork, about 15 minutes. Increase the oven temperature to broil and cook until the tops of the fillets are golden brown, about 3 minutes.

3. To serve, place 1 trout fillet on each of 6 plates, garnish with parsley, and serve immediately.

⋇Elmer's Bread Crumb Stuffing

MAKES ABOUT 1½ CUPS

This stuffing is very versatile and can be used to stuff different foods—from Trout Elmer and Stuffed Artichokes (page 218) to butterflied shrimp and tomatoes. The stuffing can be made in advance and kept refrigerated in an airtight container for up to three days.

¼	cup olive oil	1	bay leaf
¾	cup chopped green onions (green parts only), about 1 bunch,	1	teaspoon Worcestershire
1	ounce anchovy fillets packed in oil, chopped, with their oil	1	teaspoon A1 Steak Sauce
		½	teaspoon hot sauce
		¾	cup fine dry bread crumbs

1. Heat the oil in a small skillet over medium heat. Add the green onions and cook, stirring, until the onions are very soft, about 2 minutes. Add the anchovies with their oil and continue to cook, stirring, for 1 minute.

2. Add the bay leaf, Worcestershire, steak sauce, and hot sauce and cook, stirring, for 2 minutes. Transfer the mixture to a mixing bowl, add the bread crumbs, and mix well. Remove and discard the bay leaf. Let sit until cool enough to handle.

Pompano en Papillote *on a* Bed of Vegetable Ribbons *with* Emeril's Lemon Butter Sauce

MAKES 4 SERVINGS

Many old-line New Orleans restaurants featured dishes cooked *en papillote* (in a bag), a simple cooking method that steams food inside its parchment paper package. For some reason the dish became rather passé for a time but I reintroduced it on our menu because it's a great way to cook fish. The fish and vegetables steam in the bag, which, while cooking, puffs up into a dome. When the bag is opened tableside, it makes a dramatic presentation. Of course, since I love butter, we serve it with a lemony butter sauce!

1 large zucchini, peeled and trimmed	Four 8-ounce skinless pompano fillets
1 large carrot, peeled and trimmed	2 teaspoons olive oil
3 tablespoons cold unsalted butter, cut into slivers	Four 16 x 24-inch pieces parchment paper
1 tablespoon minced shallots	2 teaspoons fresh lemon juice
1¾ teaspoons herbes de Provence	1 large egg white, lightly beaten
½ teaspoon minced garlic	1 recipe Emeril's Lemon Butter Sauce (recipe follows)
¾ teaspoon salt	4 sprigs fresh parsley, for garnish
½ teaspoon freshly ground black pepper	

1. Preheat the oven to 400°F. Lightly oil a large baking sheet and set aside.

2. Cut the zucchini and carrot into thin, wide ribbons using a wide-blade vegetable peeler. Place the ribbons in a bowl and toss with 1 tablespoon of the butter slivers, the shallots, ¾ teaspoon of the herbes de Provence, the garlic, ¼ teaspoon of the salt, and ¼ teaspoon of the pepper. Set aside.

3. Rub the fish fillets on both sides with the olive oil and season with the remaining ½ teaspoon salt and ¼ teaspoon pepper.

4. Fold each parchment sheet in half lengthwise and using scissors, cut each folded sheet into a large heart shape, as if making a valentine. Open the sheets flat and arrange one-quarter of the vegetable mixture in the center of the bottom portion of each sheet and top with 1 fish

Pompano are a flat fish found in the temperate and tropical waters of the western Atlantic and also are caught throughout the year in the Gulf of Mexico, with major fishing occurring in the spring. The fish range in size from 1¼ to 4 pounds, with most averaging about 2 pounds. Pompano has long been a favorite fish on New Orleans menus and it's easy to see why—the flesh is firm and moist, and the flavor is rich and buttery.

fillet. Sprinkle each fillet with ¼ teaspoon of the remaining herbes de Provence, ½ teaspoon of the lemon juice, and dot with ½ tablespoon of the remaining butter slivers. Fold the top section of parchment over the fish and roll the edges together to seal the fish tightly in the bags.

5. Place the bags on the prepared baking sheet and using a pastry brush, paint the tops with the egg white. Bake until the fish is opaque and the vegetables are tender, about 15 minutes.

6. Place the fish packets on 4 large plates. Using scissors, cut along the top of each bag and roll it back with a fork to expose the fish. Spoon the lemon butter sauce over the fish, garnish each plate with 1 parsley sprig, and serve immediately.

*{Emeril's Lemon Butter Sauce

MAKES 1½ CUPS

This sauce is a bit different from the standard French butter sauce, or *beurre blanc*. We've added cream to ours as a stabilizer and to give the sauce a slightly richer flavor. It's also different from the old rerstaurant's Delmonico Lemon Butter Sauce on page 117, which includes Worcestershire sauce and is boiled briefly.

You'll find this is tasty paired with just about any poached or roasted fish, as well as with simply cooked vegetables, like Blanched Asparagus (page 254).

1	cup dry white wine	½	pound (2 sticks) cold unsalted butter, cut into pieces
3	lemons, peeled and quartered		
1	tablespoon minced shallots	1	teaspoon salt
1	tablespoon minced garlic	⅛	teaspoon freshly ground black pepper
½	cup heavy cream	1	tablespoon finely chopped fresh parsley

1. Combine the wine, lemons, shallots, and garlic in a medium saucepan and bring to a boil. Reduce the heat to medium-low and simmer until reduced in volume by half, about 20 minutes, stirring occasionally and mashing the lemons with the back of a spoon to break them up. Add the cream and cook until reduced by half, about 3 minutes.

2. Whisk in the butter, 1 tablespoon at a time, adding each piece before the previous one has been completely incorporated and removing the pan from the heat periodically to prevent the sauce from getting too hot and breaking; it should be thick enough to coat the back of a spoon. Whisk in the salt and pepper.

3. Strain the sauce through a fine-mesh strainer into a saucepan or bowl, pressing against the solids with the back of a spoon to extract as much liquid as possible. Fold in the parsley and cover to keep warm until ready to serve, stirring occasionally.

Gulf Seafood—Stuffed Flounder, Choron Sauce, and Cornmeal Fried Shrimp

MAKES 4 SERVINGS

Flounder, sole, and halibut are all flatfish. Because we are able to get flounder fresh from the Gulf of Mexico, we like to use it whenever we can. Stuffed flounder has been a New Orleans classic for years, but when I decided to put it on the menu I wanted to put my mark on it by not only stuffing the flounder but also topping it with crispy-fried shrimp, also from the Gulf. The addition of the Choron sauce (béarnaise sauce to which tomato puree has been added) is a New Orleans touch that I wanted to include.

Adapt this stuffing to suit your taste, or to the seafood that's available in your area. For a stronger seafood flavor, use a combination of shrimp, crabmeat, and fish.

2	teaspoons unsalted butter	1/2	teaspoon filé powder
2	tablespoons olive oil	1/4	teaspoon salt
1/3	cup finely chopped yellow onions	1/2	cup Shrimp Stock (page 267),
1/3	cup finely chopped green bell peppers		Fish Stock (page 259), or bottled clam juice
1/3	cup finely chopped celery	1/2	cup finely chopped green onions
1	teaspoon minced garlic	1	tablespoon chopped fresh parsley
12	ounces assorted fresh seafood, to include fresh Gulf fish, such as amberjack, mahi mahi, lemon fish, cobia, trout, redfish, drum, or lump crabmeat or Gulf shrimp, cut into 1/2-inch cubes, or a combination	2	teaspoons fresh lemon juice
		1	teaspoon Worcestershire
		1	teaspoon hot sauce
		Four	14 to 16-ounce flounders, boned, heads and fins removed, tails on
2	teaspoons Emeril's Original Essence or Creole Seasoning (page 260)	1	recipe Choron Sauce (recipe follows)
2	cups crumbled day-old Cornbread (recipe follows)	1	recipe Cornmeal Fried Shrimp (recipe follows)

1. Preheat the oven to 350°F. Grease 2 baking sheets with 1 teaspoon of the butter each and set aside.

2. Heat the oil in a large skillet or sauté pan over medium-high heat. Add the yellow onions, bell peppers, and celery and cook, stirring, until soft, 3 to 4 minutes. Add the garlic and cook, stirring, until fragrant, 30 seconds. Add the seafood and 1 teaspoon of the Essence and cook, stirring, until the fish are just opaque, 3 to 4 minutes. Add the cornbread, filé powder, and salt and stir to blend. Add the shrimp stock, green onions, parsley, lemon juice, Worcestershire, and hot sauce, stir to blend, and remove from the heat. Let sit until cool enough to handle.

3. Season the flesh side of each fish with ¼ teaspoon of the remaining Essence. Place the fish, flesh side up, on the prepared baking sheets. With a sharp boning knife, cut along the center bone of the fish. Carefully peel open the fish, pulling the flesh back to form a pocket. Place about ¾ cup of the stuffing in the middle of each. Lay the flaps back over the stuffing and gently press into place. Bake until the fish are opaque and the stuffing is firm, about 15 minutes.

4. Arrange 1 fish in the center of each of 4 large plates. Spoon the Choron sauce over the fish and top each portion with 3 fried shrimp. Serve immediately.

⁕{ Cornbread

MAKES ONE 9-INCH ROUND OR 4 CUPS CRUMBLED

This is a good, all-around cornbread to serve at the dinner table, or use for a stuffing. For a finer crumb and more pronounced corn flavor, eliminate the flour and increase the amount of cornmeal to two cups, as they do in my wife Alden's family. Let the cornbread go stale overnight before using it in a dressing.

¼ cup plus 1 tablespoon vegetable oil	1 teaspoon salt
1 cup yellow cornmeal	¼ teaspoon cayenne
1 cup all-purpose flour	1 cup buttermilk
2 teaspoons baking powder	1 large egg, beaten

1. Preheat the oven to 400°F. Pour 1 tablespoon of the vegetable oil into a 9-inch-round baking pan or heavy cast-iron skillet. Place the pan in the oven to preheat for at least 10 minutes.

2. Combine the cornmeal, flour, baking powder, salt, and cayenne in a large mixing bowl and stir with a wooden spoon. Add the buttermilk, the remaining ¼ cup oil, and the egg and stir well to blend.

3. Pour the batter into the preheated pan and bake until lightly golden brown and set, about 25 minutes. Remove from the oven and let cool 10 minutes before cutting.

⁕{ Choron Sauce

MAKES ABOUT 1¾ CUPS

Choron sauce is a béarnaise sauce to which tomato puree and finely diced tomatoes have been added. It is named for the nineteenth-century French chef Choron who created it, and it is classically paired with seafood, chicken, meats, and even poached eggs. The sauce also can be used as an alternate for Pan-Fried Crab Cakes (page 40), Individual Beef Wellingtons (page 174), Baby Lamb Chops (page 190), and New York Strip Steaks (page 168).

¼ cup white wine vinegar	1 tablespoon tepid water, as needed
¼ cup dry vermouth	¼ cup tomato puree or canned tomato sauce
2 tablespoons chopped shallots	2 tablespoons peeled, seeded, and
4 sprigs fresh tarragon, plus 1 tablespoon chopped fresh tarragon	chopped tomatoes
2 teaspoons black peppercorns	½ teaspoon salt
2 large egg yolks	⅛ teaspoon hot sauce or cayenne,
¾ cup melted Clarified Butter (page 257) or 12 tablespoons (1½ sticks) unsalted butter, melted	or to taste

1. Combine the white wine vinegar, vermouth, shallots, tarragon sprigs, and peppercorns in a small saucepan, bring to a boil, and cook until reduced to 4 teaspoons. Strain through a fine-mesh sieve and let cool.

2. Whisk the egg yolks and reduced wine mixture in the top of a double boiler (or in a medium bowl set over a pot of barely simmering water) until they are thick and pale yellow.

3. Remove the double boiler (or bowl and saucepan) from the heat and gradually add the butter, whisking constantly to thicken. Add enough tepid water to thin to pouring consistency. Add the tomato puree, tomatoes, 1 tablespoon chopped tarragon, salt, and hot sauce and whisk well to blend. Adjust the seasoning to taste.

4. Serve immediately or cover to keep warm for up to 10 minutes, whisking occasionally to keep from separating.

*{Cornmeal Fried Shrimp

We've given instructions in this recipe only for frying enough shrimp to serve as a garnish to the stuffed flounder, but double or triple this recipe to suit your needs.

These lightly breaded shrimp become a shrimp po-boy—that favorite New Orleans sandwich— when served on French bread with shredded lettuce, sliced tomatoes, and a slather of Caper-Herb Dressing (page 79) substituting for tartar sauce, or homemade Mayonnaise (page 264). Or pass these as hors d'oeuvres with dipping sauce on the side.

There are two secrets to successfully frying seafood. First, fill the pot only halfway with oil, and preheat the oil to the correct temperature before adding the shrimp.

Vegetable oil, for frying	12 medium shrimp, peeled and deveined,
½ cup yellow cornmeal	with tails left on
1½ teaspoons Emeril's Original Essence or Creole Seasoning (page 260), plus more for dusting	

1. Heat enough vegetable oil to come halfway up the sides of a medium pot to 350° to 360°F.

2. Meanwhile, combine the cornmeal and 1½ teaspoons Essence in a medium bowl. Add the shrimp in batches and toss to coat evenly, shaking to remove any excess.

3. Add the shrimp in 2 batches to the hot oil, turning occasionally, and cook until golden brown and the shrimp float to the top, 2½ to 3 minutes.

4. Remove with a slotted spoon and drain on paper towels. Season lightly with additional Essence and serve immediately.

Fillet of Snapper Rome

This dish was named for Ernest "Jitterbug" Rome, who began working for the LaFranca family in 1939 and served as chef for Delmonico Restaurant until the family closed the restaurant in 1997, a span of nearly sixty years. While the preparation may seem complicated, this is a very straightforward dish to make and the end result is impressive and delicious. To simplify matters, you can prepare the béchamel-crabmeat mixture and the butter sauce ahead of time, and then cook the fish at the last minute.

The crabmeat topping makes Snapper Rome a very rich dish, so I suggest simpler side dishes to accompany it, such as Broccoli (page 214) and boiled small new potatoes tossed with a little melted butter and parsley.

12 tablespoons (1½ sticks) plus 1½ teaspoons unsalted butter	1 cup lump crabmeat, picked over for shells and cartilage
¼ cup fresh lemon juice	1½ teaspoons all-purpose flour
¼ teaspoon Worcestershire	½ cup half-and-half
¼ cup fine dry bread crumbs	8 thin strips green bell peppers
Four 8-ounce skinless red snapper fillets	2 teaspoons chopped fresh parsley (optional), for garnish
1 teaspoon salt	
¼ teaspoon plus a pinch of ground white pepper	

1. Preheat the oven to broil and adjust the rack 3 to 4 inches below the top heat element. Line a baking sheet with aluminum foil and set aside.

2. Combine 1 stick of the butter, the lemon juice, and Worcestershire in a small saucepan and cook over medium heat, stirring, until the butter is melted and the mixture is warm, about 4 minutes. Pour half of the butter mixture into a small heatproof bowl, add the bread crumbs, stir well, and set aside.

3. With a pastry brush, lightly coat the baking sheet with some of the butter mixture remaining in the saucepan. Place the fillets on the baking sheet and brush lightly with more of the butter mixture. Season the top of each fillet with ⅛ teaspoon of the salt and a pinch of the white pepper and broil, basting twice, until lightly golden brown and just cooked through, 4 to 5 minutes. Remove from the oven and leave the oven on broil.

4. Melt 4 tablespoons of the butter in a medium skillet over medium heat. When foamy, add the crabmeat and cook, stirring and being careful not to break up the lumps, until warmed through, about 3 minutes. Remove from the heat.

5. Melt the remaining 1½ teaspoons butter in a medium saucepan over medium heat. Add the flour and cook, stirring constantly with a heavy wooden spoon, to make a light roux, 1 to 2 minutes. Gradually add the half-and-half, stirring constantly, and bring to a boil. Reduce the heat to medium-low and cook, stirring, until thickened, 2 to 3 minutes. Add the remaining ½ teaspoon salt, pinch white pepper, and the crabmeat mixture and stir well to combine. Remove from the heat.

6. Divide the crabmeat mixture among the fillets, spreading evenly over the tops, and sprinkle each with the bread crumb mixture. Place 2 bell pepper strips in the shape of an X on each fillet and broil until the tops are golden brown and the fish is heated through, 2 to 3 minutes.

7. Place 1 fillet in the center of each of 4 large plates and spoon any remaining butter mixture over the tops. Garnish each portion with ½ teaspoon of the parsley and serve immediately.

Pan-Seared Branzino Fillets *with* Gulf Shrimp, Roasted Onions *and* Fennel, *and* Emeril's Lemon Butter Sauce

MAKES 4 SERVINGS

Branzino is Mediterranean sea bass, known in France as *loup de mer* or sea wolf due to the fish's habit of hunting in packs. It makes many appearances on American restaurant menus today; however, it was relatively rare on this side of the Atlantic until just recently.

It's a sweet, moist, and tender white fish that traditionally is cooked and served whole, with the head on, and its delicate flavor doesn't require much seasoning. On the Delmonico dinner menu, we offer the fish whole with the head removed, while fillets are served at lunch.

1 medium red onion (about 10 ounces), peeled, ends trimmed, and cut into 6 thick rings

1 fennel bulb (about 18 ounces), cut in half and then cut into ½ inch x 1½-inch strips

6 tablespoons extra virgin olive oil

¾ teaspoon salt

¼ teaspoon freshly ground black pepper

½ cup all-purpose flour

Four 4-ounce branzino fillets, skins on, scaled

12 large shrimp, peeled and deveined

½ recipe Emeril's Lemon Butter Sauce (page 132)

4 ounces baby peashoots or watercress, rinsed and dried

1. Preheat the oven to 350°F.

2. Toss the onion rings and fennel strips with 2 tablespoons of the oil, ¼ teaspoon of the salt, and a pinch of the pepper in a 2-quart baking dish. Cover tightly with aluminum foil and roast until the vegetables are tender, about 45 minutes. Set aside, covered, to keep warm.

3. Combine the flour with ¼ teaspoon of the salt and ⅛ teaspoon of the pepper. Dredge the fish in the seasoned flour on both sides, shaking to remove any excess.

4. Place the shrimp in a medium bowl and toss with the remaining ¼ teaspoon salt and pinch pepper. Set aside.

5. Heat the remaining ¼ cup oil in a large sauté pan or skillet over medium-high heat. When the oil begins to lightly smoke, add the fish fillets, skin side down, gently press flat with the back of a fish turner or spatula, and cook until the skin is crisp, 2 to 2½ minutes. Turn and cook until just cooked through, 45 seconds to 1 minute. Transfer the fish to a platter and tent to keep warm.

6. Add the shrimp to the fat remaining in the pan and cook, turning, over medium-high heat until the shrimp are pink and just cooked through, 2 to 3 minutes. Remove from the heat.

7. Spoon 2 tablespoons of the sauce into the center of 4 large plates and arrange the vegetables on the sauce with the peashoots on top. Lay the fish fillets, skin side up, over the vegetables and top each fillet with 3 shrimp. Drizzle 1 tablespoon of the remaining sauce over each portion and serve immediately.

POULTRY:
MASTERS OF THE GAME

Old cookbooks and menus dating back to the late 1800s and early 1900s featured a great variety of poultry—turkey, chicken, squab, duck, goose, guinea fowl, capon, and yes, even pigeon. The common preparations included baking, braising, roasting, broiling, as well as using them in savory pies, casseroles, and in cold or warm daubes.

I learned early in my career that all types of poultry are versatile and in New Orleans that lesson is well confirmed. Just about anything that flies can be used in gumbos, stews, and jambalaya, but elegant poultry dishes have been and still are *au courant* in restaurant and home kitchens. I offer you our favorite selections.

Chicken Delmonico

We naturally chose Chicken Delmonico when planning the first Emeril's Delmonico menu, as it was a signature dish of the old restaurant and a beloved local favorite. In the beginning, our version consisted of a roasted whole chicken for two servings, which was carved tableside by the dining room captains, and then topped by this creamy mushroom and artichoke sauce.

The recipe has been simplified for this cookbook, and calls for chicken breast halves instead of whole chickens. You'll find, however, that the sauce is as rich as ever!

1 recipe Boiled Artichokes (page 255)	1 tablespoon chopped garlic
Four 6 to 7-ounce boneless, skinless chicken breast halves	3/4 pound assorted exotic mushrooms, such as shiitakes, chanterelles, and black trumpets, steamed, wiped clean, and sliced (about 4 cups)
2 tablespoons plus 1/2 teaspoon Emeril's Original Essence or Creole Seasoning (page 260)	
1/2 cup plus 2 tablespoons all-purpose flour	1/2 teaspoon salt
1 cup fine dry bread crumbs	1/4 teaspoon ground white pepper
1 large egg beaten with 1 tablespoon milk to make an egg wash	1/4 cup dry white wine
	1 cup Chicken Stock (page 254), or canned low-sodium chicken broth
2 tablespoons olive oil	1/2 cup heavy cream
4 tablespoons (1/2 stick) unsalted butter, cut into pieces	1 tablespoon fresh lemon juice
	2 tablespoons chopped green onions
1/4 cup minced yellow onions	1 tablespoon minced fresh parsley

1. Preheat the oven to 350°F. Line a baking sheet with aluminum foil and set aside.

2. Remove the large outer leaves from the artichokes, and discard or reserve for another use. Remove and discard the spiky inner leaves. Scrape the hairy choke from each heart and discard, trim the hearts and cut them into 1/4-inch-thick slices. Set aside.

3. Season each chicken breast half with 1/2 teaspoon of the Essence and set aside.

4. Combine 1/2 cup of the flour with 1 1/2 teaspoons of the Essence in a shallow bowl. In another shallow bowl, combine the bread crumbs with the remaining tablespoon Essence. Put the egg wash in a third bowl.

5. Dredge the chicken first in the flour, shaking to remove any excess, then in the egg wash, letting any excess drip off, and then in the bread crumbs.

6. Heat the oil and melt 1 tablespoon of the butter in a large skillet or sauté pan over medium-high heat. Add the chicken in 2 batches and cook until golden brown, 1½ to 2 minutes per side. Transfer the chicken to the prepared baking sheet and roast until cooked through, 15 to 18 minutes.

7. Meanwhile, heat 2 tablespoons of the butter over medium-high heat in a large clean skillet. Add the yellow onions and cook, stirring, until soft, about 3 minutes. Add the garlic and cook, stirring, until fragrant, about 30 seconds. Add the mushrooms and cook until soft and they give off their liquid, about 4 minutes. Add the salt and pepper and stir. Add the remaining 2 tablespoons flour, stir to incorporate, and cook until the mixture is thick, about 1 minute. Add the wine and cook, stirring, until evaporated, 30 seconds to 1 minute. Add the chicken stock, stir well to incorporate, and simmer until the mixture is thickened, about 2 minutes. Add the cream, bring to a simmer, and cook until the mixture is thickened enough to coat the back of a spoon, about 2 minutes. Add the sliced artichoke hearts and lemon juice and stir to incorporate. Remove from the heat and stir in the remaining tablespoon butter, the green onions, and parsley. Adjust the seasoning to taste.

8. To serve, place 1 chicken breast in the center of each of 4 large plates and top each with an equal portion of the sauce. Serve immediately.

⁑ Delmonico Sauce

MAKES 3 CUPS

This is the famous Delmonico Sauce that was a local favorite throughout the years the LaFranca family owned Delmonico. It's a bit different from the one we currently prepare in the restaurant, but I wanted to include it here so that you could have a choice.

To serve, follow the chicken preparation methods outlined in the previous Chicken Delmonico recipe and spoon this delicious sauce on top. Or, try this on top of pan-fried fish or veal scallops. This amount is enough for four generous portions or the recipe doubles well.

3	tablespoons unsalted butter	¼	pound button mushrooms, wiped clean, stems trimmed, and thinly sliced
¼	cup chopped green onions		
¼	teaspoon minced garlic	One-half	14-ounce can artichoke hearts, quartered, and their liquid
2	tablespoons all-purpose flour		
1	tablespoon LeGoût Chicken Base or other thick chicken base	2	tablespoons dry white wine
		2	drops yellow food coloring, optional
2	cups water		

1. Melt the butter in a saucepan over medium-high heat. When the butter is foamy, add the onions and garlic and cook, stirring, until soft, 1 to 2 minutes. Add the flour and, stirring constantly with a wooden spoon, cook to make a light blond roux, about 2 minutes. Add the chicken base and stir to incorporate. Add the water, bring to a boil, and cook, stirring occasionally until the mixture thickens, about 3 minutes. Reduce the heat to medium-low, add the mushrooms and simmer, stirring, for 1 minute. Add the artichoke hearts and their liquid and cook, stirring occasionally, for 4 minutes. Add the white wine and food coloring, if desired, stir well, and return to a boil. Reduce the heat and simmer until the sauce is thickened, 7 to 9 minutes.

2. Remove from the heat and serve immediately.

Chicken Pontalba

Chicken Pontalba is typical of the signature dishes served at old-line New Orleans Creole restaurants. This dish was created in New Orleans by chef Paul Blangé in the early days of Brennan's in the French Quarter and was a well-established local favorite when we reopened Delmonico. The recipe is very similar to chicken Clemenceau, but without the inclusion of green peas.

The name Pontalba denotes richness, as the dish is named for Baroness Micaela Almonester de Pontalba, a wealthy Parisian who in 1850 built the opulent Pontalba buildings that still flank Jackson Square in the historic French Quarter. Considered the oldest apartments in the country, the buildings continue to house elegant residences upstairs and fine retail shops downstairs.

One	2¾ to 3-pound chicken, rinsed and patted dry	8	ounces fresh white button mushrooms, stems removed, wiped clean, and thinly sliced
¾	teaspoon salt	¼	cup chopped green onions (green parts only)
¼	teaspoon plus ⅛ teaspoon ground white pepper	¼	cup dry white wine
1	tablespoon olive oil	1	recipe Brabant Potatoes (page 201)
2	tablespoons unsalted butter	1	tablespoon chopped fresh parsley
1	tablespoon minced garlic	1	recipe Béarnaise Sauce (recipe follows)
1	cup small-diced boiled ham		

1. Preheat the oven to 400°F.

2. Cut the chicken into 6 pieces, 2 breasts, 2 thighs, and 2 legs, and remove the bones from the breasts. Season the chicken pieces on both sides with ½ teaspoon of the salt and ¼ teaspoon of the pepper.

3. Heat the oil in a large ovenproof skillet or sauté pan over medium-high heat. Add the chicken pieces and cook until golden brown, 4 minutes on the first side and 3 minutes on the second side. Transfer the pan to the oven and roast until the chicken is cooked through, 18 to 20 minutes.

4. Meanwhile, melt the butter in a large skillet or sauté pan over medium-high heat. Add the garlic and cook, stirring, until fragrant, about 30 seconds. Add the ham, mushrooms, green onions, and the remaining ¼ teaspoon salt and ⅛ teaspoon pepper and cook, stirring, until the mushrooms give off their liquid and start to turn golden brown, 3 to 4 minutes. Add the wine and bring to a boil, stirring to deglaze the bottom of the pan. Reduce the heat to medium and

simmer until the mixture is thickened, 4 to 5 minutes. Add the Brabant potatoes and parsley, tossing gently to mix, and cook until the potatoes are warmed through, 1 to 2 minutes.

5. To serve, place equal amounts of the vegetable mixture in the center of 4 large plates and top with the chicken. Spoon the béarnaise sauce over the chicken and serve immediately.

⁂ Béarnaise Sauce

MAKES ABOUT 1½ CUPS

¼ cup white wine vinegar
¼ cup dry vermouth
2 tablespoons chopped shallots
4 sprigs fresh tarragon, plus 1 tablespoon chopped fresh tarragon
2 teaspoons black peppercorns
2 large egg yolks

¾ cup melted Clarified Butter (page 257) or 12 tablespoons (1½ sticks) unsalted butter, melted
1 tablespoon tepid water, as needed
½ teaspoon salt
⅛ teaspoon hot sauce or cayenne, or to taste

1. Combine the vinegar, vermouth, shallots, tarragon sprigs, and peppercorns in a small saucepan, bring to a boil, and cook until reduced to 4 teaspoons. Strain through a fine-mesh sieve and let cool.

2. Whisk the egg yolks with the wine mixture in the top of a double boiler (or in a medium bowl set over a pot of barely simmering water) until thick and pale yellow. Remove the double boiler (or bowl and saucepan) from the heat and gradually add the butter, whisking constantly to thicken. Add enough tepid water to thin to pouring consistency. Add the 1 tablespoon chopped tarragon, salt, and hot sauce and whisk well to blend. Adjust the seasoning to taste.

3. Serve immediately or cover and keep warm for up to 10 minutes, whisking occasionally to keep from separating.

Chicken Rochambeau

Leave it to a New Orleans chef to make an over-the-top dish like this by serving it with two rich sauces—Marchand de Vin and Hollandaise—on the same plate. I understand this dish was created at Antoine's restaurant in the French Quarter as homage to Count Rochambeau, one of the more important French military commanders to assist the Americans during the American Revolution.

Since it's an old New Orleans favorite, I offered my version at the restaurant to honor our Creole heritage.

4 slices ½-inch-thick white sandwich bread	1 tablespoon olive oil
1 tablespoon unsalted butter, melted	½ recipe Marchand de Vin Sauce (recipe follows)
Four ⅛-inch-thick slices boiled ham, such as Cure 81	2 tablespoons cold unsalted butter, cut into pieces
Four 6-ounce boneless, skinless chicken breast halves	1 recipe Hollandaise Sauce (page 261)
2 teaspoons Emeril's Original Essence or Creole Seasoning (page 260)	2 teaspoons chopped fresh parsley, for garnish

1. Toast the bread until light golden brown on both sides. Trim the toast using a 4-inch round cookie cutter and, using a pastry brush, lightly coat one side of the toast with the melted butter. Set aside on a wire rack to crisp.

2. Preheat the oven to 400°F. Line a small baking sheet with aluminum foil and set aside.

3. Trim the ham slices to the same size as the chicken breast halves, reserving the trimmings for another use.

4. Season each chicken breast half on both sides with ½ teaspoon of the Essence.

5. Heat the oil in a large sauté pan or skillet over medium-high heat. Add the chicken in batches and sear until lightly colored, 1 to 1½ minutes per side. Transfer the chicken to the prepared baking sheet and roast until cooked through, about 15 minutes.

6. Remove the chicken from the oven and cover to keep warm.

7. Meanwhile, add the ham to the same sauté pan or skillet and cook on both sides until warmed through, about 2 minutes. Transfer to a plate and cover to keep warm. Add the Marchand de Vin Sauce to the pan and bring to a boil, stirring to deglaze the pan, and simmer for 1 minute. Reduce the heat to low and add the butter, 1 piece at a time, stirring, until the sauce is thick and all the butter is incorporated. Remove from the heat.

8. Place 1 toast round in the center of each of 4 large plates and top each with a slice of warm ham. Spoon ¼ cup of the Marchand de Vin onto each ham slice and top with a chicken breast half. Spoon ¼ cup of the Hollandaise Sauce over each chicken breast half and garnish each portion with ½ teaspoon of the parsley. Serve immediately.

⁕{ Marchand de Vin Sauce

MAKES 2 CUPS

This rich sauce is most commonly paired with roasted or grilled meats, particularly steaks. However, in New Orleans, where rich food is the norm, it also is common to find Marchand de Vin accompanying poultry dishes, such as Chicken Rochambeau.

½	pound meat from beef shanks or oxtails, cut into ½-inch cubes	1	cup dry red wine
1	teaspoon salt	1	bay leaf
1	teaspoon freshly ground black pepper	1	sprig fresh thyme
1	teaspoon olive oil	4	cups Reduced Veal Stock (page 265) or demi-glace
¼	cup roughly chopped shallots	1	tablespoon cold unsalted butter, cut into pieces
½	teaspoon chopped garlic		

1. Season the meat evenly with ½ teaspoon each of the salt and pepper.

2. Heat the oil in a medium heavy pot over medium-high heat. Add the meat and cook, stirring, until evenly browned, about 6 minutes. Add the shallots and garlic and cook, stirring, until soft, about 1 minute. Add the red wine and stir to deglaze the pan. Bring to a boil, add the bay leaf, thyme, and the remaining ½ teaspoon each of salt and pepper, and cook until reduced to ¼ cup, about 10 minutes. Add the veal stock and bring to a boil. Reduce the heat to medium-low and simmer, stirring occasionally, until reduced by half and the mixture coats the back of a spoon, about 1 hour.

3. Strain the sauce through a fine-mesh strainer into a clean saucepan, reserving the meat for another use. Over low heat, add the butter, 1 piece at a time, whisking constantly to incorporate. Remove from the heat and adjust the seasoning to taste. Serve immediately. The sauce will keep stored in an airtight container, refrigerated, for up to 5 days, and in the freezer for up to 3 months.

Chicken à la King *on* Herb Biscuits

MAKES 4 SERVINGS

Chicken à la King was on the menu at the old Delmonico as well as on the Emeril's Delmonico menu when the restaurant initially reopened, and it continues to make frequent menu appearances. The old staff served it on toast with either a side of buttered beets and green peas, or with French fries. The popularity of this dish at Delmonico Restaurant in New Orleans is only fitting, as some accounts attribute the creation of Chicken à la King to the illustrious original Delmonico's in New York in the 1890s.

Chicken à la King is a rich dish and this recipe makes a generous four cups; depending upon your appetite, you'll probably have leftovers.

4 tablespoons (½ stick) unsalted butter	2 teaspoons chopped fresh tarragon
4 ounces button mushrooms, wiped clean, stems trimmed, and thinly sliced	¾ teaspoon salt
¼ cup chopped yellow onions	½ teaspoon ground white pepper
¼ cup chopped green bell peppers	3 large egg yolks
1 teaspoon minced garlic	1 recipe Quick Cooked Chicken (recipe follows), or 2½ cups shredded or diced cooked chicken
¼ cup all-purpose flour	
¼ cup plus 2 tablespoons dry sherry	1 teaspoon chopped fresh parsley
1½ cups milk	½ teaspoon fresh lemon juice
½ cup heavy cream	4 Herb Biscuits (recipe follows), split in half
½ cup Chicken Stock (page 254) or canned low-sodium chicken broth	16 thin strips pimiento or roasted red bell pepper

1. Melt the butter in a large saucepan over medium-high heat. Add the mushrooms, onions, and bell peppers and cook until the vegetables are soft and the mushrooms give off their liquid, about 5 minutes. Add the garlic and cook, stirring, until fragrant, 30 seconds. Add the flour and cook, stirring constantly with a wooden spoon to make a light roux, about 2 minutes. Add ¼ cup of the sherry and cook until nearly all evaporated, about 1 minute. Add the milk and cream in 3 additions, stirring and returning to a boil before adding each addition. Add the chicken stock, return to a boil, and cook, stirring occasionally, until the sauce thickens, about 3 minutes. Add the tarragon, salt, and white pepper and stir well to incorporate. Remove from the heat.

2. Whisk the egg yolks in a medium bowl until pale yellow and frothy, about 2 minutes. Add about ½ cup of the hot milk sauce to the yolks, whisking constantly. Slowly add the egg yolk mixture to the sauce in the pan, stirring until well blended. Add the remaining 2 tablespoons sherry, stir well, and return to medium heat. Fold in the chicken, parsley, and lemon juice and cook, stirring occasionally, until the chicken is warmed through, 2 to 3 minutes.

This recipe is an ideal way to use up leftover roasted chicken. Or use our simple Quick Cooked Chicken method, which doesn't require poaching liquid and roasts the chicken in the oven while you prepare the other ingredients.

Pimiento strips also are easy to make at home. Simply roast a red bell pepper on top of the gas flame or under the broiler until the skin is uniformly charred, allow it to cool in a paper or plastic bag, and then remove the charred skin and seeds. Wipe the pepper clean and cut into strips.

3. To serve, arrange 2 biscuit halves on each of 4 large plates. Spoon ¼ cup of the sauce over each biscuit half and arrange 2 strips of pimiento in the shape of an X on each. Serve immediately.

❧ Quick Cooked Chicken

MAKES 1 POUND, OR ABOUT 2½ CUPS SHREDDED OR DICED MEAT

This method of roasting chicken with vegetables in a foil pouch gives it a rich flavor as well as a moist, tender texture. A variation on the French method of cooking *en papillote* (such as we do the pompano on page 130), it also is an easy way to cook chicken for other dishes, such as chicken salad or pasta.

1 **carrot, coarsely chopped**	¼ **teaspoon salt**
1 **stalk celery, coarsely chopped**	⅛ **teaspoon freshly ground black pepper**
½ **medium yellow onion, coarsely chopped**	
1 **pound boneless, skinless chicken breast halves**	

1. Preheat the oven to 350°F.

2. Arrange the vegetables in the center of a large piece of heavy aluminum foil.

3. Lightly season the chicken breast halves on both sides with the salt and pepper and place on top of the vegetables. Fold over the sides of the aluminum foil to tightly seal, place on a baking sheet, and bake until the chicken is cooked through, 30 to 35 minutes, depending upon the size of the breasts.

4. Carefully unwrap the foil packet and let sit until the chicken is cool enough to shred or dice.

❧ Herb Biscuits

MAKES SIX 3-INCH BISCUITS

We use several soft herbs in our version of these biscuits, but if you prefer, use only one or two. This biscuit recipe also can be made without herbs for a breakfast treat.

The secret to great biscuits is not handling the dough more than necessary. Overhandling develops the gluten in the flour, which makes biscuits (or any baked goods, for that matter) tough. For that reason, the dough here is patted out on a board instead of being formed with a rolling pin. Another secret is not to twist the biscuit cutter when making the rounds; instead, firmly press the cutter into the dough and lift up.

2 cups all-purpose flour
1 tablespoon baking powder
¾ teaspoon salt
¼ teaspoon baking soda
¼ cup cold vegetable shortening

2 tablespoons cold butter, cut into small pieces
¾ cup plus 2 tablespoons buttermilk
1 tablespoon chopped assorted soft herbs, such as chives, basil, parsley, and chervil

1. Preheat the oven to 425°F.

2. Sift the flour, baking powder, salt, and baking soda into a large bowl. Cut in the shortening and butter and work with your fingertips or a pastry blender until the mixture resembles coarse crumbs.

3. Whisk together the buttermilk and herbs in a small bowl, add to the dry ingredients, and blend just until the dough is moist and pliable, being careful not to overwork.

4. Turn out the dough onto a lightly floured surface and using floured hands, pat into a ¾-inch-thick rectangle. Using a floured 3-inch biscuit cutter, cut into rounds, gathering, repatting, and cutting the dough scraps until all the dough is used.

5. Place the rounds on an ungreased baking sheet and bake until the biscuits are set and the tops are light golden brown, 12 to 14 minutes. Serve hot.

Chicken Anthony

Named for Anthony LaFranca, the longtime owner of Delmonico, this dish is very similar to the classic veal or chicken *cordon bleu*. The *cordon bleu* (blue ribbon) was worn by members of the highest order of knighthood instituted by Henry III of France in 1578. Through the years, the term has been applied to food prepared to a very high standard.

In this preparation, a slice of ham and a slice of Swiss cheese are inserted inside a thinly pounded whole chicken breast. The stack is then breaded and sautéed until golden brown. It was one of the most popular dishes on the menu in the 1940s and 1950s, and it was served either with the Lemon Butter Sauce (page 117) or béarnaise or Mornay sauces, depending on the customer's request.

¼ cup heavy cream	Pinch of freshly grated nutmeg
3 tablespoons unsalted butter	2 whole chicken breasts
1 tablespoons plus ½ cup all-purpose flour	(about 1½ pounds), patted dry
¾ cup milk	Two 1¼ ounce thin slices ham
3 tablespoons grated Swiss cheese	Two 1¼ ounce thin slices Swiss cheese
2 teaspoons Worcestershire	½ cup fine dry bread crumbs
2 teaspoons dry sherry	1 large egg beated with 1 tablesppon water to make an egg wash
¾ teaspoon salt	2 tablespoons vegetable oil
⅛ teaspoon dry mustard	1 tablespoon chopped fresh parsley,
Pinch plus ¼ teaspoon ground white pepper	for garnish

1. Gently warm the heavy cream in a small saucepan over medium heat. Remove from the heat and set aside.

2. Melt 1 tablespoon of the butter in a small saucepan over medium heat. When the butter is foamy, add the 1 tablespoon flour and cook, stirring constantly with a wooden spoon to make a light roux, 2 minutes. Gradually add the milk, whisking constantly to completely incorporate and bring to a boil. Reduce the heat to low and simmer until the mixture is thick, stirring occasionally with a wooden spoon, about 5 minutes. Add the warm cream, cheese, Worcestershire, sherry, ¼ teaspoon of the salt, mustard, pinch of the white pepper, and nutmeg and stir to incorporate. Remove from the heat and cover to keep warm until ready to serve, stirring occasionally.

3. Place each chicken breast between 2 sheets of plastic wrap. Using the flat side of a mallet, pound each slice very thin, about ⅛ inch thick.

4. Arrange 1 slice of the ham and 1 slice of the cheese on one half of each flattened chicken breast and fold the other chicken breast half over to sandwich the ham and cheese inside, pressing firmly to seal. Season both sides of each chicken breast with ¼ teaspoon of the remaining salt and ⅛ teaspoon of the remaining white pepper.

5. Place the remaining ½ cup flour in a shallow bowl, and the bread crumbs in another bowl.

6. Dredge each filled chicken breast in the beaten egg mixture, then in the flour, and then in the bread crumbs, shaking to remove any excess breading.

7. Heat the oil and melt the remaining 2 tablespoons butter in a large heavy skillet. Add the chicken breasts and cook until golden brown and cooked through, 3 to 4 minutes per side. Remove from the heat and drain on paper towels.

8. To serve, cut each chicken breast in half and place one half on each of 4 large plates. Spoon the cream sauce over the chicken, garnish with the chopped parsley, and serve immediately.

Jitterbug's Stewed Chicken

Miss Angie remembers, "We served the stewed chicken with rice on the side, with most of the gravy on the chicken and a little gravy on the rice. But every customer was special, and we'd serve it the way they wanted it. We'd also serve this with a side vegetable—green peas, collards, or spinach."

2 pounds boneless chicken breasts with skin, rinsed and patted dry (about 4 half breasts)
3/4 teaspoon salt
1/2 teaspoon freshly ground black pepper
1/4 cup olive oil
3/4 cup finely chopped yellow onions
6 tablespoons finely chopped celery
6 tablespoons finely chopped green bell peppers

2 teaspoons minced garlic
1/4 cup all-purpose flour
1 quart Chicken Stock (page 254) or canned low-sodium chicken broth
1 tablespoon Kitchen Bouquet
2 teaspoons LeGoût Chicken Base or other thick chicken base
3 cups White Rice (page 121)

1. Preheat the oven to 350°F.

2. Season both sides of the chicken with the salt and black pepper.

3. Heat the oil in a Dutch oven or large heavy pot over medium-high heat. When the oil is hot, add the chicken in batches, skin side down, and cook until golden brown, 3 to 4 minutes on the first side, and 1 to 2 minutes on the second side. Transfer to a plate.

4. Reduce the heat to medium and add the onions, celery, and bell peppers to the fat remaining in the pan and cook, stirring, until soft, about 3 minutes. Add the garlic and cook, stirring, until fragrant, about 30 seconds. Add the flour and cook, stirring constantly with a wooden spoon to make a light roux, 1½ to 2 minutes. Stirring constantly, slowly stir in the stock. Add the Kitchen Bouquet and the chicken base and stir well. Return the chicken to the pot and bring the liquid to a boil. Remove from the heat and cover. Carefully transfer the pot to the oven and bake until the chicken is tender, about 30 minutes.

5. To serve, transfer the chicken to 4 large plates and spoon the rice along the side. Spoon the gravy over the chicken and the rice, as desired, and serve immediately.

Hickory Roasted Duck *with* White Cheddar Grits, Collard Greens, *and* Dried Cherry Cane Syrup Reduction

MAKES 2 SERVINGS

This duck is a celebration of the Southern table with two classic sides—grits and greens—and a sauce flavored by Lousiana pure cane sugar. You can't beat this!

2½ cups kosher salt	12 cups ice cubes
1 pound light brown sugar	One 4 to 5-pound duck, giblets and neck
3 quarts water	removed, well rinsed and patted dry
2 medium oranges, cut in half	1 recipe White Cheddar Grits (recipe follows)
2 bay leaves	½ recipe Collard Greens (recipe follows)
¼ cup black peppercorns	1 recipe Dried Cherry Cane Syrup
¼ cup whole cloves	Reduction (recipe follows)

1. To make the brining liquid, combine the salt, sugar, water, oranges, bay leaves, peppercorns, and cloves in a large heavy pot and bring to a boil. Remove from the heat and add the ice.

2. When the brine mixture is cool, add the duck and weight with 2 small plates to submerge it. Refrigerate for 24 hours, turning the duck occasionally.

3. Line a large baking sheet with aluminum foil and place a wire rack on top.

4. Remove the duck from the brine, rinse well under cold running water, and pat dry. Discard the brine. Place the duck on the prepared wire rack and refrigerate uncovered for 24 hours.

We use a commercial smoker at Emeril's Delmonico to completely smoke the ducks for this popular dinner item. When adapting this recipe for the home cook, we recognized that most people wouldn't have a large smoker. So, we used a stovetop smoker initially to infuse the duck with the hickory scent and then finished it in the oven. These smokers are available at cooking stores and through online retailers, which also sell different hardwood chips. The smokers are very simple to use; follow the manufacturer's instructions.

If you don't want to use a smoker, increase the oven cooking time and roast the duck until it reaches an internal temperature of 165°F.

This recipe calls for 1 duck for 2 servings. You could certainly double this recipe, and cook 2 ducks, 1 at a time, in the stovetop smoker. Also note that the brining liquid should be enough for 2 ducks, depending upon the size of your container.

5. Remove the duck from the refrigerator and let come to room temperature.

6. Preheat the oven to 300°F.

7. Arrange hickory chips in the bottom of a stovetop smoker and place over medium heat, leaving the lid barely ajar. When the chips begin to smoke, place the duck on the rack in the smoker, close the lid tightly, and smoke for 45 minutes.

8. Remove the duck from the stovetop smoker and place on a clean rack over a foil-lined large baking sheet. Roast until a deep mahogany-brown color and an instant-read thermometer registers an internal temperature of 165°F, 2½ to 3 hours. (Alternatively, if using a freestanding smoker, preheat to 260°F, according to the manufacturer's instructions. Smoke the duck until tender and an instant-read thermometer registers an internal temperature of 165°F, about 6 hours.)

9. Remove from the oven and let rest for 15 minutes.

10. With poultry shears, cut the duck along either side of the backbone and remove the backbone. With a sharp knife, cut through the breastplate and remove the rib cage.

11. To serve, spoon the grits in the center of 2 large plates and place one half of the duck in the center of each serving. Spoon the greens to the side of the duck and drizzle 2 tablespoons of the syrup onto each duck. Serve immediately, passing additional sauce at the table, as desired.

❧White Cheddar Grits

MAKES 2 SERVINGS

Grits are a staple of breakfast and brunch tables across the southern United States. But they also are a fitting side to poultry and meat dishes for dinner, particularly with the addition of cheese! Serve these with the Herb Biscuits (page 156) and you've got a real southern breakfast or midnight supper.

2 cups milk	½	cup quick-cooking (not instant) grits
½ teaspoon salt	4	tablespoons (½ stick) unsalted butter
⅛ teaspoon freshly ground black pepper	½	cup grated white Cheddar

1. Combine the milk, salt, and pepper in a small heavy saucepan and bring to a simmer over medium heat. Add the grits slowly, stirring constantly until thoroughly combined. Reduce the heat to medium-low and simmer uncovered, stirring frequently, until thickened, 12 to 15 minutes. Add the butter and stir to incorporate. Add the cheese and stir until melted.

2. Serve immediately or cover to keep warm until ready to serve, stirring occasionally.

⊶{ Collard Greens

Usually greens are cooked in great quantities in a large pot, serving many. We've made this recipe as small as possible, yet you still will have leftovers. The greens will keep, refrigerated, for up to four days.

2 ounces bacon, diced	¹/₂ teaspoon freshly ground black pepper
¹/₂ cup thinly sliced yellow onions	Pinch of crushed red pepper
¹/₂ teaspoon minced garlic	³/₄ teaspoon rice wine vinegar
1 tablespoon packed dark brown sugar	¹/₄ cup lager beer
1 pound collard greens, or mustard or	1¹/₂ teaspoons molasses or cane syrup
kale, well rinsed and stems removed	Pinch of salt

1. Cook the bacon in a medium pot over medium-high heat until crisp, 4 to 5 minutes. Add the onions and cook, stirring, until soft, about 3 minutes. Add the garlic, and cook, stirring, until fragrant, 20 to 30 seconds. Add the sugar and cook, stirring, until dissolved.

2. Add the greens and the remaining ingredients, and cook, stirring occasionally, until starting to wilt, 5 to 8 minutes. Lower the heat to medium, cover, and cook, stirring occasionally, until very tender, 30 to 45 minutes. Remove from the heat and adjust the seasoning to taste. Cover to keep warm until ready to serve. (The greens will keep refrigerated in an airtight container for up to 4 days.)

⊶{ Dried Cherry Cane Syrup Reduction

The tart sweetness of this sauce offsets the duck beautifully. It is delicious on other poultry and game, from chicken to quail.

2 teaspoons olive oil	2 teaspoons Steen's 100% Pure Cane Syrup
1 tablespoon minced shallots	(see Source Guide)
¹/₂ teaspoon minced garlic	2 teaspoons cold unsalted butter,
¹/₂ cup dry red wine	cut into pieces
¹/₄ cup dried cherries	¹/₄ teaspoon salt
1¹/₂ cups Duck Stock (page 258) or	¹/₈ teaspoon freshly ground black pepper
Rich Chicken Stock (page 256)	

1. Heat the oil in a medium saucepan over medium heat. Add the shallots and garlic and cook, stirring, until fragrant, 30 seconds. Add the wine, increase the heat to medium-high, and cook, stirring, to deglaze the pan. Add the cherries and cook, stirring occasionally, until the wine is reduced to about 2 tablespoons, about 3 minutes. Add the stock and cane syrup and bring to a boil. Reduce the heat to medium-low and simmer, stirring occasionally, until the mixture is reduced to 1 cup, 8 to 10 minutes.

2. Remove from the heat and whisk in the butter, salt, and pepper. Adjust the seasoning to taste and serve immediately. (The sauce will keep refrigerated in an airtight container for up to 4 days. Reheat gently to serve.)

MEET THE MEATS

Meats—beef, veal, pork, and lamb—have been a significant part of all Delmonico menus.

The original Delmonico's Restaurant in lower Manhattan was the first to offer a Delmonico steak, but there has been much discussion as to the original cut of beef. Whatever it was, it was touted as the "best steak available," and I'm sure they sold literally tons. Today, a Delmonico steak is defined as a boned New York strip, although the rib-eye sometimes is called Delmonico. And I boast every chance I get about the New York strip steak that's currently on our menu, which we dry-age on the premises.

The LaFranca family offered Kansas City beef on their menus for years, which at the time was the top of the line. Their Calf's Liver and Onions was one of the most popular menu items. And Italian-style veal dishes such as veal parmigiana and the old classic Veal Chops Chasseur remained on the menu until they closed.

Today, we have beef and veal as well as pork and lamb to round out the menu.

New York Strip Steaks *with* Emeril's Worcestershire Sauce *and* Overstuffed Twice-Baked Potatoes

MAKES 4 SERVINGS

If you're a steak and potato lover, I highly recommend this absolutely incredible dish.

Our guests at Delmonico are given a choice of sauces for their steaks—Maître d'Hotel butter (a compound butter very similar to the one used with the Escargots, page 46, which is thinly sliced and placed on the hot meat), Emeril's Worcestershire Sauce, or Béarnaise Sauce (page 150). Choron Sauce (page 135) would be a tasty choice, too.

Use a dry skillet to sear these steaks on top of the stove if you're not up to grilling them outside. But be forewarned: you'll need a good exhaust fan as the steaks will give off a bit of smoke initially.

4 teaspoons olive oil	½ cup Emeril's Worcestershire Sauce (recipe follows), or an alternate sauce
Four 12 to 14-ounce New York strip steaks, trimmed of excess fat	4 Overstuffed Twice-Baked Potatoes (recipe follows)
4 teaspoons salt	
2 teaspoons freshly ground black pepper	

1. Preheat the grill to medium-high and preheat the oven to 450°F.

2. Lightly rub ½ teaspoon oil on each side of the steaks, and season on each side with ½ teaspoon of the salt and ¼ teaspoon of the pepper.

3. Place the steaks on the hot grill and cook for 4 minutes on each side for medium-rare, turning each steak one-quarter turn after 2 minutes to make grill marks. (Alternatively, a grill pan or large skillet over medium-high heat can be used.) Transfer to a large baking sheet and roast for 4 to 6 minutes for medium-rare, or until an instant-read meat thermometer registers an internal temperature of 140°F.

4. Place 1 steak on each of 4 plates and drizzle each with 1 to 2 tablespoons of the Worcestershire sauce. Place 1 baked potato on each plate and serve immediately.

ꗋ Emeril's Worcestershire Sauce

MAKES 3 PINTS

While the commercially available sauce is delicious, this one is really worth the effort—just be sure to safely hot pack and process it, and allow it to age for at least two weeks before serving. Use it as you would a commercial sauce—on meat and to kick up cocktails and sauces.

After opening, store this in an airtight container in the refrigerator.

2	tablespoons olive oil	2	quarts distilled white vinegar
6	cups coarsely chopped yellow onions	4	cups water
4	jalapeños, with stems and seeds, chopped	4	cups dark corn syrup
2	tablespoons minced garlic	2	cups Steen's 100% Pure Cane Syrup (see Source Guide)
Four	2-ounce cans anchovy fillets	2	tablespoons salt
2	medium lemons, skin and white pith removed	2	teaspoons freshly ground black pepper
³/₄	pound fresh horseradish, peeled and grated	¹/₂	teaspoon whole cloves
		3	pint-sized canning jars

1. Combine the oil, onions, and jalapeños in a large stockpot over high heat and cook, stirring, until the onions are slightly soft, 2 to 3 minutes. Add the garlic, anchovy fillets, lemons, horseradish, vinegar, water, corn syrup, cane syrup, salt, pepper, and cloves and bring to a boil. Reduce the heat and simmer, uncovered, stirring occasionally, until the mixture barely is reduced to about 6 cups and just coats the back of a wooden spoon, about 6 hours. Strain through a fine-mesh strainer into a clean container.

2. Sterilize three 1-pint jars and their lids according to the manufacturer's instructions. Spoon the hot mixture into the jars, filling to within ½ inch of the rims. With a clean, damp towel, wipe the rims and fit with hot lids. Screw on the metal rings.

3. Place the jars, without touching one another, on a rack in a canning kettle or large stockpot filled with enough rapidly boiling water to cover by 1 inch. Boil and process for 15 minutes.

4. Using tongs, transfer the jars to a towel and let cool completely. Test the seals and tighten the rings as needed. Store in a cool, dark place for at least 2 weeks before using. After opening, store in the refrigerator for up to 1 month.

❈ Overstuffed Twice-Baked Potatoes

MAKES 4 SERVINGS

These are so large and filling we have customers who order this as their entrée. The reason we call them overstuffed is that we add an extra baked potato to the stuffing mixture. But if these seem too large for you, then bake and mash only four (instead of the five used here) for restuffing into the potato shells, or use smaller potatoes.

These are the perfect complement to a steak, but you can make a meal out of them served with just a salad on the side.

5 large Idaho baking potatoes, about 1 pound each	2 cups grated sharp Cheddar cheese (8 ounces)
1 tablespoon olive oil	1 cup sour cream
1¾ teaspoons salt	4 tablespoons (½ stick) butter, at room temperature
¾ teaspoon ground white pepper	2 tablespoons snipped fresh chives
4 ounces bacon, chopped	

1. Preheat the oven to 400°F. Line a large baking sheet with aluminum foil.

2. Rub the potatoes with the oil and season with ½ teaspoon of the salt and ⅛ teaspoon of the pepper. Place on the prepared baking sheet and bake until fork tender, 1 hour to 1 hour and 10 minutes. Let sit until cool enough to handle. (The potatoes can be cooked 1 day in advance and kept wrapped in the refrigerator up to this point.)

3. Cook the bacon in a medium skillet over medium heat, stirring occasionally, until crisp and the fat is rendered, 5 to 6 minutes. Drain on paper towels.

4. Peel 1 potato completely, discard the skin, and place the pulp in a large bowl. Cut the top quarter from each of the remaining 4 potatoes and using a spoon, scoop the pulp from the potatoes into the bowl, leaving a ¼-inch layer of pulp around the skin. Return the potato shells to the baking sheet.

5. Mash the potato pulp until smooth using a handheld masher. Add 1 cup of the cheese, the sour cream, butter, bacon, chives, and the remaining 1¼ teaspoons salt and ½ teaspoon plus ⅛ teaspoon pepper and mash until smooth. Spoon the potato mixture back into the potato shells, top with the remaining cheese, and bake until hot and the cheese is melted, about 15 minutes.

6. Serve hot.

Dry-aging beef is a very old method of introducing flavor into and tenderizing beef. As a matter of fact, long ago butchers used to cover the sides of beef with cotton shrouds during the aging process. We have special dry-aging rooms at both Emeril's Delmonico and the Delmonico Steakhouse in Las Vegas for aging our New York strips and rib-eyes. (Filet mignon typically is not aged, as there is no fat covering to protect it from spoilage during the process.)

Several factors are essential to dry-aging beef: temperature, humidity, air circulation, and an immaculately clean environment. The process also must be slow in order to be effective—we've found that 2 to 3 weeks' aging yields the best flavor and texture.

It is not advised to dry-age beef at home, as maintaining a constant temperature of 32° to 36°F is essential for food safety. The meat will spoil if the temperature becomes too warm, and it will freeze (thus arresting the process) if it becomes too cold. Also, a constant level of 85 percent humidity must be maintained. Typically there is a 20 percent loss of weight overall, which represents a loss of moisture.

Steak Diane

When planning the Delmonico reopening, we wanted to bring back the tableside service that was so popular in dining rooms long ago. Steak Diane is one of those dishes we were proud to include in this tableside repertoire.

Supposedly named for the Roman goddess of the hunt, Diana (or Diane) style was originally a way of serving venison. Through the years, the preparation has come to mean sautéing thinly sliced or pounded filet mignon in butter and then flambéing and basting it in a rich cognac sauce.

Steak Diane takes me back to my Commander's Palace days, when this was a favorite lunch dish of proprietor Dick Brennan. Once we put it on the menu at Delmonico, it quickly became a favorite of a new generation of New Orleanians, including one of our regular diners, Glenn Vesh. Serve this with Creamed Spinach (page 212) and Brabant Potatoes (page 201) for a classic combination.

These filets are cooked to medium-rare. If you want your meat more done, slightly increase the initial cooking times.

Four **3-ounce filet mignon medallions**	2 teaspoons **Dijon mustard**
½ teaspoon **salt**	¼ cup **heavy cream**
¼ teaspoon **freshly ground black pepper**	¼ cup **Reduced Veal Stock (page** 265)
1 tablespoon **unsalted butter**	2 teaspoons **Worcestershire**
4 teaspoons **minced shallots**	2 drops **hot sauce**
1 teaspoon **minced garlic**	1 tablespoon **finely chopped green onions**
1 cup **sliced white mushroom caps**	1 teaspoon **minced fresh parsley**
¼ cup **cognac or brandy**	

1. Season the beef medallions on both sides with the salt and pepper.

2. Melt the butter in a large skillet over medium-high heat. Add the meat and cook for 45 seconds on the first side. Turn and cook for 30 seconds on the second side. Add the shallots and garlic to the side of the pan and cook, stirring, for 20 seconds. Add the mushrooms and cook, stirring, until soft, 2 minutes. Place the meat on a plate and cover to keep warm.

3. Tilt the pan toward you and add the cognac. Tip the pan away from yourself and ignite the cognac with a match. (Alternatively, remove the pan from the heat to ignite, and then return to the heat.) When the flame has burned out, add the mustard and cream, mix thoroughly and cook, stirring, for 1 minute. Add the veal stock and simmer for 1 minute. Add the Worcestershire and hot sauce and stir to combine. Return the meat and any accumulated juices to the pan and turn the meat to coat with the sauce.

4. Remove from the heat and stir in the green onions and parsley. Divide the medallions and sauce between 2 large plates and serve immediately.

Individual Beef Wellingtons *with* Périgourdine Sauce

MAKES 4 SERVINGS

When First Lady Jackie Kennedy had then White House chef René Verdon prepare beef Wellington for a Christmas party in the 1960s, the dish became a popular dinner party entrée across the country. The dish is named for the Duke of Wellington, the nineteenth-century English statesman and military officer. The name is not due to his gourmet tastes but that the final dish is said to resemble the shiny dark military boots he wore.

Beef Wellington traditionally is a two to four-pound beef tenderloin topped with mushroom duxelles and foie gras pâté, then encased in puff pastry. We've simplified the preparation by instead wrapping individual beef filets. This recipe makes four servings, but it easily can be doubled or halved.

Four **6-ounce thickly cut filet mignons**
1 **teaspoon salt**
½ **teaspoon freshly ground black pepper**
1 **tablespoon olive oil**
One-half **17 ¼-ounce package puff pastry**
    (1 sheet), thawed
1 **recipe Mushroom Duxelles**
    (recipe follows)

Four **1-ounce slices store-bought**
    country-style pork or goose liver pâté
1 **large egg beaten with 2 teaspoons water**
    to make an egg wash
1 **recipe Périgourdine Sauce**
    (recipe follows)

The filets need to be cut about 1½ inches thick to ensure that the meat doesn't dry out or become overcooked while roasting in the oven. If the meat is cut thinner, reduce the oven cooking time appropriately. And if your filets are greater than 6 ounces, the puff pastry will need to be cut into a larger square in order to envelop the meat completely. If this is the case, you may need 2 sheets of puff pastry instead of the 1 called for here.

Also, this cooking time plus resting time is for meat that's served medium-rare. If you like your meat more done, increase the initial cooking time in the skillet by another minute or 2, and monitor the doneness of the meat from the oven with an instant-read thermometer.

Both Marchand de Vin Sauce (page 153) and Béarnaise Sauce (page 150) would be delicious accompaniments to these little Beef Wellingtons, as would the Brabant Potatoes (page 201) and the Creamed Spinach (page 212).

1. Preheat the oven to 425°F. Line a baking sheet with parchment paper and set aside.

2. Season both sides of each filet with ¼ teaspoon of the salt and ⅛ teaspoon of the pepper. Heat the oil in a large heavy skillet over medium-high heat. Add the filets and sear for 1 minute on each side for medium-rare. Transfer to a plate to cool completely.

3. Roll out the puff pastry on a lightly floured surface to a 14-inch square, and cut into four 7-inch squares.

4. Spread one-quarter of the mushroom duxelles on top of each filet and top with 1 slice of the pâté, pressing to flatten. Place 1 filet, pâtè side down, in the center of a puff pastry square. Using a pastry brush or your finger, paint the inside edges of the pastry with egg wash. Fold the pastry over the filet as though wrapping a package and press the edges to seal. Place the packages seam side down on the prepared baking sheet. Brush the egg wash over the tops and sides of each package and bake until the pastry is golden brown and an instant-read thermometer registers 140°F for medium-rare, about 20 minutes.

5. Remove from the oven and let rest for 10 minutes before serving.

6. Spoon the sauce into the center of 4 large plates and arrange the beef Wellingtons on the sauce. Accompany with the vegetables of choice.

Mushroom Duxelles

MAKES ABOUT ½ CUP

This classic French preparation involves cooking chopped mushrooms with butter, shallots, and seasonings into a paste to later flavor other dishes and sauces.

At Emeril's Delmonico, duxelles are found in the eggs erato on the weekend brunch menu. Duxelles also make an easy canapé when spread on toast points or crackers with a little blue or goat cheese crumbled on top.

1 tablespoon unsalted butter	¼ teaspoon salt
2 tablespoons minced shallots	⅛ teaspoon ground white pepper
½ teaspoon minced garlic	2½ tablespoons dry white wine
10 ounces button mushrooms, wiped clean, stemmed, and finely chopped	

Melt the butter in a medium skillet over medium-high heat. Add the shallots and garlic and cook, stirring, for 30 seconds. Add the mushrooms, salt, and pepper, reduce the heat to medium, and cook, stirring, until all the liquid has evaporated and the mushrooms begin to caramelize, about 12 minutes. Add the wine and cook, stirring to deglaze the pan, until all the liquid has evaporated. Remove from the heat and let cool before using.

❧ Périgourdine Sauce

This sauce may very well be the richest thing you've ever eaten, but, hey, you only live once—go for it!

The name of this sauce pays tribute to the Périgord region of southwestern France, supplier of two of France's great delicacies: foie gras (fatted goose liver) and black truffles. The black truffles that grow underground in the Périgord are rare and must be found with specially trained dogs or sows. Any gourmet, however, will tell you that the truffle's special aromatic qualities more than compensate for their high price. Both truffle peelings and canned truffles are available at some gourmet markets or by special order, and are considerably less expensive than the fresh ones.

---

2 cups Reduced Veal Stock (page 265)
1 tablespoon unsalted butter
1 fresh black truffle, approximately 1 inch in diameter, washed, peeled, very thinly sliced, 1 canned truffle, very thinly sliced, or 2 tablespoons truffle peelings

4 ounces cold fresh goose or duck liver, cut into ½-inch cubes
½ teaspoon salt
⅛ teaspoon ground white pepper
½ cup dry Madeira wine

---

1. Place the veal stock in a small saucepan and warm gently over medium heat. Set aside.

2. Melt the butter in a medium sauté pan over medium heat. Add the truffle slices to the pan and gently cook for 1 minute. Add the liver, salt, and pepper, swirl the pan, and cook for 45 seconds. Add the Madeira, increase the heat to medium-high, stirring to deglaze the pan, and cook for 2 minutes to slightly reduce the volume. Add the veal stock, stirring well to incorporate, and cook over low heat until warmed through, 30 seconds.

3. Serve immediately.

Grilled Steak Burgers *on* Homemade Buns *with* Caramelized Onions *and* Red Bliss Potato Chips

MAKES 2 SERVINGS

I realize that most everyone thinks that a hamburger is about as American as apple pie, but I've done a little homework. I found that some food historians believe the hamburger on a bun made its debut at the world's fair in St. Louis in 1904. Well, that may be true, but in Charles Ranhofer's book *The Epicurean* he gives a recipe for beef steak, Hamburg style (*Bifteck à la hambourgeoise*). Don't you love it? There is no mention of serving it on a bun; rather, it was dished up with a thick brown gravy.

I knew I had to have an over-the-top burger on our menu and I think you'll agree that's just what we created. It's a biggy made with top-of-the-line ground sirloin for incredible flavor in every bite.

2 **Homemade Buns (recipe follows), split in half**	4 **strips applewood-smoked bacon, cooked until crisp, and drained**
1 **pound ground top sirloin**	1 **recipe Caramelized Onions (recipe follows)**
½ **teaspoon salt**	½ **recipe Red Bliss Potato Chips (recipe follows)**
½ **teaspoon freshly ground black pepper**	**Condiments of choice, such as ketchup,**
¼ **cup grated sharp Cheddar cheese**	**Mayonnaise (page** 264**), and mustard**
¾ **cup shredded iceberg lettuce**	

1. Preheat the grill and preheat the oven to 350°F. Arrange the buns, split side up, on a baking sheet.

2. Form the meat into 2 large patties, 5 to 6 inches in diameter, and sprinkle each side with ⅛ teaspoon of the salt and ⅛ teaspoon of the pepper. Place the patties on the grill and cook for 5 to 6 minutes. Flip, place 2 tablespoons of the grated cheese in the center of each patty, and cook for 5 to 6 minutes longer for medium-rare. (Alternatively, the patties can be cooked in a large skillet preheated over medium-high heat for the same length of time.)

3. Meanwhile, warm the buns in the oven, 4 to 5 minutes.

4. To serve, place the bottom buns on 2 large plates and top with the shredded lettuce. Place the patties on the lettuce and arrange 2 strips of bacon and ¼ cup of the caramelized onions on each patty. Place the top buns on each burger and serve with the red bliss potato chips on the side and condiments of choice.

Typical of New Orleans restaurants of the era, the original Delmonico restaurant featured no less than twenty-two sandwich choices on the menu in addition to the extensive selection of meat and seafood specialties. The sandwich variety was wide-ranging—from broiled calf's liver and broiled tenderloin of trout to fried soft-shell crab and breaded veal cutlet.

New Orleans continues to be a big sandwich-eating town, and these sizeable steak burgers are always in demand at lunch.

We use applewood-smoked bacon on our Delmonico steak burgers. It's leaner bacon than what you usually find at your local market (see Source Guide, page 270) and very flavorful from the long smoking method. Although not an essential component of this recipe, try it for the delicious rich and smoky taste.

❊⟩ Homemade Buns

At Delmonico we make our own soft hamburger buns, just as we do all our breads, and these are pretty straightforward to make. If you don't want to go to the effort though, use store-bought Kaiser rolls or large buns.

½	cup milk	1	teaspoon kosher salt
½	cup warm water (110°F)	2	tablespoons cold unsalted butter,
One	¼-ounce package (2¼ teaspoons)		cut into pieces
	active dry yeast	½	cup plus 2 teaspoons olive oil
⅛	teaspoon plus 1 tablespoon granulated	1	large egg, lightly beaten
	sugar	2	tablespoons heavy cream
3¼	cups all-purpose flour		

1. Line a baking sheet with parchment paper, sprinkle lightly with flour, and set aside.

2. Gently warm the milk in a small saucepan over medium heat. Remove from the heat.

3. Combine the water, yeast, and ⅛ teaspoon of the sugar in a small bowl, stir, and let the mixture sit until the yeast is foamy, 5 to 10 minutes.

4. Combine the remaining tablespoon sugar, the flour, and salt in a large bowl and stir to combine. Using your fingers, a fork, or a pastry blender, mix the butter into the flour mixture until it resembles coarse crumbs. Add the yeast mixture, the warm milk, and ½ cup of the olive oil and mix with a heavy wooden spoon to form a soft dough. (If the mixture is too wet, add more flour, 1 tablespoon at a time, until the dough comes together.)

5. Turn the dough out onto a lightly floured surface and knead until smooth and elastic, 3 to 5 minutes. (This dough is very soft.)

6. Grease a large bowl with the remaining 2 teaspoons olive oil and add the dough, turning to coat.

7. Cover the bowl with a clean kitchen towel or plastic wrap and set in a warm, draft-free place until the dough has doubled in size, about 1 hour.

While these buns are delicious when made exactly as in this recipe, you can experiment and add other flavors to yours while kneading. For instance, add chopped jalapeños to the dough for a real kick, or a little dried dill, or a combination of herbs to suit your tastes. Or make these into seeded buns by sprinkling either sesame or poppy seeds onto the egg-washed tops just before baking.

8. Punch the dough down in the center and turn out onto a lightly floured surface. Divide the dough into 8 equal portions, about 3½ ounces each. Gently press out each piece, roll into a ball about 4 inches in diameter, pressing to flatten slightly, and place on the prepared baking sheet.

9. Whisk together the egg and cream in a small bowl to make an egg wash. Using a pastry brush, gently paint the egg wash onto the top of each bun.

10. Position the rack in the lower third of the oven and preheat the oven to 375°F.

11. Cover the pan with a clean kitchen towel or lightly greased plastic wrap and place in a warm, draft-free place until doubled in size, about 1 hour.

12. Uncover the buns and bake until golden brown and a toothpick inserted into the dough comes out clean, 15 to 20 minutes, turning the baking sheet halfway through the cooking time.

13. Transfer the buns to a wire rack to cool completely.

14. To serve, slice the buns in half horizontally. (The buns will keep in an airtight bag at room temperature for 2 days.)

∗{ Caramelized Onions

MAKES ABOUT ½ CUP

1 tablespoon unsalted butter	½ teaspoon hot sauce
2 cups peeled and very thinly sliced yellow onions	½ teaspoon sugar
½ teaspoon Worcestershire	Pinch of salt

1. Melt the butter in a medium skillet over medium-high heat. Add the remaining ingredients, reduce the heat to medium-low and cook slowly, stirring occasionally, until the onions are golden brown and caramelized, 15 to 20 minutes.

2. Remove from the heat and serve either warm or at room temperature.

⁑ Red Bliss Potato Chips

The potatoes are tossed in malt vinegar and salt for a very English flavor that I find unbeatable. For a different flavor, toss the hot chips with one-quarter cup freshly grated Parmigiano-Reggiano and one tablespoon truffle oil, or chopped assorted fresh herbs and one tablespoon extra virgin olive oil.

As you cook these, remember that adding the potatoes to the oil will cause the temperature to drop. To cook these chips properly, have the oil hot enough before adding the potatoes and let it return to that temperature before adding each batch.

---

2 pounds red bliss potatoes, scrubbed well and patted dry	1½ teaspoons malt vinegar
6 cups vegetable oil	1¼ teaspoons salt

---

1. Using a mandoline or very sharp, heavy knife, slice the potatoes into rounds as thin as possible. Place in a large bowl of water to prevent discoloration.

2. Heat the oil in a large heavy pot to 350° to 360°F.

3. Remove the potatoes from the water, drain in a colander, and pat dry completely on paper towels. Add the potatoes to the oil in batches, cooking until golden brown, turning with a spider or long-handled slotted spoon to cook evenly, about 2 minutes. Drain on paper towels.

4. Place the potato chips in a large bowl and toss with the vinegar and salt. Serve immediately.

Veal Chops Chasseur

MAKES 4 SERVINGS

The veal chasseur that was prepared in the LaFranca kitchen was made with grilled cutlets and it was one of Anthony LaFranca's favorite dishes. The mushroom and shallot sauce, "with a trace of garlic," also was used on grilled boneless chicken breasts.

This Emeril's Delmonico version uses very large veal chops. The brown sauce not only has shallots and mushrooms but also chicken livers, brandy, red wine, and fresh herbs—typical hunter-style—for a hearty and very flavorful main course.

3 tablespoons unsalted butter, cut into pieces	2 tablespoons cognac or brandy
1 teaspoon all-purpose flour	1/4 cup dry red wine
1 tablespoon minced shallots	1 cup Rich Chicken Stock (page 256)
1 teaspoon minced garlic	1/2 cup peeled, seeded, and chopped tomatoes
3 ounces chicken livers, membranes removed and cut into 1/2-inch pieces (about 1/4 cup)	1 teaspoon chopped fresh thyme
	1/2 teaspoon chopped fresh rosemary
	1 1/8 teaspoons salt
2 tablespoons finely chopped ham	1/2 teaspoon plus 1/8 teaspoon freshly ground black pepper
4 ounces small button mushrooms, wiped clean, stems trimmed, and quartered (about 1 1/4 cups)	Four 14-ounce bone-in veal chops

1. Preheat the grill to medium-high and preheat the oven to 400°F.

2. Combine 1 teaspoon of the butter with the flour in a small ramekin and mix well to make a paste. Set aside.

3. Melt 1 tablespoon of the butter in a medium saucepan over medium heat. Add the shallots and garlic and cook, stirring, until fragrant, 30 seconds. Add the chicken livers and ham and cook, stirring, for 2 minutes. Add the mushrooms and cook, stirring, until they give off their liquid, about 2 minutes. Add the cognac, bring to a boil, and cook until the liquid is nearly evaporated, 30 seconds to 1 minute. Add the wine, bring to a boil, and cook until the wine is reduced by half, 1 to 2 minutes. Add the stock and tomatoes, bring to a boil, and cook until thickened and reduced by nearly one-half in volume, about 5 minutes.

4. Add the butter-flour paste, stir well, and cook until the sauce is thickened, 2 minutes. Add the remaining 1 tablespoon plus 2 teaspoons butter, the herbs, 1/8 teaspoon of the salt, and 1/8 teaspoon of the pepper and stir well to combine. Remove from the heat and cover to keep warm until ready to serve.

5. Season the chops on each side with ⅛ teaspoon of the remaining salt and a pinch of the pepper. Place on the grill and cook for 2 minutes. Turn each chop one-quarter turn to mark and cook an additional 2 minutes. Turn over and cook in the same manner for 4 minutes. (Alternatively, cook in a preheated large skillet over medium-high heat, turning once.)

6. Remove from the grill and place on a baking sheet. Roast until cooked to medium doneness, 8 to 10 minutes.

7. Transfer the chops to 4 large plates. Divide the sauce among the chops and serve immediately.

Chasseur, French for "hunter," is a brown sauce often served with game and other meats that includes mushrooms, shallots, and wine.

The sauce in this recipe is thickened in two ways—first by reducing the cognac, wine, and stock through simmering, and then by adding a *beurre manié*, or butter-flour paste, at the end of the sauce-making process. This paste needs to be cooked for about 2 minutes after it has been added not only to thicken the sauce but also to cook out any floury taste.

Veal Piccata *with* Angel Hair *and* Parmigiano-Reggiano

MAKES 4 SERVINGS

Piccata is a classic Milanese veal preparation, where the veal is quickly sautéed and served with a pan sauce made of stock, lemon juice, capers, and parsley. The pasta, tossed with herbs, spices, and olive oil, complements the veal perfectly and would make a satisfying meal on its own.

½ pound angel hair pasta	Eight 2½ to 3-ounce veal medallions, pounded
2 tablespoons extra virgin olive oil	¼ inch thick
2½ teaspoons salt	2 tablespoons olive oil
1¾ teaspoons freshly ground black pepper	3 tablespoons unsalted butter
3 tablespoons plus 1 teaspoon	½ cup dry white wine
chopped fresh parsley	¼ cup Chicken Stock (page 254),
2 teaspoons chopped fresh basil	or canned low-sodium chicken broth
2 tablespoons freshly grated	2 tablespoons fresh lemon juice
Parmigiano-Reggiano	2 tablespoons capers, drained
1 cup all-purpose flour	2 teaspoons minced garlic

1. Bring a large pot of salted water to the boil. Add the pasta and cook, stirring to separate the strands, until just al dente, about 4 minutes. Drain in a colander and return to the pot. Add the extra virgin olive oil, ½ teaspoon of the salt, ¼ teaspoon of the pepper, 2 tablespoons of the parsley, the basil, and cheese and toss to coat. Cover to keep warm.

2. Meanwhile, combine the flour with 1 teaspoon of the salt and 1 teaspoon of the black pepper in a shallow bowl.

3. Lightly season both sides of each medallion with ⅛ teaspoon of the remaining salt and a pinch of the remaining pepper. One at a time, dredge the medallions in the seasoned flour, shaking to remove any excess.

4. Heat the olive oil and melt 1 tablespoon of the butter in a large skillet or sauté pan over medium-high heat. Add the medallions in batches and cook until golden brown and just cooked through, 1 to 1½ minutes per side. Drain on paper towels and set aside.

5. Add the wine to the juices remaining in the pan and bring to a boil, stirring to deglaze the pan, and cook until the wine is reduced by half, 2 to 3 minutes. Add the chicken stock, lemon juice, capers, and garlic and return to a boil, stirring, until the mixture is thickened, about 4 minutes. Stir in the remaining 2 tablespoons butter and 1 tablespoon of the parsley. When the butter is melted, return the veal medallions to the pan and cook until heated through, about 1 minute.

6. To serve, divide the pasta among 4 large plates and arrange 2 veal medallions on each serving. Spoon the sauce over the veal and garnish each serving with ¼ teaspoon of the remaining parsley. Serve immediately.

For this preparation, thin veal cutlets are pounded to a ¼-inch thickness for a quick cooking time that preserves the meat's natural tenderness and flavor. We've added wine to our sauce, which gives the dish extra zest. If you can't find veal in your area, use thinly pounded boneless, skinless chicken breasts instead.

Calf's Liver *and* Onions

MAKES 4 SERVINGS

At the old Delmonico in New Orleans, calf's liver, lightly floured and pan-sautéed with onions and sometimes bacon, was a mainstay on the menu. Some customers preferred the liver as an open-faced sandwich while others preferred it as a plated dinner served with French fries or the vegetable of the day.

4 strips bacon, cut into ¼-inch-wide strips	1 cup Chicken Stock (page 254), or canned low-sodium chicken broth
2 pounds yellow onions, peeled and very thinly sliced	4 tablespoons (½ stick) cold unsalted butter, cut into pieces
1 bay leaf	Four 8-ounce slices calf's liver
1 teaspoon sugar	1 cup all-purpose flour
1¾ teaspoons salt	½ cup Clarified Butter (page 257) or vegetable oil
1 teaspoon freshly ground black pepper	
¼ teaspoon dried thyme	4 teaspoons chopped fresh parsley, for garnish
½ cup dry red wine	

1. Cook the bacon over medium-high heat in a large skillet, turning, until crisp and the fat is rendered, about 5 minutes. Remove with a slotted spoon and drain on paper towels, reserving the fat in the pan.

2. Return the bacon fat to medium heat. Add the onions, bay leaf, sugar, ¼ teaspoon of the salt, ¼ teaspoon of the pepper, and the thyme and reduce the heat to medium-low. Cook slowly, stirring occasionally, until golden brown and caramelized, about 45 minutes. Remove from the heat, discard the bay leaf, and stir in the bacon. Transfer to a bowl and cover to keep warm until ready to serve.

3. Return the skillet to medium-high heat. Add the wine and cook, stirring to deglaze the pan, until the wine is reduced to 2 tablespoons, about 5 minutes. Add the chicken stock, bring to a boil, and cook until reduced by half, about 5 minutes. Reduce the heat to low and add the unsalted butter, 1 piece at a time, stirring well to incorporate. Remove from the heat and cover to keep warm.

4. Lightly season each slice of liver on both sides with ¼ teaspoon of the salt and ⅛ teaspoon of the pepper.

5. Combine the flour, the remaining ½ teaspoon salt, and remaining ¼ teaspoon pepper in a medium shallow bowl. One at a time, dredge the liver slices in the seasoned flour, shaking to remove any excess. Place on a plate.

6. Heat the clarified butter over medium-high heat in a large clean skillet. When the butter is hot, cook the liver in 2 batches until browned, 2 minutes on each side.

7. Arrange 1 slice of liver in the center of each of 4 large plates, spoon the sauce over the top, and arrange the onion mixture over the sauce. Garnish each serving with 1 teaspoon of the parsley and serve immediately.

Calf's liver often can be purchased presliced, about ¼ inch thick, or you can ask your butcher to slice it for you. If you purchase the liver whole, freeze it until slightly firm, and then slice it yourself using a heavy, sharp knife.

Brabant Potatoes (page 201) and French fried potatoes are two good accompaniments to this dish.

Baby Lamb Chops *with* Rosemary-Parmesan Crust *and* Barolo Syrup

MAKES 4 MAIN-COURSE SERVINGS OR 8 APPETIZER SERVINGS

Very small lamb chops often are called "lollipop" lamb chops, because when passed as hors d'oeuvres, guests can pick up the chops with their fingers and eat the meat right off the bone, just as one would eat a lollipop.

Sixteen **2 to 3-ounce baby lamb chops**
2 **tablespoons Emeril's Original Essence, or Creole Seasoning (page** 260**)**
1/3 **cup Dijon mustard**
1 1/2 **cups fine dry bread crumbs**
1/2 **cup freshly grated Parmigiano-Reggiano**

2 **tablespoons olive oil**
1 **tablespoon minced garlic**
1 **tablespoon minced fresh rosemary**
1/4 **teaspoon salt**
1/4 **teaspoon freshly ground black pepper**
1 **recipe Barolo Syrup (recipe follows)**

1. Preheat the oven to 425°F. Lightly grease a large baking sheet and set aside.

2. Spread the lamb chops on a work surface covered with plastic wrap. Generously season the chops on both sides with the Essence and using your fingers, evenly spread a light coating of the mustard on both sides.

3. Combine the bread crumbs, cheese, oil, garlic, rosemary, salt, and pepper in a large shallow bowl and stir to mix well. Working one at a time, place the chops in the bread crumb mixture, turning to coat evenly on both sides and shaking to remove any excess. Place on the prepared baking sheet and bake for 8 minutes for medium-rare, or until an instant-read thermometer registers 145°F. Remove the chops from the oven, increase the temperature to broil, and adjust the oven rack to the highest position. Broil the chops until the crusts are golden brown and slightly crisp, 1 to 2 minutes.

4. To serve as an appetizer or main course, arrange the chops on either 8 small plates or 4 large plates, and, using a tablespoon, drizzle the syrup over the chops in a zigzag fashion. Serve immediately.

If you plan to offer these as hors d'oeuvres or as part of a buffet supper, purchase the smallest chops available and trim any excess fat from the sides before cooking. To serve, arrange the chops on a large platter with the bones facing out, and drizzle the syrup onto the meat in a spiral, starting at the center of the platter. Garnish with chopped parsley and sprigs of rosemary and serve.

For a main course, increase the serving size to three or four chops per person, and try the Hash Brown Cakes (page 99) or Roasted Garlic Smashed Potatoes (page 202) as a side dish.

✣ Barolo Syrup

Barolo is named for the town in Italy's Piedmont region where the wine is made from the Nebbiolo grape. Syrah, or any other hearty, full-bodied red wine, will make a fine substitute.

The wine, mirepoix, and stock are simmered initially for one hour to infuse the liquid with as much flavor as possible.

3 tablespoons cold unsalted butter, cut into pieces	One 750-ml bottle Barolo or other hearty red wine
½ cup chopped yellow onions	1 teaspoon sugar
¼ cup chopped carrots	Pinch of salt
¼ cup chopped celery	Pinch of freshly ground black pepper
1 small bay leaf	
2 cups Reduced Veal Stock (page 265) or Rich Chicken Stock (page 256)	

1. Melt 1 tablespoon of the butter in a large saucepan over medium-high heat. When the butter is foamy, add the onions, carrots, celery, and bay leaf and cook, stirring, until the vegetables are soft, 2 to 3 minutes. Add the veal stock and wine and bring to a boil. Reduce the heat to medium-low and simmer uncovered for 1 hour, using a ladle as needed to skim any impurities that rise to the top of the surface.

2. Strain through a fine-mesh strainer into a clean saucepan. Return to medium heat and simmer until the syrup is reduced to ½ cup, 6 to 8 minutes.

3. Whisk in the remaining 2 tablespoons butter, several pieces at a time. When all the butter has been incorporated, remove from the heat, stir in the sugar, salt, and pepper and serve immediately or cover to keep warm until ready to serve. The syrup will keep refrigerated in an airtight container for up to 1 week.

New Orleans–Style Stuffed Leg of Lamb *with* Garlic Wine Sauce, Mint Pesto Tossed Baby Potatoes, *and* Haricots Verts

MAKES 6 SERVINGS

This stuffed leg of lamb is served exclusively on Easter Sunday at the restaurant, but I assure you it can be served year round. The stuffing combines herbs, pancetta (that wonderful Italian bacon), artichoke hearts, cheese, and lemon zest—fantastic. The finished dish makes a wonderful table-side presentation.

½   **recipe Boiled Artichokes (page** 255)

¼   **pound pancetta or bacon, cut into ½-inch dice**

½   **cup finely chopped yellow onions**

4   **teaspoons minced garlic**

1½   **cups fine dry bread crumbs**

¾   **cup extra virgin olive oil**

1   **teaspoon salt**

¾   **teaspoon freshly ground black pepper**

    Pinch of cayenne

¼   **cup minced fresh parsley**

1   **tablespoon minced fresh oregano**

6   **tablespoons freshly grated Pecorino Romano cheese**

1   **tablespoon fresh lemon juice**

½   **teaspoon finely grated lemon zest**

1   **teaspoon Emeril's Original Essence or Creole Seasoning (page** 260)

One   **4-pound boned leg of lamb, butterflied, excess fat and sinew trimmed**

1¾   **pounds small red potatoes (about 1¼ inches in diameter), scrubbed well, or larger red potatoes, halved or quartered**

1¼   **pounds haricots verts or small, thin green beans, rinsed and ends trimmed**

1   **recipe Mint Pesto (recipe follows)**

1   **recipe Garlic Wine Sauce (recipe follows)**

1. Preheat the oven to 400°F.

2. Remove the large outer leaves from the artichokes, and discard or reserve for another use. Remove and discard the spiky inner leaves. Scrape the hairy choke from each heart and discard. Trim the hearts and cut into ½-inch dice. Set aside.

3. Cook the pancetta in a large skillet or sauté pan over medium-high heat until crisp and the fat is rendered, 5 to 6 minutes. Remove with a slotted spoon and drain on paper towels. Add the onions to the fat remaining in the pan and cook, stirring, for 3 minutes. Add the garlic and cook, stirring, until fragrant, 30 seconds. Add the bread crumbs, ½ cup of the olive oil, ½ teaspoon of the salt, ¼ teaspoon of the pepper, and the cayenne and cook, stirring, until the bread crumbs are lightly toasted and golden brown, about 3 minutes. Add the parsley and oregano, stir, and remove from the heat. Let cool.

This will make an impressive main course for a special dinner or your Easter meal. It's best to get your butcher to bone the leg of lamb and butterfly it for you. Figure that an 8-pound leg will yield a 4 to 5-pound boneless piece of meat. The recipe will yield 6 generous servings of lamb cooked to medium-rare. If you prefer your meat more done, adjust the cooking time accordingly.

4. Combine the cooled bread crumb mixture with the pancetta, artichoke hearts, cheese, lemon juice, lemon zest, and Essence in a large bowl. Add the remaining ¼ cup olive oil and stir until well blended. Adjust the seasoning to taste.

5. Spread the butterflied leg of lamb, boned side up, on a work surface covered with plastic wrap. Cover with a second sheet of plastic wrap and pound with a meat mallet to a ¾-inch thickness. Spread the bread crumb mixture evenly across the meat, leaving a ½-inch border on all sides. Roll the meat over the stuffing, jelly-roll fashion, and tuck in the ends. Tie with kitchen twine every 2 inches and season the outside of the lamb with the remaining ½ teaspoon salt and ½ teaspoon black pepper. Place in a heavy roasting pan and roast until brown and tender, and an instant-read thermometer registers 110°F for medium-rare, about 45 minutes, testing in several places, as different parts of the leg cook at different rates. Remove from the oven, wrap the roasting pan in foil, and let the meat rest for 15 to 20 minutes.

6. Meanwhile, put the potatoes in a medium pot, cover with salted water by 1 inch, and bring to a boil. Cook until the potatoes are tender, 12 to 15 minutes. Drain in a colander, place in a large bowl, and cover to keep warm.

7. Bring a medium saucepan of salted water to a boil. Add the beans and cook until just tender, 2 to 3 minutes. Transfer with a slotted spoon to an ice bath to refresh, drain, and place in the bowl with the potatoes. Add ½ cup of the pesto sauce to the vegetables and stir with a heavy wooden spoon to coat evenly. Add the remaining ¼ cup pesto sauce, as desired. Cover the vegetables to keep warm until ready to serve.

8. Transfer the lamb to a cutting board, remove the kitchen twine, and slice. Divide the meat among 6 large plates and arrange the potatoes and green beans to the side. Spoon the sauce over the meat and serve.

⁕{ Mint Pesto

MAKES ABOUT ¾ CUP

2 cups packed fresh mint leaves	1 teaspoon fresh lemon juice
¼ cup pine nuts, lightly toasted	½ teaspoon salt
¼ cup freshly grated Parmigiano-Reggiano	¼ teaspoon freshly ground black pepper
3 garlic cloves, peeled and crushed	¼ cup extra virgin olive oil

Combine the mint, nuts, cheese, garlic, lemon juice, salt, and pepper in the bowl of a food processor and process until well chopped. With the machine running, slowly add the oil through the feed tube and process to make a smooth paste, scraping down the sides as needed. Adjust the seasoning to taste and transfer to an airtight container until ready to use. (The pesto will keep in an airtight container, refrigerated, for up to 5 days.)

*{Garlic Wine Sauce

4 tablespoons (½ stick) cold unsalted butter, cut into pieces	¼ teaspoon salt
2 tablespoons finely chopped shallots	⅛ teaspoon freshly ground black pepper
1 tablespoon minced garlic	½ cup dry red wine
¼ teaspoon finely chopped fresh rosemary	1½ cups Lamb Stock (page 262) or Rich Chicken Stock (page 256)
¼ teaspoon finely chopped fresh thyme	

1. Melt 1 tablespoon of the butter in a medium saucepan over medium-high heat. Add the shallots, garlic, rosemary, and thyme and cook, stirring, for 1 minute. Add the salt and pepper and stir well. Add the red wine, bring to a boil, and simmer until reduced by half, about 3 minutes. Add the stock and bring to a boil. Reduce the heat to medium and cook at a brisk simmer until the sauce is reduced by half, about 10 minutes.

2. Reduce the heat to low and add the remaining 3 tablespoons butter, several pieces at a time, whisking to incorporate, adding more butter as the previous pieces are incorporated into the sauce.

3. Remove from the heat, adjust the seasoning to taste, and serve immediately.

Roast Rack of Pork with Slow-Braised Red Cabbage, Green Apple Jam, *and* Rosemary Pan Jus

MAKES 4 SERVINGS

This rack of pork was a standout on the menu when we first opened Emeril's Delmonico. The dining room captains would carve the meat tableside, serving it and the side dishes from a beautiful copper sauté pan. We occasionally run this as a special, and always to rave reviews.

Two 2-**bone** 24-**ounce pork chops**
1 **tablespoon olive oil**
4 **teaspoons Emeril's Original Essence or Creole Seasoning (page** 260)
¼ **cup dry red wine**
1 **tablespoon minced shallots**
½ **teaspoon minced garlic**
1½ **teaspoons Dijon mustard**
1 **cup Rich Chicken Stock (page** 256)

½ **teaspoon minced fresh rosemary**
4 **tablespoons (**½ **stick) cold unsalted butter, cut into pieces**
⅛ **teaspoon salt**
⅛ **teaspoon freshly ground black pepper**
1 **recipe Slow-Braised Red Cabbage (recipe follows)**
1 **recipe Green Apple Jam (recipe follows)**

1. Preheat the oven to 350°F.

2. Rub the chops on all sides with the oil and season with the Essence.

3. Heat a large skillet or 2 medium skillets over medium-high heat. Add the pork chops and brown on the top, bottom, and both sides for 2 minutes per side, for a total of 8 minutes cooking time. Transfer the chops to a small roasting pan or rimmed baking sheet. Drain off all but 1 tablespoon of the fat from the pan and set aside.

4. Place the chops in the oven and roast until medium and an instant-read thermometer registers 155°F, 25 to 30 minutes.

5. Place the pork chops on a cutting board or platter and let rest for 5 minutes.

6. While the baking pan is still hot, add the wine and stir, scraping, with a wooden spatula or spoon to deglaze the pan.

7. Heat the reserved 1 tablespoon fat in the large skillet used to initially cook the chops over medium-high heat. Add the shallots and garlic and cook, stirring, until soft, about 30 seconds. Add the wine and deglazed pan juices and cook until reduced by half, about 1 minute. Add the mustard and stir. Add the chicken stock and rosemary and bring to a boil. Reduce the heat to medium and cook until the liquid is reduced by one-third in volume, 1 to 2 minutes. Reduce the heat to low and add the butter, 1 piece at a time, stirring well to incorporate each addition. Season with the salt and pepper and remove from the heat.

8. To serve, cut each chop between the 2 bones into 2 separate chops and arrange on 4 large plates. Pour any accumulated juices from the meat into the sauce and stir to blend. Spoon the sauce over the chops and serve with the cabbage and jam on the side.

⁕⌇ Slow-Braised Red Cabbage

MAKES ABOUT 4 CUPS

This dish also would be good served with sausages, as they do in Alsace, or with ham or roasted veal.

1	tablespoon olive oil	¼	cup red wine vinegar
6	cups shredded red cabbage	¼	cup sugar
2½	cups thinly sliced red onions	2	tablespoons water
⅓	cup minced ham (2 ounces)	1	bay leaf
1	teaspoon finely grated orange zest	1	teaspoon salt
½	cup Ruby Port	½	teaspoon ground white pepper

1. Heat the oil in a large sauté pan over medium-high heat. Add the cabbage and onions, stir, cover, and lower the heat to medium. Cook covered, stirring occasionally, until the cabbage is wilted, 12 to 13 minutes. Uncover, add the remaining ingredients, and bring to a boil. Reduce the heat to medium and simmer uncovered, stirring occasionally, until thick and reduced nearly by one-half in volume, about 30 minutes.

2. Remove from the heat, discard the bay leaf, and adjust the seasoning to taste. Serve warm.

⁕⌇ Green Apple Jam

MAKES 1¾ CUPS

This very versatile sauce goes with everything from blinis and pancakes to roasted pork.

4	tablespoons (½ stick) unsalted butter	1	tablespoon peeled and grated fresh ginger
1¾	pounds Granny Smith apples (4 medium), peeled, cored, and diced (4½ cups)	1	bay leaf
½	cup water	One	3-inch cinnamon stick
¼	cup light brown sugar	⅛	teaspoon ground allspice
1	tablespoon apple cider vinegar	⅛	teaspoon salt

1. Melt 2 tablespoons of the butter in a large sauté pan over medium-high heat. Add the apples and cook, turning, until starting to color and soften, 8 to 10 minutes. Add ¼ cup of the water, the brown sugar, vinegar, ginger, bay leaf, cinnamon stick, allspice, and salt and stir well. Reduce the heat to medium and cook, stirring occasionally, until the apples are very tender and the mixture is thick, about 25 minutes. Add the remaining ¼ cup water and cook until nearly evaporated, 2 to 3 minutes. Add the remaining 2 tablespoons butter and stir to incorporate.

2. Remove from the heat and discard the bay leaf and cinnamon stick. Serve warm or at room temperature. (The jam will keep in an airtight container, refrigerated, for up to 1 week. Warm gently before serving or serve at room temperature.)

The pork available today is so lean that it's important not to overcook it. We cook our pork chops and racks of pork to medium temperature, which may be a little pinker than you usually eat, but this allows the meat to retain a nice juiciness. Keep in mind, too, that trichinosis is nearly nonexistent in pork today because of modern farming practices, although, if it weren't, it would be killed at 137°F (and we suggest cooking this pork to an internal temperature of 155°F).

Have your butcher cut 2 large 2-bone, 24-ounce pork chops especially for you. Or if you cannot find such chops in your area, large racks of pork can be found online at the Niman Ranch Web site (see Source Guide, page 272) or through similar reputable butchers, and you can trim them at home.

TAKING SIDES

In 1827 when the Delmonico brothers established their restaurant in New York City, they introduced new, and what then were considered exotic, vegetables such as eggplant, endive, and artichokes on their menu. Always on the cutting edge, the brothers purchased a 220-acre farm in 1834 on Long Island where they maintained a country residence and grew vegetables for their restaurant that were not otherwise available in America.

I certainly wanted to keep up that tradition by going all out with the vegetables and side dishes that we would offer at Emeril's Delmonico. With all the fresh ingredients that are available to us these days, we experimented with different recipes, old and new, to create exciting sides to offer our guests. We, of course, included some of the sides offered by the LaFranca family.

Stilton Potato Gratin

Use a good-quality blue cheese if you can't find Stilton. And although I like Gorgonzola, the creamy texture does not work for this recipe. Slice the potatoes as thinly as possible on a mandoline or other adjustable blade slicer or use a very sharp, heavy knife.

2	teaspoons unsalted butter	1	teaspoon minced garlic
2½	pounds russet potatoes	1	teaspoon fresh thyme leaves
1¼	teaspoons salt	⅔	cup crumbled Stilton cheese or other
½	teaspoon freshly ground black pepper		good-quality blue cheese
1¾	cups heavy cream	1½	teaspoons chopped fresh parsley,
1	tablespoon finely chopped shallots		for garnish

1. Preheat the oven to 350°F. Grease a 9-inch-square baking dish with the butter and set aside.

2. Peel the potatoes and cut crosswise into ⅛-inch-thick slices. Toss the potatoes in a large bowl with 1 teaspoon of the salt and the pepper. Arrange half of the potatoes, slightly overlapping, in the prepared dish.

3. Combine the cream, the remaining ¼ teaspoon salt, the shallots, garlic, and thyme in a small saucepan, bring to a simmer, and simmer for 2 minutes. Ladle half of the hot cream mixture over the potatoes in the dish, evenly distributing the shallots and thyme with the back of the ladle. Crumble half of the cheese over the cream and potatoes, and make another layer each of the remaining potatoes, cream mixture, and cheese. Cover tightly with aluminum foil and bake for 45 minutes. Carefully remove the foil and continue baking until bubbly and the top is golden brown, about 15 minutes.

4. Remove from the oven and let rest until firm enough to cut, 15 to 20 minutes. Cut into portions, garnish with the parsley, and serve hot.

Brabant Potatoes

MAKES 4 SERVINGS

Brabant potatoes are fried potato cubes that have been cooked quickly in water before frying, which gives them a light, crunchy texture. Brabants are a traditional accompaniment to a variety of classic New Orleans Creole dishes and so are often found on the plates at Delmonico.

- 4 **pounds russet potatoes, peeled**
- 4 **cups vegetable oil**
- 1 **teaspoon salt**

1. Cut each potato into an even rectangular shape by cutting off the bottom, top, and sides, then cut into ½-inch cubes. Put in a medium heavy saucepan and add enough water to cover by 1 inch. Bring to a boil and cook until the potatoes are slightly tender, about 10 minutes.

2. Remove from the heat and drain on paper towels.

3. Heat the oil in a large, deep heavy pot or an electric deep fryer to 360°F. Add the potatoes and fry until golden brown and slightly crisp, turning to cook evenly, for 3 to 4 minutes.

4. Remove and drain on paper towels. Season with salt and serve hot.

Roasted Garlic Smashed Potatoes

MAKES 5 CUPS, 4 TO 6 SERVINGS

We serve these potatoes slightly chunky at the restaurant, with the potatoes still in their skins. If you like smoother mashed potatoes, peel them before cooking and mash longer.

2	pounds small red potatoes (about 1¼ inches in diameter), scrubbed well, or medium red potatoes, halved	1	cup heavy cream
1½	teaspoons salt	8	tablespoons (1 stick) unsalted butter
		1	recipe Roasted Garlic (recipe follows)
		½	teaspoon freshly ground black pepper

1. Put the potatoes in a medium pot with ½ teaspoon of the salt and enough cold water to cover by 1 inch and bring to a boil over high heat. Reduce the heat and cook at a low boil until the potatoes are fork tender, 16 to 20 minutes, depending upon their size.

2. Meanwhile, combine the cream and butter in a small saucepan and cook over medium heat until the butter is melted. Set aside.

3. Drain the potatoes and return to the pot over medium-low heat, shaking the pan to dry the potatoes completely. Add the cream mixture, garlic, the remaining 1 teaspoon salt, and the pepper and coarsely mash the potatoes using a potato masher until well blended but still slightly chunky. Serve immediately.

⁂ Roasted Garlic

MAKES ABOUT 2 TABLESPOONS

This recipe can be increased to satisfy your garlic cravings. If you're a real garlic lover, use two heads of garlic for your potatoes—or more!

1	teaspoon olive oil	Pinch of salt
1	head garlic, upper quarter removed	Pinch of freshly ground black pepper

1. Preheat the oven to 350°F. Line a small baking dish with aluminum foil.

2. Rub the oil into the exposed cloves of the garlic and sprinkle lightly with the salt and pepper. Place the garlic in the prepared dish, cut side down, and bake until the cloves are soft and golden, 45 minutes to 1 hour. Remove from the oven and let sit until cool enough to handle.

3. Squeeze the head to expel the garlic cloves into a bowl. Mash into a paste and set aside until needed. (The roasted garlic will keep, tightly covered, in the refrigerator for up to 2 days.)

Spaghetti Bordelaise

MAKES 2 MAIN-COURSE SERVINGS OR 4 FIRST-COURSE OR SIDE SERVINGS

A traditional French bordelaise sauce is composed of red or white wine, brown stock, bone marrow, shallots, parsley, and other herbs. In New Orleans, it's made with butter, olive oil, garlic, parsley, and green onions and can be found at countless restaurants served many ways—on broiled or grilled meats, as a dipping sauce for seafood, tossed with poached oysters and linguini, or simply tossed with spaghetti, as we do here.

During the LaFranca ownership, the sauce often was served with frog's legs. (Emeril's version of Frog's Legs, with a variation on the New Orleans–style bordelaise sauce, is on page 50.)

- $\frac{1}{2}$ **pound spaghetti**
- 1 **recipe Bordelaise Sauce (recipe follows)**
- $\frac{1}{4}$ to $\frac{1}{2}$ **cup grated Parmigiano-Reggiano**

1. Bring a large heavy pot of salted water to a boil. Add the spaghetti and cook, stirring to separate the strands, until the pasta is al dente, 7 to 8 minutes for dry pasta. Drain in a colander and return to the pot. Add the warm bordelaise sauce and toss well to coat.

2. Divide the spaghetti among plates or large shallow bowls, sprinkle cheese to taste over the top of each serving, and serve immediately.

*{ Bordelaise Sauce

MAKES ABOUT $\frac{1}{2}$ CUP

6 tablespoons unsalted butter	1 teaspoon Worcestershire
1 tablespoon olive oil	Pinch of salt
2 tablespoons minced garlic	Pinch of freshly ground black pepper
2 tablespoons minced fresh parsley	Hot sauce, to taste
1 tablespoon minced green onions	

1. Combine the butter and oil in a small saucepan over medium heat. When the mixture begins to foam, add the garlic and cook, stirring, until fragrant, about 30 seconds. Add the parsley, green onions, and Worcestershire and cook, stirring, for 2 minutes. Add the salt, pepper, and hot sauce and stir to blend.

2. Serve immediately or cover to keep warm, stirring occasionally, until ready to serve.

Rosemary-Gruyère Bread Pudding

MAKES 6 SERVINGS

This savory bread pudding was first prepared for a private party several years ago as a side dish to roasted quail and it was a great hit. Try it with any game, poultry, or meat and consider it for your Thanksgiving table. For ease of preparation, soak the bread in the custard, covered, overnight in the refrigerator before baking.

1 tablespoon extra virgin olive oil	1 teaspoon salt
1 cup finely chopped yellow onions	1/2 teaspoon freshly ground black pepper
1 teaspoon minced garlic	Pinch of grated nutmeg
2 teaspoons chopped fresh rosemary	3/4 cup grated Gruyère or Swiss cheese
1 1/2 cups whole milk	5 cups 1-inch cubes French bread or
1 cup heavy cream	home-style white sandwich bread
4 large eggs, lightly beaten	

Gruyère is a Swiss cow's-milk cheese named for the village where it is produced. It is a creamy, semi-soft cheese with a nutty, slightly earthy flavor. Substitute Emmentaler or Swiss for Gruyère.

1. Heat the oil in a medium skillet over medium-high heat. Add the onions and cook, stirring, until soft, 3 to 4 minutes. Add the garlic and rosemary and cook, stirring, until fragrant, about 30 seconds. Remove from the heat and let cool.

2. Combine the milk, cream, eggs, salt, pepper, and nutmeg in a large bowl and whisk well. Add the onion mixture and cheese and stir well. Add the bread cubes and let sit, stirring occasionally, until the bread has absorbed the liquid, at least 1 hour or, covered and refrigerated, up to 12 hours.

3. Preheat the oven to 350°F. Butter an 8-inch-square baking dish.

4. Pour the bread mixture into the prepared dish and bake until the top is golden brown and puffed and the center is set, about 45 minutes. Let cool for 15 minutes before serving.

Buttermilk Onion Rings

Crunchy-fried onion rings are a must, in my book, to serve with our big hamburgers, a steak, or to munch on. You can make the rings as thin or as thick as you like. And just as when making the Red Bliss Potato Chips (page 182), successful frying depends upon the oil being at the proper temperature before adding each batch of onions.

1 cup buttermilk	2 large yellow onions, cut into
1/4 cup hot sauce	1/2-inch-thick rings
3 tablespoons Emeril's Original Essence	Vegetable oil, for frying
or Creole Seasoning (page 260)	2 cups all-purpose flour

1. Whisk together the buttermilk, hot sauce, and 2 teaspoons of the Essence in a large bowl. Add the onion rings and press to coat evenly with the buttermilk mixture. Cover and marinate in the refrigerator for 1 hour.

2. Heat enough oil to come halfway up the sides of a medium pot to 360°F.

3. Combine the flour with 2 tablespoons of the Essence in a shallow bowl. Dredge the onions in the seasoned flour, tossing to coat each ring evenly, and shake off any excess flour. Carefully add the onions to the hot oil, in batches, and fry until golden brown, turning with a spider or long-handled slotted spoon to cook evenly and prevent sticking, about 3 minutes per batch. Drain on paper towels and season with the remaining 1 teaspoon Essence.

4. Serve hot.

Spinach *and* Asparagus Soufflés

These individual soufflés make appearances from time to time at private dinner parties held at Emeril's Delmonico. We serve them as a side dish, although they also would make an appealing appetizer or light luncheon main course. They're best served right out of the oven—while still impressively puffed up—so you'll need to time your meal accordingly.

5 **tablespoons unsalted butter**	4 **large egg yolks**
2 **tablespoons fine dry bread crumbs**	$\frac{1}{2}$ **teaspoon salt**
5 **ounces fresh spinach, well rinsed**	$\frac{1}{4}$ **teaspoon ground white pepper**
and stems removed	**Pinch of cayenne**
$\frac{1}{2}$ **cup asparagus tips**	$\frac{1}{3}$ **cup coarsely grated Gruyère or**
1 **tablespoon minced shallots**	**Swiss cheese**
1 **teaspoon minced garlic**	5 **large egg whites, at room temperature**
1 **cup milk**	2 **tablespoons grated Parmesan cheese**
3 **tablespoons all-purpose flour**	

1. Preheat the oven to 375°F. Butter the bottom and sides of six 6-ounce ramekins with 1 tablespoon of the butter and coat evenly with the bread crumbs, tapping out any excess. Place the ramekins on a small baking sheet and set aside.

2. Bring a medium saucepan of salted water to a boil. Add the spinach and cook until wilted and tender, 2 minutes. Drain in a fine-mesh strainer, pressing with a large spoon to release as much water as possible. Finely chop enough spinach to yield $\frac{1}{2}$ cup. Set aside.

3. Bring a small saucepan of salted water to a boil. Add the asparagus tips and cook until tender, 1 to 2 minutes, depending upon their thickness. Drain and transfer to an ice bath to stop the cooking; drain and set aside.

4. Melt 1 tablespoon of the butter in a medium skillet over medium-high heat. Add the shallots and garlic and cook, stirring, until soft, about 1 minute. Add the asparagus tips and spinach and cook until the spinach is completely dry, about 1 minute. Remove from the heat and cool slightly.

5. Place the milk in a small saucepan and scald over medium heat. Set aside.

6. Melt the remaining 3 tablespoons butter in a medium saucepan over medium-high heat. Add the flour, reduce the heat to low, and cook, stirring constantly with a wooden spoon, until it forms a light roux, 2 minutes. Gradually add the hot milk, whisking constantly, and cook until thick and smooth, 1 to 2 minutes.

7. Remove from the heat and add the egg yolks, one at a time, whisking after each addition. Add the spinach mixture, salt, pepper, and cayenne and stir well.

8. Place the mixture in the bowl of a food processor and pulse until smooth. Transfer to a large bowl and stir in the cheese.

9. Whip the egg whites in a large clean bowl until stiff peaks form. Stir one-quarter of the beaten egg whites into the spinach mixture to lighten. In 3 additions, gently fold the remaining whites into the spinach mixture.

10. Divide among the prepared ramekins, filling to just below the lip of each ramekin. Sprinkle the top of each soufflé with 1 teaspoon of the Parmesan cheese and bake until the tops are risen and golden brown and the centers are just set, 16 to 20 minutes, being careful not to open the oven door for the first 10 minutes of the cooking time.

11. Serve immediately in the ramekins.

Caramelized Onion *and* Bacon–Smothered Exotic Mushrooms

MAKES 4 TO 6 SERVINGS

This recipe may look simple but the flavor is incredible, making this an often-requested recipe from Delmonico diners. The mushrooms are initially roasted to intensify their flavor as well as to prevent them from getting mushy. Serve these mushrooms alongside steak or chicken.

1¼ pounds assorted exotic mushrooms (such as shiitake, crimini, and oyster), wiped clean and stems removed	2 strips bacon, chopped
3 tablespoons olive oil	5 tablespoons unsalted butter
½ teaspoon salt	1 pound yellow onions, thinly sliced
¼ teaspoon freshly ground black pepper	⅓ cup Chicken Stock (page 254), or canned low-sodium chicken broth

1. Preheat the oven to 400°F.

2. Place the mushrooms in a large bowl, drizzle with 2 tablespoons of the olive oil, and toss to coat with the salt and pepper. Spread the mushrooms on a large baking sheet and roast for 10 minutes. Set aside to cool.

3. Cook the bacon in a small skillet over medium heat, stirring occasionally, until crisp and the fat is rendered, 4 to 5 minutes. Drain on paper towels.

4. Heat 4 tablespoons of the butter in a large heavy skillet over medium-high heat. Add the onions, reduce the heat to medium-low, and cook slowly, stirring occasionally, until golden brown and caramelized, about 35 minutes. Remove from the heat and set aside.

5. Heat the remaining 1 tablespoon olive oil in another large skillet over medium-high heat. Add the mushrooms and cook, stirring, until tender, about 4 minutes. Add the caramelized onions and bacon and cook until heated through, about 1 minute. Add the chicken stock and cook, stirring to deglaze the pan, about 1 minute. Add the remaining 1 tablespoon butter and cook, stirring, for 30 seconds.

6. Serve immediately.

Creamed Spinach

I love this version of the steak house classic so much that I could eat it at almost every meal. It's rich and very satisfying so you don't need a large serving—but, hey, do whatever makes you happy.

$\frac{1}{2}$	teaspoon unsalted butter	2	tablespoons milk
$1\frac{1}{4}$	pounds fresh baby spinach, rinsed as necessary	5	tablespoons grated Parmigiano-Reggiano
1	cup heavy cream	$\frac{1}{2}$	teaspoon salt
1	tablespoon cornstarch	$\frac{1}{8}$	teaspoon ground white pepper
		$\frac{1}{3}$	packed cup grated sharp or medium Cheddar

1. Preheat the oven to 400°F. Lightly grease a 2-cup baking dish or ramekin with the butter and set aside.

2. Place the spinach and enough water to cover the bottom of a large skillet or sauté pan over medium heat, cover tightly, and cook, stirring occasionally, until completely wilted, 5 to 7 minutes. Drain in a colander and set aside.

3. Bring the cream to a low boil in a medium saucepan. Remove from the heat.

4. Whisk the cornstarch and milk in a small bowl until smooth to make a slurry. Add the slurry to the hot cream and return to medium heat, whisking until the mixture thickens and starts to boil, about 1 minute. Add the Parmesan, salt, and pepper and whisk until smooth. Add the cooked spinach and stirring constantly with a wooden spoon, return to a boil, about 1 minute. Remove from the heat.

5. Pour the spinach into the prepared baking dish, sprinkle the Cheddar evenly over the top, and bake until the cheese is melted, 5 to 6 minutes.

6. Serve hot.

We use baby spinach to make our creamed spinach—it is much cleaner than the larger variety, the stems are tender and do not need to be removed, and it does not need to be chopped for the final preparation. If you use larger spinach leaves, remove the tough stems and wash the leaves well; also, you will need to chop the cooked leaves before adding them to the cream mixture.

Creamy Cabbage Alfredo

MAKES 3½ CUPS, 4 TO 6 SERVINGS

Napa cabbage, also called Chinese cabbage, is delicately mild compared to the common cabbage, which has a more distinctive flavor. I think you'll be surprised, but happy, with this unusual combination of the Napa cabbage and creamy sauce. Serve this as an alternative to creamed spinach, or with pork or fish.

2 tablespoons unsalted butter	1 cup heavy cream
2¾ pounds Napa cabbage, finely sliced (12 cups)	½ cup grated Parmigiano-Reggiano
	¾ teaspoon salt
¾ cup peeled and finely sliced or grated carrots	¼ teaspoon freshly ground black pepper

1. Melt the butter in a large skillet or sauté pan over high heat. Add the cabbage and carrots and cook, stirring, until the cabbage is wilted, about 25 minutes.

2. Drain in a colander, return to the pan, and place over medium-high heat. Add the remaining ingredients and cook until the mixture is thick, stirring occasionally, about 5 minutes.

3. Serve immediately.

Broccoli with Hollandaise Sauce

MAKES 4 SERVINGS

This classic vegetable dish was on the old Delmonico menu and continues to be a favorite of New Orleans diners. Serve this with Trout Delmonico (page 126) or Fillet of Snapper Rome (page 138) for a timeless pairing.

1   large bunch broccoli (about 1½ pounds), tough stems removed, trimmed, and cut into flowerets

1   recipe Hollandaise Sauce (page 261)

1. Bring a large pot of salted water to a boil. Add the broccoli, reduce the heat to a gentle boil, and cook until tender, 7 to 8 minutes.

2. Drain the broccoli and then transfer to a serving dish. Drizzle the broccoli with the warm hollandaise sauce and serve immediately.

Green Beans Creole

In the old days, entrées always came with a side or two. Green beans smothered with ham, onions, and tomatoes were a menu staple. You'll find that these go well with just about any of the dishes from the old Delmonico repertoire.

2 tablespoons unsalted butter	3 cups water
2 slices bacon, chopped	1 teaspoon salt
¼ cup chopped ham	½ teaspoon freshly ground black pepper
1 cup chopped yellow onions	1¼ pounds fresh green beans, ends
½ cup diced canned tomatoes, with their juices	trimmed and cut in half

1. Melt the butter in a medium saucepan over high heat. Add the bacon and ham and cook, stirring, for 2 minutes. Add the onions and cook, stirring until soft, about 4 minutes. Add the tomatoes and their juice and cook, stirring, for 4 minutes. Add 2 cups of the water, the salt, pepper, and the beans. Reduce the heat to medium and cook, stirring occasionally, until the beans begin to soften, about 20 minutes. Add the remaining 1 cup water and cook until the beans are very tender, about 10 minutes.

2. Serve hot.

Delmonico's Famous Eggplant Casserole

MAKES 4 TO 6 SERVINGS

This dish, created by Elmer Decquir, indeed was famous. It appeared on the menu for years and no one dared to take it off due to its high demand.

2 medium eggplants (about 2 pounds), peeled and cut into large chunks	1½ cups diced canned tomatoes, with their juice
1¼ teaspoons salt	½ pound peeled and deveined small shrimp, minced
2 tablespoons unsalted butter	1 tablespoon plus 1 teaspoon LeGoût Chicken Base or other thick chicken base
1½ cups chopped yellow onions	
½ cup seeded and chopped green bell peppers	½ cup chopped green onions
½ cup chopped celery	1 teaspoon freshly ground black pepper
1 teaspoon chopped fresh garlic	⅓ cup fine dry bread crumbs
2 small bay leaves	

1. Preheat the oven to 350°F. Lightly grease a 7 x 11-inch baking dish and set aside.

2. Place the eggplants in a large pot, season with ¼ teaspoon of the salt, cover with water by 1 inch, and bring to a boil. Reduce the heat slightly and cook at a gentle boil until the eggplants are tender and very soft, about 30 minutes. Remove from the heat and drain well, reserving 3 tablespoons of the cooking liquid. Set aside.

3. Melt the butter in a medium pot or Dutch oven over medium heat. Add the yellow onions, bell peppers, celery, garlic, and bay leaves and cook, stirring occasionally, until the vegetables are soft and golden, about 10 minutes. Stir in the reserved 3 tablespoons eggplant cooking liquid and the tomatoes and their juices and allow the mixture to simmer gently for 5 minutes. Add the shrimp and cook for 10 minutes, stirring frequently to keep from sticking.

4. Add the chicken base, reserved eggplants, green onions, the remaining 1 teaspoon salt, and the black pepper and cook for 2 minutes, stirring. Remove from the heat and discard the bay leaves. Spoon the mixture into the prepared baking dish, sprinkle the bread crumbs over the top, and bake until the bread crumbs are lightly browned and the mixture is bubbly, about 30 minutes.

5. Remove from the oven and let cool slightly before serving.

Stuffed Artichokes

MAKES 4 SERVINGS

Stuffed artichokes are a very common New Orleans menu item, typical of the city's Italian heritage. Recipes differ from family to family and restaurant to restaurant. Some stuffings are simply a combination of bread crumbs, garlic, herbs, and olive oil, while others include seafood, sausage, or meat. This recipe incorporates Elmer's flavorful Bread Crumb Stuffing. The size of the artichokes will determine the amount of time needed to cook them; start checking for doneness after forty minutes.

1 recipe Boiled Artichokes (page 255)	4 teaspoons olive oil
1 recipe Elmer's Bread Crumb Stuffing (page 128)	½ recipe Lemon Butter Sauce (page 117)

1. Remove the stems of the artichokes so that they sit flat. Cut off about 1 inch from the tops with a sharp knife and trim the sharp points of the artichoke leaves with kitchen shears.

2. Preheat the oven to 350°F.

3. Gently press back the center leaves on the artichokes so the inner choke and prickly leaves are revealed. Pull out the core of undeveloped white leaves in the center of each artichoke and gently scrape out the hairy choke with a teaspoon so as not to damage the heart.

4. Gently press the artichoke leaves outward to make space between the leaves and fill with the stuffing. Place the artichokes in a baking dish and add enough water to cover the bottom of the pan by ½ inch. Drizzle each artichoke with 1 teaspoon of the oil, cover the pan with aluminum foil, and bake until the artichoke leaves come out easily when pulled and the hearts are tender, 45 minutes to 1 hour, adding more water as necessary.

5. Transfer the artichokes to 4 large artichoke plates or dinner plates and drizzle with the lemon butter sauce. Serve hot.

SWEET SUCCESS

A meal without dessert is unfinished, as far as I'm concerned. Something as simple as a chocolate-covered coconut bonbon or a chocolate sundae is more than enough to satisfy one's craving for a sweet note on which to end the meal. On the other hand, there are those of us who enjoy something more extravagant, like crêpes served with warm chocolate sauce and strawberries flambéed with liqueur tableside, a creamy bread pudding topped with rich rum sauce, or a luscious lemon pie topped with silky meringue.

We have a dessert menu that offers classics but we have given them a spin. Check out the Brown Sugar Baked Alaska, Bananas Foster Bread Pudding, and Profiteroles filled with house-made ice cream. Perhaps the Apple Pie, Velvet Chocolate Torte, or the Warm Chocolate Praline Tart will strike your fancy.

My advice: do as our Delmonico guests—pick one or two treats and enjoy a sweet ending to your meal!

Velvet Chocolate Torte *with* Clear Orange–Caramel Sauce

MAKES ONE 10-INCH TORTE, 12 SERVINGS

The chocolate mousse that is the filling for this torte is light and airy, smooth and slightly sweet— perfect in my book—and the orange-caramel sauce provides just the right complement to it. This dessert is very straightforward to make, with the filling requiring only six ingredients.

¾ cup pecans	1 teaspoon pure vanilla extract
¾ cup walnuts	1½ cups cold heavy cream
¼ cup light brown sugar	2 tablespoons Kahlúa, Tia Maria,
6 tablespoons unsalted butter, melted	or other coffee-flavored liqueur
12 ounces semisweet chocolate	1 recipe Clear Orange–Caramel Sauce
4 large egg whites	(recipe follows)
¾ cup confectioners' sugar	

1. Preheat the oven to 350°F.

2. Spread the pecans and walnuts on a small baking sheet and bake until fragrant and lightly toasted, about 8 minutes. Let cool.

3. Place the nuts and brown sugar in the bowl of a food processor and with the machine running, add the melted butter in a slow stream through the feed tube and process until combined. Reserve 2 tablespoons of the nut mixture for the topping and press the remaining mixture evenly across the bottom of a 10-inch springform pan.

4. Place the chocolate in the top of a double boiler or in a heatproof bowl set over barely simmering water and stir until melted. Set aside.

5. To make the meringue, combine the egg whites, confectioners' sugar, and vanilla in a large bowl and whip with an electric mixer until stiff peaks form. Set aside.

6. In a clean bowl using clean beaters, whip the cream with the Kahlúa until stiff peaks form, being careful not to overbeat.

7. Place the chocolate in a large bowl and add one-third of the meringue, stirring until well combined. Fold in the remaining meringue in 2 additions, being careful not to overmix. Fold the whipped cream into the chocolate mixture, being careful not to deflate the mixture, and pour into the prepared pan. Sprinkle the reserved 2 tablespoons of the nut mixture over the top, wrap the pan with plastic wrap, and refrigerate overnight.

8. To serve, slice the cake using a thin, sharp knife dipped in warm water and arrange on 12 plates. Drizzle the orange-caramel sauce to the side of each slice and serve.

✤{ Clear Orange–Caramel Sauce

1½ **cups sugar**	1 **tablespoon fresh lemon juice**
½ **cup water**	¾ **cup fresh orange juice**
1 **tablespoon grated orange zest**	

1. Combine the sugar, water, orange zest, and lemon juice in a medium heavy saucepan and cook over medium-high heat, stirring constantly, until the sugar dissolves. Once the sugar dissolves, stop stirring and continue to cook until the mixture thickens and turns golden brown, 10 to 15 minutes.

2. Remove from the heat and add the orange juice (the mixture will bubble up). Return to medium-high heat and cook, stirring constantly, for 1 minute.

3. Remove from the heat and let cool slightly. Strain through a fine-mesh strainer into a bowl and cool to room temperature before serving. (The sauce will thicken as it cools.)

Here are two quick kitchen secrets—egg whites whip better at room temperature, while heavy cream achieves the best peaks when whipped cold.

Warm Chocolate Praline Tart *with* Caramel *and* Chocolate Sauces *and* Vanilla Ice Cream

MAKES ONE 10-INCH TART, 8 SERVINGS

New Orleans is known for its pralines, the sweet concoction made primarily of sugar and pecans, which were peddled in the streets of the French Quarter many years ago. Today there are several shops in the Quarter that make the candies on the premises and the aroma is intoxicating. I love using them in desserts and this one is absolutely the best.

1 recipe Chocolate Tart Crust (recipe follows)	½ teaspoon pure vanilla extract
6 tablespoons granulated sugar	¼ teaspoon salt
6 tablespoons light brown sugar	2 cups coarsely crumbled Chocolate Pralines (recipe follows)
1 tablespoon all-purpose flour	
3 large eggs, lightly beaten	1 recipe Caramel Sauce (page 228)
¼ cup dark corn syrup	1 recipe Chocolate Sauce (recipe follows)
¼ cup light corn syrup	1 recipe Vanilla Ice Cream (page 250),
1 tablespoon dark rum	or good-quality store-bought ice cream

1. On a lightly floured surface, roll the dough out to a 12-inch circle, about ⅛ inch thick. Gently fit the dough into a 10-inch fluted tart pan with a removable bottom, easing the pastry gently into the bottom and sides. Trim the edges of the dough so that they overhang slightly over the edge of the tart pan, then fold this excess dough over the sides so that the outer edges are almost twice as thick as the bottom of the crust. Press so that the edges are flush with the top of the pan. Cover and refrigerate for at least 30 minutes or overnight.

2. Preheat the oven to 350°F and position a rack in the center of the oven.

3. Line the tart shell with parchment paper and pie weights, beans, or rice and bake until set and the edges just begin to firm up, about 15 minutes. Remove the parchment and weights and bake until completely set, 10 to 12 minutes. Cool completely on a wire rack.

4. Reduce the oven temperature to 325°F.

5. To prepare the tart filling, combine the granulated sugar, brown sugar, and flour in a large bowl and stir to blend. Add the eggs, dark and light corn syrups, rum, vanilla, and salt and whisk well to blend.

6. Crumble the pralines evenly over the bottom of the prepared tart shell and pour the filling over the pralines. Bake until the tart is set, 1 hour and 10 minutes to 1 hour and 20 minutes.

7. Cool completely on a wire rack.

8. To serve, cut the tart into 8 slices. Spoon about 1½ tablespoons of the caramel sauce onto the center of 8 dessert plates and arrange the slices on top. Drizzle each slice with about 3 tablespoons of the chocolate sauce and arrange a scoop of ice cream to the side. Serve immediately.

✳{Chocolate Tart Crust

MAKES ONE 9 OR 10-INCH TART CRUST

1¼ **cups all-purpose flour**	8 **tablespoons (1 stick) cold unsalted**
¾ **cup confectioners' sugar**	**butter, cut into pieces**
¼ **cup unsweetened cocoa powder**	1 **large egg, lightly beaten**
Pinch of salt	

Sift the flour, sugar, cocoa, and salt into a large bowl. With your fingers, incorporate the butter pieces into the dry ingredients until the mixture resembles coarse crumbs. Mix in the egg to make a soft dough. Flatten the dough into a disk, wrap tightly in plastic wrap, and place in the refrigerator to rest for at least 1 hour before using.

✳{Chocolate Pralines

MAKES ABOUT 3 CUPS CRUMBLED PRALINES

This recipe makes slightly more than is needed for the tart filling. However, these pralines make a great lunch box treat or crunchy ice cream topping when crumbled. Or double the recipe and make large pralines for holiday gift giving.

½ **cup light brown sugar**	2 **tablespoons unsalted butter**
½ **cup granulated sugar**	¾ **cup chopped pecans**
¼ **cup heavy cream**	2 **ounces semisweet chocolate chips**

1. Line a large baking sheet with parchment paper or aluminum foil and set aside.

2. Combine the brown sugar, granulated sugar, heavy cream, and butter in a large heavy saucepan and cook over medium-high heat, stirring, until the sugars have dissolved, about 3 minutes. Continue to cook until the mixture reaches the softball stage, 238° to 240°F on a candy thermometer, 3 to 4 minutes.

3. Remove from the heat, add the pecans and chocolate chips, and stir vigorously until the pecans remain suspended in the mixture, about 2 minutes. Spoon onto the prepared baking sheet, spreading with the back of a spoon to form a thin layer of uniform thickness. Cool completely and then crumble as needed. (Alternatively, make individual pralines by dropping the hot praline mixture by the spoonful onto the prepared baking sheet, let cool, and then remove with a thin knife.)

❊{Chocolate Sauce

MAKES 1½ CUPS

This sauce is very versatile and can be made either with the semisweet chocolate that we prefer at the restaurant or with bittersweet or milk chocolate pieces. It's delicious served simply on top of ice cream or drizzled over your favorite pie, the Warm Chocolate Praline Tart, or the Chocolate-Strawberry Crêpes (page 245). For a more sophisticated flavor, substitute one tablespoon of your favorite liqueur or brandy for the vanilla extract.

¾ cup half-and-half	½ pound semisweet chocolate chips (1⅓ cups)
1 tablespoon unsalted butter	¼ teaspoon pure vanilla extract

1. Scald the half-and-half and butter in a small heavy saucepan over medium heat. Remove from the heat.

2. Place the chocolate and vanilla in a medium heatproof bowl. Add the hot half-and-half and let sit for 2 minutes, then whisk until smooth. Serve slightly warm. (The sauce can be kept refrigerated in an airtight container for up to 3 days; rewarm gently before serving.)

Brown Sugar Baked Alaska *with* Chocolate-Hazelnut Ice Cream, Flaming Frangelico-Rum Sauce, *and* Candied Hazelnuts

MAKES 8 TO 10 SERVINGS

This spectacular dessert is one we served when Delmonico first reopened, and is another dessert that was presented and then finished tableside for two. After presentation, the waiter would cut the small Baked Alaska in half with a heated knife and place one-half on each plate. The waiter then would make a hot caramel-rum sauce (similar to the sauce for Bananas Foster but without the cinnamon) and drizzle it flaming over both halves.

The showy presentation makes this ideal for special occasions, so we've increased the size of this dessert to serve a party. As with the Lemon Meringue Pie (page 242), we use a blowtorch at the restaurant to brown meringues. However, in this case, because of the height of the meringue, a torch really is necessary, unless you have a very large oven with a broiler element at the top.

Traditionally, Baked Alaska is assembled on a white genoise or sponge cake. But at Delmonico, we wanted to make this the ultimate chocolate dessert, and so we used a chocolate cake for our base.

¼ cup hazelnuts	8 large egg whites, at room temperature
1 recipe Chocolate-Hazelnut Ice Cream (recipe follows) or good-quality store-bought chocolate ice cream, softened	1 cup packed light brown sugar
	1 recipe Caramel Sauce (recipe follows)
	¼ cup Frangelico or dark rum
1 recipe Chocolate Cake (recipe follows)	1 tablespoon cold unsalted butter

1. Preheat the oven to 350°F.

2. Spread the hazelnuts on a small baking sheet and bake until the skins are cracked and the nuts are deep golden brown, 8 to 10 minutes. Place the nuts in a towel and rub them to remove the skins. Let cool.

3. Line a 1½-quart 9-inch metal bowl with plastic wrap, leaving an 8-inch overhang. Spoon the softened ice cream into the bowl, spreading evenly. Fit the cake over the ice cream, pressing to adhere, and wrap with the overhanging plastic. Freeze until the ice cream is hardened, at least 4 hours.

4. Place the egg whites in a large bowl fitted with an electric mixer and beat until soft peaks form. Gradually add the sugar, beating until the whites become stiff and a glossy meringue forms, about 5 minutes.

5. Uncover the cake and invert onto a metal or ovenproof platter, or a 9 or 10-inch diameter tart bottom. Working quickly, pipe or spread the meringue over the cake and out to the edges to seal. Freeze uncovered for at least 30 minutes and up to 12 hours.

6. Using a blowtorch, brown the meringue evenly on all sides. Arrange on a platter.

7. Combine the caramel sauce and hazelnuts in a medium saucepan and warm over medium heat. Once the sauce starts to bubble, remove the pan from the heat and add the Frangelico. Return the pan to the heat and carefully tilt the edge of the pan toward the flame to ignite the liquor. (Alternatively, light the mixture off the heat using a match and return to medium heat.) Once the flame dies out, swirl the cold butter into the sauce. Remove from the heat.

8. Drizzle the sauce over the top of the Baked Alaska and serve immediately.

⁕{ Caramel Sauce

MAKES A GENEROUS ¾ CUP

We serve this sauce with many desserts at Delmonico, including the Bananas Foster Bread Pudding (page 235) and Warm Chocolate Praline Tart (page 224).

¾ **cup granulated sugar**	½ **cup heavy cream**
2 **tablespoons water**	2 **tablespoons to** ¼ **cup milk**
½ **teaspoon lemon juice**	

Combine the sugar, water, and lemon juice in a medium heavy saucepan. Place over medium-high heat and cook, stirring, until the sugar dissolves. Let boil without stirring until the mixture becomes a deep amber color, 2 to 3 minutes, watching closely so it doesn't burn. Carefully add the cream or it may splatter, whisk to combine, and remove from the heat. Add the milk, 2 tablespoons at a time, until the desired consistency is reached. Remove from the heat and allow to cool before using.

Chef Charles Ranhofer of the original Delmonico's in New York is credited with creating the first Baked Alaska in 1867 to celebrate the American purchase of Alaska that year. A recipe for individual desserts, with ice cream and meringue baked on a cookie base, appears in his 1867 cookbook, *The Epicurean.*

There are written references to earlier ice cream desserts that were very similar to the Baked Alaska. These ranged from *omelette surprise* (created in 1804) and the Norwegian omelet (another reference to a frozen landscape), to one concocted by the chef of the Grand Hotel in Paris in 1866. These desserts probably all sprang from the earlier gourmet fascination with molded ice cream *bombes.*

TOP: Pipe the merigue in rows to completely cover the ice cream. BOTTOM: The meringue is browned evenly with a blowtorch before serving.

☙ Chocolate-Hazelnut Ice Cream

MAKES ABOUT 1 QUART

If you're familiar with Nutella chocolate spread, then you're familiar with the rich flavor of Gianduja, a hazelnut-flavored chocolate candy that originated in Turin in the Piedmont region of Italy. This is what we use in the Delmonico pastry kitchen to make this rich ice cream.

And while this aromatic chocolate can be found in some gourmet markets or from chocolate wholesalers, we re-created the flavor for this recipe using hazelnuts and semisweet chocolate, and an infusion of the hazelnut-flavored liqueur, Frangelico. If you'd prefer, make a chocolate ice cream instead by omitting the nuts and liqueur, and adding an extra two ounces of chocolate to the custard base.

½ cup hazelnuts	½ pound semisweet chocolate, chopped
2 cups heavy cream	3 tablespoons Frangelico or other
1 cup milk	nut-flavored liqueur
6 large egg yolks	1 teaspoon pure vanilla extract
½ cup granulated sugar	

---

1. Preheat the oven to 350°F.

2. Spread the hazelnuts on a small baking sheet and bake until the skins are cracked and the nuts are deep golden brown, 8 to 10 minutes. Place the nuts in a towel and rub them to remove the skins. Let cool and roughly chop.

3. Combine the cream and milk in a medium heavy saucepan and bring to a gentle boil over medium heat. Remove from the heat.

4. Beat the egg yolks with the sugar in a medium bowl until frothy and lemon colored, about 2 minutes. Whisk 1 cup of the hot cream into the egg yolks in a slow, steady stream. Gradually add the egg mixture to the hot cream, whisking constantly. Cook over medium-low heat, stirring occasionally, until the mixture thickens enough to coat the back of a spoon, about 5 minutes.

5. Remove from the heat, add the chocolate, hazelnuts, Frangelico, and vanilla and stir until the chocolate is melted. Cover with plastic wrap, pressing it directly against the surface of the mixture to keep a skin from forming. Refrigerate until well chilled, about 2 hours.

6. Pour the mixture into an ice cream maker and freeze according to the manufacturer's instructions. Transfer to an airtight container and freeze until ready to serve.

❊{Chocolate Cake

This all-around chocolate cake would be great topped with fresh fruit and sweetened whipped cream, or cut into layers and frosted.

6 tablespoons unsweetened cocoa poweder	¼ teaspoon plus ⅛ teaspoon salt
¾ cup hot water	¾ cup buttermilk
1½ cups sugar	2 large eggs
1½ cups all-purpose flour	½ cup plus 1 tablespoon vegetable oil
1¼ teaspoons baking soda	½ teaspoon vanilla extract

1. Preheat the oven to 350°F. Butter and lightly flour a 9-inch cake pan, knocking out the excess flour, and set aside.

2. Place the cocoa in a medium bowl and slowly add the hot water, whisking to dissolve. Set aside.

3. Sift together the sugar, flour, baking soda, and salt into a large mixing bowl and set aside. In a separate bowl, whisk the buttermilk, eggs, oil, and vanilla until well combined. Add the wet ingredients to the dry ingredients and fold in the cocoa. Stir just until all the ingredients are combined.

4. Pour the batter into the prepared cake pan and bake until set in the center and a tester comes out clean, about 20 minutes.

5. Cool the cake in the pan for 15 minutes, then turn out onto a wire rack to finish cooling.

Profiteroles *with* Vanilla Ice Cream *and* Chocolate Sauce

MAKES 16 PROFITEROLES, 4 TO 8 SERVINGS

This timeless classic was on the dessert menu when we first opened the restaurant and makes special appearances now and then with different flavors of ice cream. Profiteroles (or cream puffs) are made of choux paste, which magically rises in the oven to leave a hollow pastry for filling. And while I've always liked fiddling around with them, using different fillings and toppings, I always return to this classic presentation.

1 **cup milk**	1 **teaspoon water**
6 **tablespoons unsalted butter**	½ **recipe Vanilla Ice Cream (page** 250) **or**
1 **teaspoon sugar**	**1 recipe Sweetened Whipped Cream**
Pinch of salt	**(page** 251)
¾ **cup all-purpose flour**	**Confectioners' sugar, for garnish**
5 **large eggs, at room temperature**	1 **recipe Chocolate Sauce (page** 226)

1. Preheat the oven to 425°F. Line a large baking sheet with parchment paper and set aside.

2. Combine the milk, butter, sugar, and salt in a medium saucepan and bring to a slow boil over medium heat and cook until the butter is melted. Remove from the heat and add the flour all at once, stirring with a heavy wooden spoon. Return the pan to medium-low heat and stir briskly until the mixture becomes a smooth paste and pulls away from the sides of the pan in a ball, 1 to 2 minutes.

3. Remove from the heat and let cool slightly, 1 to 2 minutes. Stirring constantly with a heavy wooden spoon, add 4 of the eggs, one at a time, beating well after the addition of each, and mix until smooth. Let the dough cool.

4. Beat the remaining egg with the water in a small bowl to make an egg wash.

5. Transfer the dough to a pastry bag fitted with a plain ¾-inch tip and pipe out 16 ping-pong-ball-sized rounds onto the prepared sheet, about 2 inches apart. (Alternatively, spoon onto the baking sheet with a large spoon.) Lightly brush the egg wash on the tops and sides of the dough using a pastry brush and bake until doubled in size, 14 to 15 minutes. Reduce the temperature to 375°F and bake until the balls are golden brown, firm to the touch, and hollow inside, 6 to 7 minutes. Turn off the oven and leave the oven door ajar for 10 minutes for the puffs to dry.

6. Cool completely on a wire rack. Cut each profiterole in half and scoop out the doughy centers with a small spoon.

7. To serve, fill the bottom halves with a small scoop (about 1 ounce) of the ice cream (or fill with 2 tablespoons of the whipped cream) and cover with the tops. Place 2 to 4 profiteroles on each dessert plate and sift the confectioners' sugar over the profiteroles and decoratively onto the plates. Drizzle each profiterole with warm chocolate sauce and serve immediately.

Other items made from *pâte à choux* paste (or choux) include éclairs and cheesy gougères. Profiteroles traditionally are stuffed with a pastry cream (or thick custard), ice cream, or sweetened whipped cream, and then drizzled with chocolate or caramel sauce.

Profiteroles also can be made savory by omitting the sugar, increasing the salt slightly, and adding chopped fresh herbs or seasonings, as desired. Fill savory profiteroles with light seafood mousses, such as shrimp mousse, or lobster or crabmeat salad for elegant cocktail or lunch fare.

Delmonico Fluff

This simple but very satisfying chocolate sundae was well loved by the many families who were regular Delmonico customers. Large scoops of a good-quality vanilla ice cream were topped with thick chocolate syrup, a big spoonful of whipped cream, and sprinkles of toasted coconut and almond slivers.

¼ **cup sweetened coconut flakes**
¼ **cup blanched, slivered almonds**
⅓ **cup cold heavy cream**
2 **teaspoons confectioners' sugar**

1 **recipe Vanilla Ice Cream (page** 250) **or good quality store-bought vanilla ice cream**
½ **cup chocolate syrup or Chocolate Sauce (page** 226)

1. Preheat the oven to 350°F. Line a small baking sheet with parchment paper.

2. Spread the flaked coconut on the prepared baking sheet and bake until golden brown, 4 to 5 minutes. Let cool on the baking sheet.

3. Spread the almond slivers on a clean small baking sheet and bake until fragrant and lightly toasted, 4 to 5 minutes. Let cool on the baking sheet.

4. Place the cream in a medium bowl and whisk or beat with an electric mixer until thick and frothy. Add the confectioners' sugar and beat until soft peaks form. Set aside.

5. Place 2 scoops of ice cream in each of 4 footed parfait glasses or dessert bowls. Drizzle 2 tablespoons of the syrup over each serving of ice cream and top with 2 tablespoons of the whipped cream. Sprinkle each serving with 1 tablespoon each of the toasted coconut and almonds and serve immediately.

Bananas Foster Bread Pudding *with* Vanilla Ice Cream *and* Caramel Sauce

MAKES 10 TO 12 SERVINGS

Bananas Foster was created at Brennan's, another classic New Orleans restaurant, in the 1950s when the city was a major port of entry for Central and South American bananas. The dish has become a global favorite through the years and I've enjoyed kicking it up in different preparations—from pie and ice cream to this bread pudding.

This dessert is New Orleans all the way—from the Creole-style bread pudding to the ultrarich filling and à la mode ice cream topping. Cut out the rum if you're serving this dessert to kids. And don't forget that the secret to a good bread pudding is to use day-old French bread.

9	tablespoons unsalted butter	3	cups heavy cream
1½	cups packed light brown sugar	1	cup milk
¾	teaspoon ground cinnamon	1	teaspoon pure vanilla extract
6	firm-ripe bananas, peeled and cut crosswise into ¾-inch-thick slices		Pinch of salt
		6	cups ½-inch cubes day-old French bread
¼	cup banana liqueur	1	recipe Vanilla Ice Cream (page 250) or good-quality store-bought ice cream
½	cup dark rum		
4	large eggs, lightly beaten	1	recipe Caramel Sauce (page 228)

1. Preheat the oven to 350°F. Butter a 10 x 14-inch baking dish with 1 tablespoon of the butter and set aside.

2. Melt the remaining 8 tablespoons butter in a large skillet over medium heat. Add 1 cup of the brown sugar and the cinnamon and cook, stirring, until the sugar dissolves, about 2 minutes. Add the bananas and cook on both sides, turning, until the bananas start to soften and brown, about 3 minutes. Add the banana liqueur and stir to blend. Carefully add the rum and shake the pan back and forth to warm the rum and flame the pan. (Or, off the heat, carefully ignite the pan with a match and return to the heat.) Shake the pan back and forth, basting the bananas, until the flame dies. Remove from the heat and let cool.

3. Whisk together the eggs, the remaining ½ cup brown sugar, the cream, milk, vanilla, and salt in a large bowl. Add the cooled banana mixture and bread and stir to blend thoroughly. Pour into the prepared baking dish and bake until firm, 50 minutes to 1 hour. Cool on a wire rack for 20 minutes.

4. To serve, scoop the pudding onto dessert plates. Top each serving with a small scoop of vanilla ice cream, drizzle with caramel sauce, and serve immediately.

Jitterbug's Bread Pudding
with Rum Crème Anglaise

Both Angie and Rose agree, as did their regular customers, that this bread pudding is quite different from many others. Jitterbug made a rich custard that was added to toasted bread cubes, which resulted in a lighter and moister pudding.

It was never cut into squares like most bread puddings were; rather, it was spooned out into small dessert bowls and doused with Jitterbug's custard-like rum sauce. This can be served either warm or chilled.

6 slices white bread, cut into ½-inch cubes (about 4 cups)

8 tablespoons (1 stick) unsalted butter, melted

4 large eggs

½ cup sugar

1 tablespoon dark rum

½ teaspoon pure vanilla extract

¼ teaspoon grated nutmeg

¼ teaspoon salt

2 cups whole milk, scalded

2 cups sliced canned peaches, drained, liquid reserved

1 cup chopped or crushed canned pineapples, drained, liquid reserved

2 tablespoons butter, cut into 8 thin slices

1 recipe Rum Crème Anglaise (recipe follows)

1. Preheat the oven to 350°F.

2. Toss the bread cubes with the melted butter in a large bowl, spread on a large baking sheet, and bake until lightly browned, about 10 minutes. Transfer to a 7 x 11-inch baking dish and set aside.

3. Beat the eggs in a large bowl. Add the sugar, rum, vanilla, nutmeg, and salt and whisk to combine. Slowly add the milk, whisking constantly.

4. Arrange the fruit over the toasted bread cubes. Pour the custard evenly over the mixture, dot with the sliced butter, and bake until the custard sets, about 35 minutes. Let rest for 15 minutes.

5. Spoon the pudding into dessert bowls, ladle 3 to 4 tablespoons of the rum sauce over each serving, and serve.

*⟩Rum Crème Anglaise

4	large egg yolks	2	cups milk, scalded
2	tablespoons cornstarch	¼	cup dark rum
6	tablespoons sugar	1	drop yellow food coloring, optional
2	teaspoons vanilla extract		

Whisk together the egg yolks, cornstarch, sugar, and vanilla in a medium saucepan. Slowly whisk in the warm milk and cook, stirring constantly, over medium-low heat until the mixture thickens, 3 to 4 minutes. Strain through a fine-mesh strainer into a medium bowl and stir in the rum and food coloring, if desired. Serve at room temperature or chilled.

Bourbon Vanilla Crème Brûlées

The combination of bourbon, eggs, cream, and vanilla gives these crème brûlées (burnt creams) a delicate eggnog flavor that's absolutely delicious. We've served many crème brûlée variations through the years at Emeril's Delmonico, but this one has been a dessert menu favorite for some time—you'll see why when you taste it.

These make a great dinner party dessert since they can be baked the day before and refrigerated, and then quickly topped with their sugar coating immediately before serving.

2⅓ cups heavy cream	1 teaspoon pure vanilla extract
⅔ cup milk	2 large eggs
½ cup granulated sugar	4 large egg yolks
3 tablespoons bourbon	3 tablespoons light brown sugar

1. Preheat the oven to 300°F. Arrange six 6-ounce ramekins or custard cups in a baking dish large enough to hold them without touching and set aside.

2. Combine the cream, milk, and granulated sugar in a medium saucepan and bring to a simmer over medium-high heat, stirring to dissolve the sugar. Remove from the heat and stir in the bourbon and vanilla.

3. In a medium bowl, whisk the eggs and yolks until thick and pale yellow, about 2 minutes. Gradually add the hot cream mixture to the eggs, whisking constantly. Strain through a fine-mesh strainer into a clean container.

4. Divide the custard among the prepared ramekins and fill the baking dish with enough hot water to come halfway up the sides of the ramekins. Place in the middle of the oven and bake until the custards are firm yet shake slightly, 45 to 50 minutes. Remove from the oven and cool the ramekins on a wire rack. Refrigerate until completely cool, at least 4 hours or overnight.

5. Sprinkle the top of each custard with 1½ teaspoons of the brown sugar. Using a blowtorch, caramelize the sugar. (Alternatively, preheat the broiler. Place the custards on a baking sheet and broil until the sugar melts and caramelizes, watching closely to avoid burning, and rotating the cups, 1 to 2 minutes.)

6. Place the ramekins on dessert plates and serve immediately.

Apple Pie *with* Lard Crust

Apple pie has long been a favorite at Delmonico—both at Emeril's Delmonico and the Delmonico of long ago. Chef Ernest "Jitterbug" Rome made the old restaurant's apple pie differently from this recipe. That pie consisted of cooking apple slices in butter, with cinnamon, nutmeg, and sugar. The mixture was then thickened with cornstarch and poured into a prepared piecrust and sealed with a top crust. The top crust was brushed with an egg wash, sprinkled with a cinnamon-sugar mixture, and baked until golden.

Diners then had the option of ordering apple pie à la mode (topped with a scoop of vanilla ice cream) or served warm with a slice of Cheddar cheese on top.

When I reopened Delmonico, popular demand required that we put apple pie back on the menu. Believe it or not, we used a piecrust that was made with lard! Lard, if you don't know, makes an unbelievably flaky and tender crust; it can be purchased in most supermarkets. Try this recipe for something different. Or, if you'd prefer, use the Sweet Piecrust on page 244 instead, doubling the ingredients.

1 recipe Lard Piecrust (recipe follows)	3 tablespoons all-purpose flour
6 medium Granny Smith apples (about 2¾ pounds)	½ teaspoon ground cinnamon
4 teaspoons fresh lemon juice	¼ teaspoon grated nutmeg
¾ cup plus 1 tablespoon sugar	Pinch of salt
	1 tablespoon heavy cream

1. Preheat the oven to 375°F.

2. Roll out 1 piece of the dough on a lightly floured surface to a 12-inch circle and transfer to a 9-inch pie pan, pressing gently to fit. Cover with plastic wrap and refrigerate until ready to fill. Keep the second portion of dough wrapped in the refrigerator.

3. Peel, core, and cut the apples into ¼-inch-thick slices and toss in a large bowl with the lemon juice to prevent discoloration. Add ¾ cup of the sugar, the flour, cinnamon, nutmeg, and salt and toss to coat the apples. Spoon the apple mixture into the prepared pie shell.

4. Roll out the second piece of dough to an 11-inch circle and arrange over the fruit. Trim the edges of both crusts to a ¾-inch overhang, fold under the 2 crusts to seal, and crimp the edges decoratively. With a sharp knife, cut a pattern of slits in the center of the top crust. With a pastry brush, brush the cream over the top crust and sprinkle with the remaining 1 tablespoon sugar. Bake until the crust is golden brown and the juices begin to bubble, 45 to 55 minutes.

5. Remove from the oven and cool on a wire rack for 1 to 2 hours before serving.

*{Lard Piecrust

Lard is made by boiling or rendering pig or hog fat, the highest grade of which is found around the animal's kidneys. And while the process can be done at home, lard has been commercially available for cooking purposes since the mid-1800s. Today, lard can be found in the baking section of supermarkets.

Lard is 100 percent fat, meaning it has a higher melting point and that is why it makes such a flaky crust. Although it is shelf stable, it is best used cold in pastry dough.

2½ **cups all-purpose flour**	1 **cup cold lard, cut into pieces**
2 **tablespoons sugar**	4 to 5 **tablespoons ice water, or as needed**
½ **teaspoon salt**	

1. Sift the flour, sugar, and salt into a large bowl. With your fingers, work the lard into the dry ingredients until the mixture resembles coarse crumbs. Add 4 tablespoons of the ice water and work with your fingers until the dough comes together, adding more water as needed, 1 teaspoon at a time, to make a smooth dough, being careful not to overwork the dough.

2. Divide the dough in two, form into disks, wrap tightly in plastic wrap, and refrigerate for at least 30 minutes before using.

Lemon Meringue Pie

Meringue making wasn't perfected until the early 1700s and it was supposedly the great French chef Antonin Carême who thought to use a pastry bag—as we do—for piping meringue onto pies. An American pastry chef and cooking school founder, Elizabeth Coane Goodfellow, is credited with inventing the actual lemon meringue pie in the early 1800s.

But I always say that nothing is so good it can't be improved upon. We played around with this pie until we settled on this version. The lemon custard is tart and thick, and the creamy sweet meringue is thicker than most.

1 recipe Sweet Piecrust (recipe follows)	2 tablespoons finely grated lemon zest
1¼ cups granulated sugar	1½ tablespoons Limoncello lemon liqueur
5 tablespoons cornstarch	2 tablespoons cold unsalted butter,
1 cup milk	cut into pieces
½ cup cold water	4 large egg whites, at room temperature
⅛ teaspoon salt	¼ teaspoon cream of tartar
6 large egg yolks	6 tablespoons confectioners' sugar
⅔ cup fresh lemon juice	

1. Remove the dough from the refrigerator and on a lightly floured surface, roll out to a 12-inch circle. Transfer the dough to a 9-inch pie pan, pressing gently to fit, trim the edge to within ½ inch of the pan, turn under, and crimp decoratively. Refrigerate for 30 minutes to 1 hour.

2. Preheat the oven to 375°F.

3. Line the pie shell with parchment paper and fill with pie weights, dry beans, or rice. Bake until the crust is set, about 12 minutes. Remove the parchment paper and weights and bake until lightly colored, 8 to 10 minutes. Cool on a wire rack before filling.

4. Combine the granulated sugar, cornstarch, milk, water, and a pinch of the salt in a large nonreactive saucepan, whisk to combine, and bring to a simmer over medium heat, whisking occasionally. As the mixture reaches a simmer and begins to thicken and turn clear, 4 to 5 minutes, whisk in the egg yolks, 2 at a time. Slowly add the lemon juice, whisking constantly, and add the zest and liqueur. Add the butter, 1 piece at a time, and whisking constantly, return to a simmer. Remove from the heat and pour immediately into the prepared piecrust.

At Emeril's Delmonico, we brown the meringue toppings with a blowtorch. It's a simple process, using a backward-forward motion a few inches above the pie (or the Baked Alaska). We recognize, however, that not all home cooks have this tool and so call to either broil or bake the meringue until the top is golden brown. If you do have a blowtorch, by all means use it, and note that the meringue will set best if it is added while the lemon filling still is hot.

5. Beat the egg whites, cream of tartar, and remaining pinch of salt in a large bowl with an electric mixer until soft peaks form. Beating constantly, gradually add the confectioners' sugar and beat until glossy stiff peaks form, being careful not to overbeat, as this will make the meringue difficult to spread.

6. Transfer the meringue to a pastry bag fitted with a medium star tip. Working one row at a time, pipe the meringue across the top of the hot lemon filling in a zigzag pattern, alternating direction with each row. Cover the pie filling completely, going out to the pastry edges, so the meringue does not draw up or weep during baking. (Alternatively, spread the meringue evenly over the pie filling using a rubber spatula, smoothing out to the pastry edges. Make decorative peaks in the meringue using a dull knife or the back of a spoon.)

7. To quickly cook the meringue, preheat the broiler with the rack in the highest position. Place the pie under the broiler and cook until the meringue is set and golden brown, 1 to 2 minutes, watching carefully to avoid burning. (Alternatively, the meringue can be cooked in a preheated 325°F oven until set and golden brown, 14 to 16 minutes.)

8. Transfer the pie to a wire rack to cool completely before serving.

⁂Sweet Piecrust

MAKES ONE 9- OR 10-INCH CRUST

This standard sweet crust is flaky, delicious, and easy to make. And if you're unable to obtain or unwilling to use lard, double the ingredients and make this crust instead for the Apple Pie on page 239, and bake as specified.

1¼	cups all-purpose flour	2	tablespoons cold vegetable shortening
1	tablespoon sugar	3 to 4	tablespoons ice water, or as needed
¼	teaspoon salt		
6	tablespoons cold unsalted butter, cut into pieces		

1. Sift the flour, sugar, and salt into a large bowl. With your fingers, work the butter and shortening into the dry ingredients until the mixture resembles coarse crumbs. Add 3 tablespoons of the ice water and work with your fingers until the dough comes together, adding more water as needed, 1 teaspoon at a time, to make a smooth dough, being careful not to overwork the dough.

2. Form the dough into a disk shape, wrap tightly in plastic wrap, and refrigerate for at least 30 minutes before using.

Chocolate-Strawberry Crêpes

Crêpes have long been, and continue to be, featured on the menus of fine New Orleans restaurants. Prepared tableside, they make an exciting and dramatic presentation in the dining rooms at Delmonico. Warm chocolate with strawberries makes a delectable dessert, but one that is not too overwhelming.

2 tablespoons unsalted butter
½ cup thinly sliced hulled strawberries
¼ cup sugar
2 tablespoons strawberry liqueur or kirsch

2 tablespoons brandy
½ recipe Dessert Crêpes (recipe follows) or 6 store-bought crêpes, defrosted if frozen
½ cup warm Chocolate Sauce (page 226)

1. Heat a large skillet over medium-high heat. Add the butter, swirling the pan until the butter is melted. Add the strawberries and cook, stirring, for 1 minute. Add the sugar and cook, whisking constantly, until the mixture is foamy, 1 to 2 minutes.

2. Remove the skillet from the heat, add the strawberry liqueur and brandy, and return the skillet to the heat, tilting the pan toward the flame to ignite. (Or, off the heat, carefully ignite the pan with a match, and return to the heat.) Shake the pan back and forth, basting the strawberries, until the flame dies.

3. Add the crêpes to the pan, one at a time, using a fork to fold each crêpe into quarters. After all of the crêpes have been added, swirl in the strawberry sauce to heat through and coat.

4. To serve, arrange 3 crêpes on each plate and spoon strawberry sauce over the top. Drizzle each serving with ¼ cup of the chocolate sauce and serve immediately.

Strawberry-flavored liqueur can be found in liquor stores. You could substitute other fruit-flavored liqueurs for this recipe, such as kirsch (or kirschwasser), the clear spirit made from distilling the juice of small black cherries, or the raspberry-flavored Chambord.

Remember, safety is foremost in the kitchen; please be careful when flambéing foods at home.

*}Dessert Crêpes

Making crêpes is much simpler than you might think—the secret to success is allowing the batter to rest before making them—and practice makes perfect.

We use these basic sweet crêpes to make the Chocolate-Strawberry Crêpes and Lemon Crêpes (page 248), which are prepared tableside at Emeril's Delmonico. For a simple dessert or breakfast treat, fill these crêpes with the jam or preserves of your choice, or fresh fruit, and sprinkle the tops with confectioners' sugar before serving.

¾ cup all-purpose flour	2 tablespoons sugar
3 large eggs, beaten	Pinch of salt
¾ cup plus 3 tablespoons milk	2 tablespoons melted unsalted butter

1. Whisk together the flour, eggs, milk, sugar, salt, and 1½ tablespoons of the butter in a medium bowl to form a smooth batter the thickness of heavy cream. Cover and refrigerate for at least 1 hour or overnight.

2. Heat a crêpe pan or small heavy nonstick skillet over medium-high heat. When hot, brush with a light coating of the remaining ½ tablespoon butter. Ladle about 3 tablespoons crêpe batter into the pan, tilting the skillet to evenly coat the pan with batter. Cook until golden brown on the bottom and the top begins to look dry, 1 to 2 minutes. Using a spatula, carefully turn the crêpe and cook on the second side just until the bottom colors slightly, about 30 seconds.

3. Transfer to a plate and cover loosely to keep warm. Repeat with the remaining batter. (The crêpes can be made up to 3 days in advance and refrigerated in an airtight container with layers of wax paper separating them. They also can be frozen, tightly wrapped, for up to 1 month. Defrost before using.)

Lemon Crêpes

Classic Crêpes Suzette are made with an orange-butter sauce and orange-flavored liqueur, but we wanted a different take on them. Here we use lemon juice and dark rum. You'll find these are a simple yet impressive way to end a special meal.

2 tablespoons unsalted butter	2 tablespoons dark rum
6 paper-thin crosswise, center-cut lemon slices, seeds removed	½ recipe Dessert Crêpes (page 247) or 6 store-bought crêpes, defrosted if frozen
¼ cup sugar	6 tablespoons Sweetened Whipped Cream (page 251)
6 tablespoons fresh lemon juice	
2 teaspoons finely grated lemon zest	

1. Heat a large skillet over medium-high heat. Add the butter, swirling the pan until the butter is melted. Add the lemon slices and cook, stirring, for 1 minute. Add the sugar and cook, whisking constantly, until the mixture begins to caramelize and turns light golden brown, about 2 minutes. Add the lemon juice and zest, whisk to incorporate, and cook until the mixture becomes foamy, 1 to 2 minutes.

2. Remove the skillet from the heat, add the rum and return the skillet to the heat, tilting the pan toward the flame to ignite. (Or, off the heat, carefully ignite the pan with a match and return to the heat.) Shake the pan back and forth until the flame dies.

3. Add the crêpes to the pan, one at a time, using a fork to fold each crêpe into quarters. When all of the crêpes have been added, swirl in the lemon sauce to heat through and coat.

4. To serve, arrange 3 crêpes on each plate and spoon lemon sauce over the top. Garnish each serving with 3 tablespoons of the whipped cream and serve immediately.

Chocolate Coconut Bonbons

MAKES ABOUT 2 DOZEN BONBONS

When we introduced these I couldn't eat just one; I popped them in my mouth like popcorn! They were designed to serve as a garnish for our coconut cream pie, but we also like to offer them as a final treat at private parties. And with the inclusion of white chocolate, these candies taste like a richer version of an ever-popular, commercial coconut-chocolate candy.

This recipe doubles easily for large parties or holiday gift-giving.

4 ounces white chocolate, chopped	2 tablespoons unsalted butter, at room temperature
1/2 pound sweetened coconut flakes	
1/2 cup sweetened condensed milk	1/4 teaspoon pure vanilla extract
6 tablespoons confectioners' sugar, sifted	12 ounces semisweet chocolate, chopped
	1 tablespoon vegetable shortening

1. Line a large baking sheet with parchment or wax paper and place a large wire rack on top. Set aside.

2. Melt the white chocolate in the top of a double boiler or in a medium bowl set over a pan of barely simmering water, stirring occasionally. Set aside.

3. Combine the coconut, condensed milk, confectioners' sugar, butter, and vanilla in a large bowl and stir to combine. Add the melted white chocolate and mix well. Cover and refrigerate until stiff, at least 2 hours or overnight.

4. Using a 1-inch scoop (about 1½ teaspoons), scoop the coconut mixture into balls and set on the prepared wire rack. Refrigerate the balls until firm, about 1 hour.

5. To make the chocolate coating, in the top of a double boiler or in a metal bowl set over barely simmering water, combine 8 ounces of the semisweet chocolate and the shortening. Melt over low heat, stirring, until the mixture reaches 116° to 118°F, or feels fairly warm but not hot to the touch. Remove from the heat and stir in the remaining 4 ounces of chocolate. Continue stirring until the chocolate reaches 80°F or feels cool to the touch. Return to low heat and cook, stirring, until the temperature rises to 85° to 87°F, or feels barely cool. Remove from the heat.

6. Remove the coconut balls from the refrigerator. Working one at a time, dip a ball into the melted semisweet chocolate and, using 2 forks, turn to coat completely. Lift the coated coconut ball from the chocolate with the forks, letting the excess chocolate drip off into the bowl. Place the ball on the wire rack and repeat with the remaining coconut balls. Let the chocolates set, uncovered, at room temperature or in the refrigerator, at least 1 hour.

7. Serve at room temperature or chilled. (The bonbons will keep in a tightly covered container, with the layers separated by wax paper, in a cool, dry place for up to 6 days.)

Vanilla Ice Cream

Vanilla Ice Cream is a big favorite all around. We use it for stuffing Profiteroles (page 232) and serving atop the Bananas Foster Bread Pudding (page 235) and Warm Chocolate Praline Tart (page 224). It's great on its own, or served as a sundae, like the Delmonico Fluff (page 234), or in a parfait.

2	**cups heavy cream**	1 **vanilla bean, split in half lengthwise**
2	**cups milk**	6 **large egg yolks**
¾	**cup sugar**	

1. Combine the cream, milk, sugar, and vanilla seeds and bean in a medium heavy saucepan and bring to a gentle boil over medium heat. Remove from the heat.

2. Beat the egg yolks in a medium bowl until frothy and lemon colored, about 2 minutes. Whisk 1 cup of the hot cream into the egg yolks in a slow, steady stream. Gradually add the egg mixture to the hot cream, whisking constantly. Cook over medium-low heat, stirring occasionally, until the mixture thickens enough to coat the back of a spoon, about 5 minutes.

3. Remove from the heat and strain through a fine-mesh strainer into a clean bowl. Cover with plastic wrap, pressing it directly against the surface of the mixture to keep a skin from forming. Refrigerate until well chilled, about 2 hours.

4. Pour the mixture into an ice cream maker and freeze according to the manufacturer's instructions. Transfer to an airtight container and freeze until ready to serve.

Sweetened Whipped Cream

Homemade sweetened whipped cream bears no resemblance whatsoever to the products available at your local supermarket. The airy texture and lightly sweet flavor of the real thing are simply incomparable! And if you like your cream sweeter, by all means, whip in additional sugar to suit your taste. Whipped cream also can be flavored with different extracts or liqueurs—for example, substitute one teaspoon of a nut-flavored liqueur like Nocello or Frangelico for the vanilla extract when serving sweetened whipped cream with a chocolate or nut dessert.

Cream can be beaten by hand using a balloon whisk, if your arm is up to it; the process goes more quickly than you might imagine. And you'll find it much easier to beat smaller amounts of cream by hand, such as what's needed for the Lemon Crêpes (page 248). Cream whips best when very cold, and even better when the bowl and beaters or whisk also are cold, straight from the refrigerator or freezer.

To determine how much heavy cream to beat for a recipe, figure that the cream will double in volume when whipped, or yield twice its original volume.

1 **cup cold heavy cream**
2 **tablespoons confectioners' sugar**
½ **teaspoon pure vanilla extract**

1. Place the cream in a medium bowl and beat with an electric mixer at medium speed until it becomes thick and frothy. Beating, add the confectioners' sugar and vanilla and beat until soft peaks form, being careful not to overbeat.

2. Serve immediately.

BASICS

Blanched Asparagus

MAKES 1 POUND

1   pound asparagus spears

1. With a sharp knife, remove the tough woody ends from the asparagus. Lay the asparagus flat, align the tips, and trim the spears to the same length.

2. Bring a large saucepan of salted water to a boil. Add the asparagus and cook until just tender, 1 to 2 minutes, depending upon their thickness. Drain and transfer to an ice bath to stop the cooking; drain.

Chicken Stock

MAKES 3 QUARTS

4   pounds chicken bones, such as wings, backs, carcasses, and necks, rinsed in cool water
2   cups coarsely chopped yellow onions
1   cup coarsely chopped carrots
1   cup coarsely chopped celery
3   garlic cloves, peeled and smashed
4   bay leaves
1   teaspoon black peppercorns
2   teaspoons salt
1   teaspoon dried thyme
½   teaspoon dried rosemary
½   teaspoon dried oregano

1. Put all the ingredients in a large stockpot. Add enough cold water to cover the bones by 1 inch and bring to a boil over high heat. Reduce the heat to medium-low and simmer, uncovered, for 2 to 3 hours, skimming occasionally to remove any foam that forms on the surface.

2. Remove from the heat and strain through a fine-mesh strainer. Store refrigerated in an airtight container for up to 3 days or freeze for up to 2 months.

Boiled Artichokes

MAKES 4

Artichokes are commonly found on New Orleans tables, whether as part of another dish or simply boiled and served with Mayonnaise (page 264) or Hollandaise Sauce (page 261) for dipping.

They were stuffed at the old Delmonico, and at Emeril's Delmonico we serve them in the Oyster-Artichoke Soup (page 58). And at both restaurants, artichoke hearts are a main component of the Delmonico Sauce (page 144 and page 146).

1 **gallon water**	2 **teaspoons whole black peppercorns**
4 **bay leaves**	4 **large globe artichokes,** 10 **to** 12 **ounces each**
3 **tablespoons salt**	1 **lemon, halved**

1. Bring the water, bay leaves, salt, and peppercorns to a boil in a large pot.

2. With a small, sharp knife, trim the tough outer skin from the artichoke stems and remove the bottom row of leaves. Using long-handled tongs, carefully add the artichokes and lemon to the pot and return to a boil. Place 2 small heavy plates on top of the artichokes to keep them submerged, lower the heat, and cook at a low boil until the artichokes are tender, 20 to 25 minutes. Drain in a colander and let the artichokes sit until cool enough to handle.

3. To serve whole, remove the stems of the artichokes so that they sit flat. Cut off about 1 inch from the tops with a heavy, sharp knife and trim the sharp points off the artichoke leaves with kitchen shears.

4. Gently press back the center leaves on the artichokes so the inner choke and prickly leaves are revealed. Pull out the cone of the undeveloped leaves in the center of each artichoke and gently scrape out the hairy choke with a teaspoon so as not to damage the heart. Serve with a dipping sauce of choice.

Rich Chicken Stock

MAKES 2 QUARTS

This is the way to go when you need a more intense flavor than regular chicken stock can give you. And while making this is an all-day project, the extra effort is definitely worth the end result.

4	pounds chicken bones	1	cup dry red wine
1	cup coarsely chopped yellow onions	5	sprigs fresh parsley
½	cup coarsely chopped carrots	5	sprigs fresh thyme
½	cup coarsely chopped celery	2	bay leaves
5	garlic cloves, peeled and smashed	1	teaspoon black peppercorns
One	6-ounce can tomato paste		

1. Preheat the oven to 375°F.

2. Spread the chicken bones evenly in a large roasting pan and roast for 2 hours, stirring after 1 hour. Remove from the oven and add the onions, carrots, celery, garlic, and tomato paste, stirring to mix. Roast for 45 minutes longer.

3. Remove the pan from the oven and transfer the hot vegetables and bones to a large heavy stockpot. Place the roasting pan over 2 burners on medium-high heat. Add the wine and stir with a heavy wooden spoon to deglaze and dislodge any browned bits from the bottom of the pan. Pour the hot wine mixture into the stockpot. Add the parsley, thyme, bay leaves, peppercorns, and water to cover by 1 inch.

4. Bring to a boil over medium-high heat. Reduce the heat to medium-low and simmer, uncovered, for 4 hours, skimming the surface frequently to remove any foam that forms on the surface.

5. Remove from the heat and strain through a fine-mesh strainer into a clean container and let cool completely. Store refrigerated in an airtight container for up to 3 days or freeze for up to 2 months.

Clarified Butter

MAKES ABOUT 1½ CUPS

What makes clarified butter so great is its higher smoke point. This means you can cook meats and fish at a higher temperature than you can with regular butter, making it ideal for pan-frying. At the restaurant we use it to cook a variety of meats and seafood, and even vegetables. Its neutral flavor also makes the most flavorful egg-based sauces, including hollandaise, tasso hollandaise, béarnaise, and choron sauces.

By clarifying the butter during a slow-cooking process, you're able to strain out the milk solids that burn quickly, as well as the water and salt. You'll lose about one-quarter of your original butter amount during the process.

½ **pound (2 sticks) unsalted butter, cut into pieces**

1. Place the butter in a heavy saucepan and melt slowly over low heat. Remove the pan from the heat and let stand for 5 minutes. Skim the foam from the top, and slowly pour into a clean container, discarding the milky solids in the bottom of the pan.

2. The clarified butter will keep refrigerated in an airtight container for up to 1 month.

Duck Stock

2 duck carcasses (about 4 pounds)	4 bay leaves
1 tablespoon vegetable oil	1 cup dry red wine
2 teaspoons salt	1/4 cup tomato paste
1/8 teaspoon freshly ground black pepper	12 cups cold water
3 cups chopped yellow onions	10 sprigs fresh thyme
1 cup chopped carrots	5 sprigs fresh tarragon
1 cup chopped celery	8 sprigs fresh parsley
1 head garlic, split in half	1 teaspoon black peppercorns

1. Break and crack the bones of the carcasses.

2. Heat the vegetable oil in a 6-quart stockpot over medium-high heat. Season the bones with 1 teaspoon of the salt and the black pepper. Add the bones to the pot and brown for about 10 minutes, stirring often. Add the onions, carrots, celery, garlic, bay leaves, and the remaining teaspoon salt. Cook until the vegetables are very soft, about 5 minutes, stirring often. Add the wine and tomato paste and stir to mix. Cook for 5 minutes, stirring occasionally. Add the water and stir well. Put the thyme, tarragon, parsley sprigs, and peppercorns in a piece of cheesecloth, tie it together with kitchen twine, add it to the mixture, and bring the mixture to a boil. Skim off any foam that rises to the surface. Reduce the heat to medium and simmer, uncovered, for 3 hours, skimming occasionally to remove any foam that forms on the surface.

3. Remove from the heat and strain through a fine-mesh strainer into a clean container and let cool completely. Refrigerate overnight and remove any congealed fat from the surface. The stock can be stored refrigerated in an airtight container for up to 3 days, or in the freezer for 1 month.

Fish Stock

2½ pounds fish bones and heads, from any white-fleshed fish, such as cod, pollock, grouper, snapper, or flounder (do not use bones from oily fish, such as pompano, redfish, mackerel, or bluefish)
1 cup dry white wine
1 cup coarsely chopped yellow onions
½ cup coarsely chopped celery

½ cup coarsely chopped carrots
3 garlic cloves, peeled and smashed
1 lemon, quartered
3 tablespoons fresh lemon juice
2 teaspoons salt
3 bay leaves
1 teaspoon whole black peppercorns
1 teaspoon dried thyme

1. Rinse the fish bones and heads well in a large colander under cold running water.

2. Put all of the ingredients in a stockpot, add enough cold water to cover by 1 inch, and bring to a boil over high heat. Lower the heat to medium-low and simmer, uncovered, for 1 hour, skimming occasionally to remove any foam that forms on the surface.

3. Ladle through a fine-mesh strainer into a clean container and cool completely. Cover and refrigerate. The stock can be refrigerated for up to 3 days, or freeze in airtight containers for up to 2 months.

Hard-Boiled Eggs

MAKES 3 EGGS

It's important to peel the eggs once they are cool enough to handle and while they still are warm. Once the eggs cool, the shells tend to stick more. If the eggs are still warm once they are peeled, place them in an ice-water bath to prevent discoloration, then drain, wrap in plastic, and refrigerate until needed.

This simple method will work for any number of eggs—just make sure they fit flat in one layer in the pot.

3 **large eggs**

Put the eggs in a small flat-bottomed saucepan that can hold them in 1 layer. Add enough water to cover by ½ inch, and bring to a boil over high heat. Reduce the heat to a gentle boil and cook for 10 minutes. Remove from the heat and drain. Put them in a colander under cold running water, then peel when cool enough to handle.

Creole Seasoning

MAKES ⅔ CUP

This is an all-around blend that we use to season just about everything at all of my restaurants, Emeril's Delmonico included.

2½	**tablespoons paprika**	1	**tablespoon onion powder**
2	**tablespoons salt**	1	**tablespoon cayenne**
2	**tablespoons garlic powder**	1	**tablespoon dried oregano**
1	**tablespoon freshly ground black pepper**	1	**tablespoon dried thyme**

Combine all the ingredients thoroughly and store in an airtight container for up to 3 months.

Hollandaise Sauce

The frequent appearance of hollandaise sauce on the menus of both Delmonico restaurants, as well as at the original New York location, is testament to the amazing versatility of this classic French egg-based sauce. The earliest written reference to the sauce dates to 1758, and traditionally hollandaise sauce is paired with vegetables, fish, poultry, and poached egg dishes. In this book, you'll find it atop Chicken Rochambeau (page 152), with Broccoli (page 214), and as a Tasso Hollandaise with the Eggs Pontchartrain (page 101). Or serve it as a sauce for Blanched Asparagus (page 254) and Boiled Artichokes (page 255).

The secret to successfully making hollandaise—and all egg-based sauces, for that matter—lies in slowly building the emulsion by steadily whisking the fat (in this case, butter) into the yolks. Not only does whisking cause the egg yolks to thicken, increase in volume, and provide a base for the clarified butter but the steady action allows the butter to be suspended and form the emulsion.

2 large egg yolks
1 tablespoon fresh lemon juice
2 teaspoons water
1/2 cup Clarified Butter (page 257), or 8 tablespoons (1 stick) unsalted butter, melted

1 tablespoon tepid water, as needed
1/4 teaspoon salt
1/8 teaspoon cayenne

1. In the top of a double boiler or in a medium bowl set over a saucepan of barely simmering water, whisk the egg yolks with the lemon juice and 2 teaspoons water until the egg yolks are thick and pale yellow. Remove the double boiler (or bowl and saucepan) from the heat and gradually add the butter, whisking constantly to thicken. Add enough tepid water to thin to pouring consistency. Add the salt and cayenne and whisk well to blend. Adjust the seasoning to taste.

2. Serve immediately, or cover to keep warm for up to 10 minutes, whisking occasionally to keep from separating.

Lamb Stock

MAKES ABOUT 5 CUPS

6 to 8 **pounds lamb bones, sawed into**
    2- or 3-inch pieces
2 **tablespoons olive oil**
1 **cup tomato paste**
8 **tomatoes, coarsely chopped**
2 **large onions, peeled, halved, and sliced**
2 **carrots, peeled and chopped**
2 **ribs celery, chopped**
2 **heads garlic, cut in half horizontally**
8 **quarts water, cold or at room temperature**

4 **bay leaves**
2 **teaspoons dried leaf basil**
2 **teaspoons dried leaf thyme**
2 **teaspoons dried leaf tarragon**
2 **teaspoons dried leaf oregano**
½ **cup chopped fresh parsley, stems and leaves**
1½ **teaspoons black peppercorns**
2 **teaspoons salt**
2 **cups dry red wine**

1. Preheat the oven to 425°F.

2. Place the bones in a roasting pan and toss with the oil. Roast until brown, about 15 minutes. Turn the bones, spread with the tomato paste, and roast for 10 minutes. Add the tomatoes, onions, carrots, celery, and garlic and stir to combine. Roast until the bones are a deep brown color and the vegetables are tender, about 25 minutes.

3. Remove the roasting pan from the oven, and transfer the bones and vegetables to a large stockpot. Do not discard the juices in the pan. Add the water, bay leaves, basil, thyme, tarragon, oregano, parsley, peppercorns, and salt to the pot with the bones and bring to a boil.

4. Meanwhile, place the roasting pan on top of the stove over medium heat. Add the wine and stir with a heavy wooden spoon to deglaze and scrape up the sticky brown bits clinging to the bottom. Add the contents to the pot with the bones. When the mixture returns to a boil, reduce the heat to low and simmer, uncovered, for about 3½ hours, skimming occasionally to remove any foam that forms on the surface.

5. Strain the stock through a fine-mesh strainer into a clean container, skim the surface, and let cool thoroughly. Discard the bones and vegetables. Refrigerate the stock overnight. Remove any congealed fat from the surface the next day and refrigerate for up to 3 days or freeze in 2-cup containers for up to 1 month.

Large Croutons

We use large croutons for a variety of dishes at Emeril's Delmonico—from salads to cheese courses. They're also ideal for spreading with meats, such as Morris Kahn's Steak Tartare (page 52) or pâtés, and serving alongside creamy dishes such as the Crawfish in Spicy Cream Sauce (page 44), Crabmeat Imperial (page 36), and Crabmeat Remick (page 35).

Cut your toasts thick or thin as you like. And for an extra garlicky treat with your Caesar Salad (page 86), rub these with a split garlic clove before toasting them, then chop fresh from the oven.

One 12 to 15-inch loaf French or Italian
     bread, cut into ¼-inch to ½-inch slices
¼   cup olive oil

¼   teaspoon salt
⅛   teaspoon freshly ground black pepper

1. Preheat the oven to 400°F.

2. Place the bread slices on a large baking sheet and brush one side of each slice with the olive oil, then lightly season with the salt and pepper. Bake until light golden brown, about 8 minutes.

3. Cool slightly on the baking sheet before handling or serving.

Mayonnaise

Homemade mayonnaise gives a bright flavor to the Pan-Fried Crab Cakes (page 40), Crabmeat Remick (page 35), and Miss Hilda's Asparagus and Crabmeat Salad (page 92). It's also delicious as a dip for Boiled Artichokes (page 255), or a simple sandwich spread.

1 large egg	$\frac{1}{2}$ teaspoon salt
1 large egg yolk	$1\frac{1}{4}$ cups vegetable oil
2 teaspoons fresh lemon juice	$\frac{1}{4}$ cup olive oil
1 teaspoon Dijon mustard	$\frac{1}{8}$ teaspoon cayenne, optional
2 tablespoons water	

1. Place the egg, egg yolk, lemon juice, mustard, 1 tablespoon of the water, and salt in the bowl of a food processor or blender. Process on high speed for 20 seconds. With the motor running, pour the oil in a thin stream through the feed tube and process until the mixture begins to thicken. When half of the oil has been incorporated, add the remaining tablespoon water. With the motor running, add the remaining oil in a thin stream, and process on high until all the oil is incorporated.

2. Adjust the seasoning to taste with salt and cayenne, if desired.

3. Chill and use as needed. It will keep, stored in an airtight container in the refrigerator, for up to 1 day.

Reduced Veal Stock

4 pounds veal bones with some meat attached, sawed into 2-inch pieces (have the butcher do this)	¼ cup tomato paste
2 tablespoons olive oil	6 quarts water
2 cups coarsely chopped yellow onions	4 bay leaves
1 cup coarsely chopped carrots	1 teaspoon dried thyme
1 cup coarsely chopped celery	1 teaspoon salt
5 garlic cloves, peeled and smashed	1 teaspoon whole black peppercorns
	2 cups dry red wine

1. Preheat the oven to 375°F.

2. Spread the bones evenly in a large roasting pan and toss with the oil. Roast, turning occasionally, until golden brown, about 1 hour.

3. Remove from the oven and spread the onions, carrots, celery, and garlic over the bones. Smear the tomato paste over the vegetables and return the pan to the oven. Roast for another 45 minutes. Remove from the oven and pour off the fat from the pan.

4. Transfer the bones and vegetables to a large stockpot. Do not discard the juices in the roasting pan. Add the water, bay leaves, thyme, salt, and peppercorns to the stockpot and bring to a boil.

5. Meanwhile, place the roasting pan over 2 burners on medium-high heat. Add the wine and stir with a heavy wooden spoon to deglaze and dislodge any browned bits clinging to the bottom of the pan. Add the contents to the stockpot. When the liquid returns to a boil, reduce the heat to low and simmer, uncovered, for 8 hours, skimming occasionally to remove any foam that rises to the surface.

6. Ladle the stock through a fine-mesh strainer into a large clean pot. Bring to a boil, reduce to a gentle boil, and cook, uncovered, until reduced to 6 cups, about 1 hour. Let cool, then cover and refrigerate overnight.

7. Remove any congealed fat from the surface of the stock. The stock can be stored, covered, in the refrigerator for up to 3 days or frozen in airtight containers for up to 2 months.

Vegetable Stock

MAKES ABOUT 2 QUARTS

1 tablespoon olive oil	2 ears corn, kernels scraped off, kernels
1 large yellow onion, peeled, halved,	and cobs reserved
and sliced	1/2 pound mushroom stems, rinsed
1 carrot, peeled and chopped	4 bay leaves
1 rib celery, chopped	1 teaspoon chopped fresh basil
3 heads garlic, cut horizontally in half	1 teaspoon chopped fresh thyme
4 quarts water	1 teaspoon chopped fresh tarragon
1 green bell pepper, cored, seeded,	1 teaspoon chopped fresh oregano
and chopped	1 teaspoon chopped fresh parsley
2 tomatoes, coarsely chopped	1 teaspoon chopped fresh chives
	1/2 teaspoon black peppercorns

1. Heat the oil in a large stockpot over high heat. Add the onion, carrot, celery, and garlic and cook, stirring occasionally, until the onions are soft, 3 to 4 minutes. Add the remaining ingredients and bring to a boil. Reduce the heat to low and simmer, uncovered, for 1¾ hours.

2. Remove from the heat and strain through a fine-mesh strainer into a clean container. Let cool completely.

3. The stock can be stored, covered, in the refrigerator for up to 3 days or frozen in airtight containers for up to 2 months.

Shrimp Stock

When you peel uncooked shrimp, reserve the shells and heads in a heavy plastic bag in the freezer until you have enough to make this aromatic stock. About two and a half pounds of shrimp will yield one pound of shells and heads for this purpose.

1 pound shrimp shells and heads	3 bay leaves
1 cup coarsely chopped yellow onions	1 teaspoon black peppercorns
1/2 cup coarsely chopped celery	1 teaspoon dried thyme
1/2 cup coarsely chopped carrots	2 teaspoons salt
3 garlic cloves, peeled and smashed	

1. Place the shrimp shells and heads in a large colander and rinse under cold running water.

2. Place all the ingredients in a heavy 6-quart stockpot. Add 1 gallon of water to cover, and bring the mixture to a boil over high heat, skimming with a slotted spoon to remove any foam that rises to the surface. Reduce the heat to medium-low and simmer, skimming occasionally, for 45 minutes.

3. Remove the stock from the heat and strain through a fine-mesh strainer into a clean container. Store the stock in an airtight container for up to 3 days, refrigerated, or freeze for up to 2 months.

Emeril's Restaurants

EMERIL'S RESTAURANT
800 Tchoupitoulas Street
New Orleans, LA 70130
504-528-9393

NOLA
534 St. Louis Street
New Orleans, LA 70130
504-522-6652

EMERIL'S DELMONICO
1300 St. Charles Avenue
New Orleans, LA 70130
504-525-4937

EMERIL'S NEW ORLEANS FISH HOUSE
at the MGM Grand Hotel and Casino
3799 Las Vegas Boulevard South
Las Vegas, NV 89109
702-891-7374

DELMONICO STEAKHOUSE
at the Venetian Resort and Casino
3355 Las Vegas Boulevard South
Las Vegas, NV 89109
702-414-3737

EMERIL'S ORLANDO
6000 Universal Boulevard
at Universal Studios City Walk
Orlando, FL 32819
407-224-2424

EMERIL'S TCHOUP CHOP
at Universal Orlando's Royal Pacific Resort
6300 Hollywood Way
Orlando, FL 32819
407-503-2467

EMERIL'S ATLANTA
One Alliance Center
3500 Lenox Road
Atlanta, GA 30326
404-564-5600

EMERIL'S MIAMI BEACH
at Loews Miami Beach Hotel
1601 Collins Avenue
Miami Beach, FL 33139
305-695-4550

Web Sites

Chef Emeril Lagasse
www.emerils.com
The official Web site for everything Emeril. Here you will find listings for all his restaurants, shows, merchandise, and in-depth background and insight into Emeril's culinary world, as well as weekly menus with recipes, kitchen tips, fun food talk, and lots of great information . . . Bam!

The Emeril Lagasse Foundation
www.emeril.org
The foundation seeks to inspire and enable young people to realize their full potential by supporting programs that create developmental and educational opportunities within the communities where Emeril's restaurants operate.

All-Clad Cookware
www.emerilware.com
The cookware that Chef Emeril believes in. Here you will find the entire range of Emerilware by All-Clad—from skillets to sauté pans.

B&G Foods
www.bgfoods.com
If you want to kick up your kitchen a notch, look for Emeril's original spice blends, salad dressings, marinades, hot sauces, and pasta sauces distributed by B&G Foods and available at supermarkets nationwide.

Food Network
www.foodtv.com
Log on to the Food Network's site for all recipes and scheduling information for *Emeril Live* and *The Essence of Emeril* shows, and ticket information for *Emeril Live*.

Good Morning America
abcnews.go.com
Wake up to Chef Emeril on Friday mornings on ABC, when he shares his culinary creations with America.

HarperCollins Publishers
www.harpercollins.com
This informative site offers background on and chapter excerpts of all of Chef Emeril's best-selling cookbooks.

New Orleans Fish House
www.nofishhouse.com
Emeril's Gulf Shrimp are certified Wild American Shrimp packaged and distributed by New Orleans Fish House.

Pride of San Juan
www.prideofsanjuan.com
Emeril Lagasse and Pride of San Juan have partnered to bring you fresh high-quality produce. Emeril's Gourmet Produce brand launches with an innovative selection of prepackaged salads and herb packs.

Sanita Clogs
www.sanitaclogs.com
Emeril and Sanita Clogs have teamed up to provide you with a new clog especially made for Emeril and you! Sanita Clogs have produced quality Danish clogs since 1907.

Sara Lee Foods
www.emerilsgourmetmeats.com
Emeril's Gourmet Meats offer bold, full-flavored meat products with consistent top quality. It will take your dinner to a whole new level.

Waterford/Wedgewood
www.wwusa.com
The world's leading luxury lifestyle group produces Emeril at Home, a classic addition to the home kitchen.

Wüsthof Knives
www.wusthof.com
Emerilware Knives gift and block sets, made to Emeril's specifications by one of the world's foremost manufacturers of quality cutlery.

Source Guide

Emeril's Homebase
829 St. Charles Avenue
New Orleans, LA 70130
Tel: 800-980-8474
     504-558-3940
www.emerils.com
Emeril's cookware, cookbooks, specialty
food products, chefware, and more

Steen's Syrup
119 North Main Street
Abbeville, LA 70510
Tel: 800-725-1654
Fax: 337-893-2478
www.steensyrup.com
100% pure cane syrup, dark and light molasses

New Orleans Fish House
821 S. Dupre Street
New Orleans, LA 70125
Tel: 800-839-3474
     504-821-9700
www.nofh.com
Full line of fresh and frozen seafood, including
shrimp, gumbo crabs, crabmeat, crawfish, and fish,
and turtle meat.

Zatarain's
82 First Street
New Orleans, LA 70053
Tel: 504-367-2950
Fax: 504-362-2004
www.zatarain.com
Spices and seasonings including file powder, crab
and shrimp boil mixes, Creole mustard. Available
at supermarkets nationwide.

Niman Ranch
1025 East 12th Street
Oakland, CA 94606
Tel: 510-808-0340
www.nimanranch.com
Dry-aged beef, including New York steaks, rib eyes,
and prime rib roast. Non-aged beef cuts include
Chateaubriand and beef short ribs. Other meats
include pork chops, pork tenderloins, Applewood
smoked bacon and slab bacon, lamb loin chops,
and lamb shanks.

INDEX